FAITH IN HUMAN RIGHTS

FAITH IN HUMAN RIGHTS

Support in Religious Traditions for a Global Struggle

Robert Traer

Georgetown University Press
Washington, D.C.

Library of Congress Cataloging-in-Publication Data

Traer, Robert.
    Faith in human rights : support in religious traditions for a
global struggle / Robert Traer.
        p.   cm.
    ISBN 0-87840-491-0 : $19.95. -- ISBN 0-87840-492-9 (pbk.) : $9.95
    1. Human rights--Religious aspects. I. Title.
BK65.H78T72 1991
291.1'77--dc20   90-41971
                                                             CIP

"faith throws a new light on everything"

Gaudium et Spes

Table of Contents

PREFACE

Almost forty years ago, as a boy, I climbed the steps of the Lincoln Memorial in Washington, D.C. and stood before the massive statue of Abraham Lincoln. Then I turned and read on the walls of the Memorial the words of the Gettysburg and Second Inaugural Addresses. I was especially taken by the Gettysburg Address and vowed to learn it by heart, as soon as I returned home. I can still recite most of it today.

In the midst of the carnage of the Civil War, Lincoln urged the living to rededicate their lives to the great unfinished work begun in a "nation, conceived in liberty, and dedicated to the proposition that all men [people] are created equal." He asked for increased devotion to the cause for which so many had given their lives: "that this nation, under God, shall have a new birth of freedom; and that government of the people, by the people, for the people, shall not perish from the earth."

Lincoln's resolve cost him his life. However, his challenge lived on in me, as I went through the motions of saying the Pledge of Allegiance at school and praying to God in church.

Twelve years later his words took on new meaning when, as a civil rights worker, I sang freedom songs and spirituals in the rural churches of Mississippi. It was in these same churches that the call of Jesus became clear and compelling, and I returned from the South to prepare for the Christian ministry. However, as I studied the Bible and church history, I continued to work for civil rights. I marched for open housing in Chicago with Martin Luther King, Jr. and, because of my commitment to nonviolent love, I opposed the war in Vietnam.

In 1969 I accepted a call to a small, suburban church where I tried to develop both a pastoral and prophetic ministry. I spoke out from the pulpit and in public, in support of civil rights and in opposition to the war in Vietnam. After several members left the church and revenues fell, I began to see that I was failing to communicate my faith. I left the church with the realization that I had a long way to go before I made sense of Christ and Lincoln, grace and freedom, salvation and civil rights.

A year of teaching in Japan left me pondering the peace I experienced while meditating in Buddhist temples. And two years of living in community at Grailville, a Roman Catholic retreat center, introduced me to contemplative prayer in the Christian tradition, the mass, and the saints. I continued to probe my heritage as a law student. I organized a "Hired Gun" seminar to reflect on ethical issues in the practice of law. And in a course on international law, I became aware of human rights law but failed to comprehend its global impact.

Once admitted to the bar, I renewed my effort to realize the biblical and democratic imperatives of our tradition. For ten years I organized nonprofit corporations to help people secure adequate housing, food, and health care. I was elected to the school board on a reform platform. Later I ran for and nearly won a seat in the state senate. I spoke out against the death penalty, supported nuclear disarmament, and lobbied for economic justice—unpopular positions in my community.

In short, by the grace of God, I tried to live my faith, as a Christian and an American. I tried to embrace the life that Martin Luther King, Jr. affirmed in his "I Have a Dream" address before the Lincoln Memorial in 1963.

King described his dream as "deeply rooted in the American dream that one day this nation will rise up and live out the true meaning of its creed—we hold these truths to be self-evident, that all men [people] are created equal." He also described his dream in the imagery of biblical faith: "I have a dream that one day every valley shall be exalted, every hill and mountain shall be made low, the rough places shall be made plain, and the crooked places shall be made straight and the glory of the Lord will be revealed and all flesh shall see it together."

"With this faith," he proclaimed, "we will be able to hew out of the mountain of despair a stone of hope. . . . With this faith we will be able to work together, to pray together, to struggle together, to go to jail together, to stand up for freedom together, knowing that we will be free one day. This will be the day when all of God's children will be able to sing with new meaning—'my country 'tis of thee; sweet land of liberty; of thee I sing; land where my fathers died, land of the pilgrim's pride; from every mountain side, let freedom ring'. . . ."

"And when we allow freedom to ring," King concluded, "we will be able to speed up that day when all of God's children . . . will be able to join hands and to sing in the words of the old Negro spiritual, 'Free at last, free at last; thank God Almighty, we are free at last'."

I have fallen far short of the challenge raised by Lincoln and the call voiced by Jesus and the dream articulated by King. Yet they are fundamental to my life and our heritage, and renew faith within me. The Spirit, like the wind, "blows where it will" (John 3:8). And so, despite the

injustices and the tragedies of our time, I continue to trust in the love of God.

In a world shaped by different cultures and religious traditions, the ferment of faith is everywhere. There are many who have been called to realize justice and peace in community. Their convictions are rooted in diverse histories and traditions. Yet, as I have discovered through my research, they share a faith in freedom, democracy, and human rights.

What follows is my initial attempt to articulate this global faith. In addition, I am working with others to organize a global interfaith effort in support of human rights. We are calling all persons of good will: to act on a shared faith in freedom, democracy, and human rights to secure the conditions for human dignity, to join with women and men of different traditions in the struggle for justice and peace, and to ground action and reflection in our traditions of faith.

We are aware that the institutions of the religious communities of the world have often aided the social, economic, and political interests which violate human dignity. However, we are convinced that freedom, democracy, and human rights are and can be and must be rooted in the deepest convictions of our various cultures and religious traditions, if we are to build a world community in which the differences among peoples are respected.

In the words of those gathered at the 1987 World Congress of the International Association for Religious Freedom: "We reaffirm the requirement laid upon us by our religious commitment to participate in work for peace, mutual understanding, human rights and the alleviation of suffering. We pledge our cooperation at all levels with those who are working for these goals out of a personal commitment which may be other than ours."

In the development of this effort, as in the writing of this book, I am indebted to many people. The work of Robert Bellah long ago challenged me to bring together in my thinking what in *Habits of the Hearts* he refers to as the biblical and republican traditions of America. And I am mindful of his counsel that emphasizing rights may reinforce the individualistic bias in American life which works against the creation of a good society.

Harold Berman's brief book, *The Interaction of Law and Religion*, inspired me while I was still in law school to pursue related questions of theology and jurisprudence. The writings of Wilfred Cantwell Smith have shaped my understanding of faith and the religious traditions of the world, and critical comments by Mark Juergensmeyer, John Coleman, and James Gordley have been extremely helpful.

Frank Newman's dogged determination, to make sure that the law helps people, continues to move me; and the proddings of Hugh White and Harlan Stelmach have kept me working on the problems that remain in translating this faith into action. The faith of the women of the Grail,

the patient counsel of my wife, Nancy, and the understanding of my five children have been a constant reminder of the power and mystery of love.

What follows, of course, is my responsibility and not theirs. However, I am deeply grateful for the continuing guidance and inspiration which I have received from so many. Finally, I give thanks for the life and witness of Martin Luther King, Jr., who more than any other contemporary person, has shown me the way.

Robert Traer

INTRODUCTION

Louis Henkin suggests that today "all the major religions proudly lay claim to fathering" human rights.[1] If this is so, it is remarkable in at least two respects. First, human rights are a central topic of legal and political discussion. It is by no means obvious that human rights are a matter of religious concern, much less that they are rooted in religious faith. Second, as each religious tradition is defined by different beliefs and practices, it seems unlikely that there would be any consensus about human rights among the participants in these traditions.

However, I intend to show that Henkin's claim is essentially correct. Within the major religious traditions of the world today there are many leaders who have embraced human rights as an expression of their faith. This support for human rights is global, cutting across cultures as well as systems of belief and practice. How this has happened and what it might mean for our world is the subject of this investigation.

Clearly, something new is occurring when women and men[2] of different faith traditions join with those of no religious tradition to champion human rights. Faith in human rights is becoming global.

What Are Human Rights?

Abdul Aziz Said suggests that today "Human rights may be difficult to define but impossible to ignore."[3] Human rights are impossible to ignore, because they are widely asserted. However, human rights are hard to define because they are not simply derived from philosophical arguments. Rather, human rights are the result of experience and history: "while the struggle to assure a life of dignity is probably as old as human society itself, reliance on human rights as a mechanism to realize that dignity is a relatively recent development."[4]

With the adoption of the Universal Declaration of Human Rights in 1948, the expression "human rights" replaced in international law the term "rights of man," an expression adopted during the nineteenth century to refer to the traditional affirmations of "natural rights" made popular by the English, American and French Revolutions.[5]

> Because of this historical development, the term "human rights" has tended to convey a broader meaning than the expression "rights of man." "Human rights" thus connotes economic and social as well as civil and political rights, equality of the sexes and the rights of the individual on an international as well as a national plane.[6]

Thus the expression "human rights" refers to the law of human rights which has been and is being developed to protect and promote human dignity. Or more simply, human rights are "what the laws say" they are.[7]

The foundation of human rights law is the Universal Declaration of Human Rights, which is now part of the customary law of nations and thus binding on all states.[8] This Declaration is cited in most international human rights legal instruments and is affirmed by human rights scholars and advocates. Human rights law includes international, regional and bilateral treaties, and through constitutional provisions has been incorporated into the law of most states. Human rights law makes the welfare of individual human beings a matter of international concern: "No nation can any longer claim not to know what human rights are; nor can any nation now assert that the manner in which it treats its own nationals is free from international scrutiny."[9]

Human rights include the self-determination of peoples, fundamental freedoms involving integrity rights for the individual and freedom of action, political rights, social and economic rights, and cultural rights involving the right to cultural identity and continuity and the right to participate in the cultural life of society and to enjoy the benefits of that activity.[10] Today it is widely accepted, as stated by the International Commission of Jurists, that the

> Rule of Law requires the establishment and observance of certain standards that recognize and foster not only the political rights of the individual but also his economic, social and cultural security. It is endangered by the continued existence of hunger, poverty and unemployment, which tend to make a truly representative form of government impossible and promote the emergence of systems of government opposed to the principles of the Rule of Law.[11]

Admittedly, no single theory of law neatly accounts for all these rights, nor does any single strategy assure their balanced realization. Moreover, there continues to be vigorous debate over international human rights law.

Thus human rights law is and continues to be a process of developing global consensus. The Universal Declaration of Human Rights not only laid the cornerstone for the content of human rights but also established the manner in which the whole structure of human rights law is being built. When Louis Henkin refers to human rights as "simply those moral-political claims which, by contemporary consensus, every human being has or is deemed to have upon his society and government,"[12] he is affirming the tradition of human rights law which has developed since the Universal Declaration of Human Rights.

Religious Opposition to Human Rights

Abba Hillel Silver admits that "Religion was not only tardy in championing human rights; at times it was actually retarding and reactionary."[13] Certainly, this was true of the Christian tradition. Despite all the present discussion of human rights in the churches, Erich Weingärtner suggests:

> It is perhaps premature to speak of any "Christian tradition" of human rights, especially in view of the fact that the Christian church has not historically been in alliance with the pioneers of human rights, whatever their tradition.[14]

On behalf of the early church, Tertullian did argue with the Roman proconsul Scapula that worship according to one's convictions "is a fundamental right, a privilege of nature."[15] However, soon after Constantine made Christianity legal in the Roman empire, Augustine articulated a justification for "the spiritual utility of civil coercion" which gave the authorities "the right to restrain the freedom of dissenters."[16]

It is not surprising then that Pius VI, as early as the brief *Quod aliquantum* in 1791, criticized the French Revolution's Declaration of the Rights of Man for supporting freedom of opinion and communication.[17] Many saw the French Declaration as a threat to religious and spiritual authority and not merely as a rejection of traditional political authority. Thus Lamennais called for a Declaration of the Rights of God rather than a Declaration of the Rights of Man.[18] At stake in this struggle was the notion of rule by divine right, the dominant form of political theory in Europe after the fourth century.

In 1864 Pius IX in the *Syllabus of Errors* struggled to preserve the privileged position of the Roman Catholic Church. Among the ideas *condemned* in this desperate effort are the following:

> 55. The Church should be separated from the State and the State from the Church.

77. In this age of ours it is no longer expedient that the Catholic religion should be treated as the sole State religion and that any other forms of religious worship should be excluded.

78. Hence those States, nominally Catholic, who have legally enacted that immigrants be permitted to have free exercise of their own particular religion, are to be praised.[19]

Until very recently, the Roman Catholic Church has resisted the human rights movement "as an alien force."[20]

Of course, this was always "clear" to Protestants, who tend to see their own history "as a series of successes in emancipating people for the enjoyment of greater freedom," and Roman Catholicism as "a perennial Inquisition":

Catholic history is depicted as unrelieved servitude in subjection to hierarchical authority, freedom of conscience being stifled by the imposition of unreasonable, outrageously dogmatic restraints upon children, women, and men.[21]

Similarly, Protestants tend to see Eastern Orthodoxy, especially the notorious early Byzantine and the Russian traditions, as equally flawed and oppressive.

However, in fact it was only the "left-wing" Christians of the Reformation in the sixteenth century who consistently advocated freedom, against oppression by either princely or priestly power.[22] Luther's support of civil authority over against the rights of the common people is well documented, as is the Calvinist bent toward theocracy and the suppression of personal liberties used to enforce it.

Thus the development of human rights in the West may be seen as a central dimension of what social theorists now call "secularization." Max Stackhouse writes:

For at least two centuries in the West, the fact that established Christianity has relinquished, or been forced to relinquish, control over key public institutions of civilization as well as over the habits of the modern mind has not only been described as historical fact, but has been celebrated as the triumph of freedom, human rights, and democracy.[23]

Stackhouse notes that many observers of "secularization" see it as a kind of "banishment of religion by modern progress," but he suggests that it might better be understood as "the triumph of some kinds of religion" over others.[24]

It is understandable then why members of traditional cultures may resist the Western values associated with human rights, for many leaders

in the religious traditions of the West have similarly been wary. In both instances human rights affirmations are seen to involve beliefs and practices which seem to undermine revered traditions.

Specifically, faith in human rights seems to undercut the sense of duty which is so much a part of traditional culture in both its Eastern and Western forms. Elaine Pagels writes that the concept of human rights "does not occur in ancient rabbinic Judaism,"[25] and Louis Henkin observes: "Judaism knows not rights but duties, and at bottom, all duties are to God."[26] Clearly, the Bible "stressed not rights but duties,"[27] and the early Christian tradition

> tends to focus more on duties and responsibilities than on rights, more on the call to achieve our human potential by overcoming sin and distortion in life through a synergy of Divine Grace and the exercise of spiritual self-discipline than by claiming it as a right to be granted by others. The tradition emphasizes the idea that love more often than not requires sacrifice of one's "rights" than the insistence upon them, and forgiveness of their violation by others than insistence upon their fulfillment.[28]

Within such a tradition "rights," when they are identified as necessary to protect those who are victimized by others, tend to be derived from the duties one has to God.

In the words of Carl F. H. Henry, evangelical Protestant theologian and founder of *Christianity Today:*

> The Bible does not teach that human beings simply on the basis of existence have inherent or a priori rights, or that they have absolute rights accruing from sociological or political considerations. The Bible has a doctrine of divinely imposed duties; what moderns call human rights are the contingent flipside of those duties.[29]

Moreover, Henry asserts that the God of the Bible "formulates human duties as an obligation to God, not as conferring tangible rights or benefits upon humanity *per se*."[30]

This emphasis on duty rather than rights is not unique to traditional Christian faith. Kana Mitra writes: "Like most other religions of the world, Hinduism emphasizes the duties of humans rather than their rights."[31] Thus human rights were readily seen by members of traditional cultures and religious traditions as part of an alien faith.

The Universal Declaration of Human Rights

Support for human rights developed during World War II. As early as 1941, Hersch Lauterpacht asserted: "The protection of human personality and of its fundamental rights is the ultimate purpose of all law, national and international."[32] That same year President Franklin D. Roosevelt was to give "human rights" perhaps their first official articulation, in a message to Congress calling for the upholding of the "Four Freedoms" or "four essential human freedoms." Roosevelt declared that "Freedom means the supremacy of human rights everywhere."[33] And the following year Prime Minister Winston Churchill spoke of the time "when this world's struggle ends with the enthronement of human rights."[34]

Thus the founding texts of the modern international order were based on an affirmation of fundamental human rights which Louis Henkin describes as "a declared article of faith," and which he suggests may be understood as "a self-evident truth."[35] This affirmation of faith was to usher in "a revolution in the theory and practice of international law," in the words of John Humphrey, who suggests "that there has been no more radical development in the whole history of international law than this bursting, as it were, of its traditional boundaries."[36]

In international law the treatment of the citizens of a state had never before been subject to review by an international authority. However, under human rights law the fundamental rights of persons clearly transcend the authority of the state.

Much of the leadership for this revolution in law came from nongovernmental organizations which participated in the drafting of the United Nations Charter and the Universal Declaration of Human Rights. Forty-two private organizations were present at the UN Conference at San Francisco in April 1945. This was the first time in history that citizens' groups had participated in a conference on international law. The Dumbarton Oaks Proposal—developed in 1944 by representatives of the governments of the United States, Britain, the Soviet Union, and China—had asserted that the United Nations should "promote respect for human rights and fundamental freedoms."[37] However, it was largely through the lobbying efforts of nongovernmental organizations that this single reference to human rights was expanded to seven references in the final draft of the UN Charter and also that nongovernmental organizations were given a role within the structure of the United Nations to assist in the promotion and protection of human rights.[38]

Only a few representatives of religious institutions were among the human rights advocates at this stage. In particular, Lutheran theologian O. Frederic Nolde of the Federal Council of Churches lobbied very effectively for inclusion of human rights in the UN Charter and later for specific

provisions in the Universal Declaration of Human Rights. While Roosevelt had spoken of the "Four Freedoms" and Churchill of "the enthronement of human rights," the governments of the United States and Britain were at "first rather cool towards taking up the question of human rights."[39] Representatives of the governments of Chile, Cuba and Panama took the lead in urging that the UN Charter include specific provisions concerning human rights.[40] In fact, the great powers did not consider human rights issues central to the development of the United Nations until the atrocities committed during the war in the concentration camps of Eastern Europe were widely publicized.[41]

By 1945 there was substantial pressure to develop an international bill of human rights. That same year Hersch Lauterpacht published a draft bill and an argument for its enactment. He began his essay by quoting Churchill's now memorable phrase:

> In the course of the second World War "the enthronement of the rights of man" was repeatedly declared to constitute one of the major purposes of the war. The great contest, in which the spiritual heritage of civilization found itself in mortal danger, was imposed upon the world by a power whose very essence lay in the denial of the rights of man as against the omnipotence of the state. That fact added weight to the conviction that an international declaration and protection of the fundamental rights of man must be an integral part of any rational scheme of world order.[42]

He began his draft bill by asserting that "the enthronement of the rights of man has been proclaimed to be the purpose of the war waged by the United Nations. . . ."[43]

On 10 December 1948 the General Assembly of the United Nations affirmed the Universal Declaration of Human Rights without dissenting vote, with forty-eight nations voting in favor, eight nations abstaining, and two nations absent.[44] A new era had begun.

The Universal Declaration affirms that human beings, "born free and equal in dignity and rights," are entitled to human rights "without distinction of any kind, such as race, color, sex, language, religion, political or other opinion, national or social origin, property, birth or other status." The rights set forth are primarily civil and political rights and include the rights to life, liberty, security, protection against torture and arbitrary arrest, equal protection of the law, freedom of movement, participation in government, religion, freedom of opinion and expression, freedom of assembly and association, and ownership of property.

However, the Universal Declaration of Human Rights also affirms social and economic rights. For everyone "is entitled to realization, through national effort and international co-operation and in accordance with the organization and resources of each State, of the economic, social and

cultural rights indispensable for his dignity and the free development of his personality."

Therefore, the Declaration proclaims "the right to work, to free choice of employment, to just and favorable conditions of work and to protection against unemployment," as well as the rights to leisure time and education. Moreover, it affirms that: "Everyone has the right to a standard of living adequate for the health and well-being of himself and of his family, including food, clothing, housing and medical care and necessary social services, and the right to security in the event of unemployment, sickness, disability, widowhood, old age or other lack of livelihood in circumstances beyond his control."

Humphrey remarks that adoption of the Declaration was a far greater achievement than anyone could have imagined in 1948: "For while its adoption by the General Assembly gave it great moral and political authority, it is its subsequent history which has given the Declaration the unique status it now possesses in international law and politics."[45] Eighteen years later the texts of the two covenants designed to implement the Universal Declaration would be adopted without dissenting vote by a General Assembly more representative of the world's peoples, with one hundred nations voting in favor and only Portugal and South Africa abstaining.[46]

These covenants were developed because the Universal Declaration was intended as a standard or first stage, to be followed not only by covenants but also by institutional machinery for implementation. Gerald Draper has described the Universal Declaration as "a transitional instrument somewhere between a legal and a moral ordering,"[47] for

> During the years since its adoption the Declaration has come, through its influence in a variety of contexts, to have a marked impact on the pattern and content of international law and to acquire a status extending beyond that originally intended for it. In general, two elements may be distinguished in this process—first, the use of the Declaration as a yardstick by which to measure the content and standard of observance of human rights; and, second, the reaffirmation of the Declaration and its provisions in a series of other instruments. These two elements, often to be found combined, have caused the Declaration to gain a cumulative and pervasive effect."[48]

In 1974 Humphrey was able to assert as the accepted opinion of legal scholars that, regardless of the intentions of its authors, "the Universal Declaration is now part of the customary law of nations and therefore binding on all states."[49]

Although its legal status has changed, from the very beginning the Universal Declaration was affirmed in language suggesting the highest credibility and authority. In her final speech at the plenary session of the

General Assembly, Eleanor Roosevelt, who chaired the Commission on Human Rights which drafted the Declaration, suggested that the Declaration "may be the Magna Carta for all humanity."[50] Already in 1949 Arthur Holcombe was comparing the Universal Declaration with the American Declaration of Independence, whose principles "remain a source of continuing inspiration to us."[51]

The search has been "for some notion of law which should transcend the positive law of the state—that positive law which had so often been manipulated for tyrannical purposes—to seek for a law which might afford a basis for essential human rights. . . ."[52] More than a generation after the Universal Declaration was adopted, Senator Edward Kennedy suggested that

> The lesson of the Holocaust was etched in the Universal Declaration; the sovereignty of the state is no longer immune to the claims of our common humanity. The higher law of human rights transcends the often heedless engines of political power.[53]

To find the Nazis guilty of crimes against humanity required finding some authoritative law above that of the German state. The Universal Declaration of Human Rights was the expression of that standard. It was declared to be not merely international, representing agreement among states, but universal in that it set forth a morality transcending that of any particular tradition or culture.[54]

In the words of Myers McDougal and Gertrude Leighton, the Universal Declaration

> represents the converging and integration on a global scale of many movements, movements hitherto restricted in a real diffusion but centuries-old and rooted deep in universal human nature and civilized culture. It is heir to all the great historic democratic movements—for constitutionalism, freedom, equality, fraternity, humanitarianism, liberalism, enlightenment, peace, opportunity, and so on. It is the contemporary culmination of man's long struggle for all his basic human values. . . .[55]

Sir Muhammed Zafrulla Khan of Pakistan, a Muslim and a member of the International Court of Justice for many years, gave this tribute to the Universal Declaration:

> It stands as a shining milestone along the long, and often difficult and weary, paths trodden by man down the corridors of history, through centuries of suffering and tribulations towards the goal of freedom, justice and equality. It is the first comprehensive formulation, based upon consensus, of the values which are designed to secure the dignities of man.[56]

This "consensus" has been described as the "practical point of convergence of extremely different theoretical ideologies and spiritual traditions."[57]

Religious Support for Human Rights

James W. Nickel argues that: "The formulation by the United Nations in 1948 of the Universal Declaration of Human Rights made possible the subsequent flourishing of the idea of human rights."[58] Whatever the reasons, clearly human rights are a central topic today in both international law and contemporary moral and religious discourse.

Despite their denial in practice, human rights are universally accepted in principle. Louis Henkin argues:

> For natural law today, it is human rights that claim to be the natural, higher law, not the divine right of kings or the sovereignty of the state, not the inferiority of women or races. In positive law today, it is human rights that are national and international law, not the laws of Hitler or some other "jurisprudence of terror." And it is individual civil-political and economic-social rights that are accepted as law, not unmitigated collectivism or laissez-faire. The idea of human rights is accepted in principle by all the governments regardless of other ideology, regardless of political, economic, or social condition.[59]

The enforcement of human rights is certainly inadequate and at times hypocritical, yet no government overtly denies the standards of international human rights law.

As early as 1951, Jacques Maritain referred to this notion of an international consensus as a kind of "secular faith."[60] What I will show in the following chapters is that this human rights consensus is embraced and affirmed by leading members of the major religious traditions of the world.

In fact, human rights are at the center of a global moral language that is being justified, elaborated, and advocated by members of different religious traditions and cultures. This is true not merely in the West but also in Africa and Asia. It is true not only in the First and Second Worlds, where liberal and socialist human rights theories have evolved, but in the Third World as well. Jews, Christians, Muslims, Hindus, Buddhists, and advocates of religious traditions indigenous to Africa and Asia fundamentally agree about human rights.

In what follows I will show that this is so. In Part One I will examine different positions within the Christian tradition. Liberal Protestants fundamentally agree with Roman Catholics and evangelical Protestants about human rights, despite quite different theological approaches.

Moreover, Christians all over the world are involved within their own cultures in the struggle to secure human rights. This new witness and consensus on human rights within the global Christian community is a striking development that deserves greater recognition.

In Part Two I will examine the human rights arguments and advocacy of leaders in other religious traditions. Jews and Muslims read their scriptures to justify support for human rights. Hindus believe that their tradition values human rights as well as sacred duties. Buddhists affirm that human rights may express the relational reality of all life. Africans and Asians assert that the traditional values of their cultures provide the conditions for human dignity which in modern parlance are identified as human rights.

In Part Three I will argue that disparate notions of human rights are being forged into a new synthesis or global faith in our time, particularly in the crucible of the Third World. There the denial of human rights is flagrant and brutal. Nonetheless, the witness to human rights is as passionate as it is dangerous. Throughout the Third World men and women have rallied around the Universal Declaration of Human Rights and have supported human rights affirmations which are rooted in the cultures of the First and Second Worlds as well as in their own traditional cultures.

Thus one may discern a common faith at the heart of the human rights movement which increasingly is shared by people all around the globe.

Notes

1. Louis Henkin, *The Rights of Man Today* (Boulder, Colo.: Westview Press, 1978), xii.

2. To verify the explicit use of human rights language, I quote many persons in this study, some of whom do not use inclusive language. However, at all times by "human rights" I mean the human rights of women and men.

3. Abdul Aziz Said, "Preface," in *Human Rights and World Order*, ed. Said (New York: Praeger Publishers, 1978), xi.

4. Rhoda E. Howard and Jack Donnelly, "Introduction," in *International Handbook on Human Rights*, ed. Donnelly and Howard (Westport, Conn.: Greenwood Press, 1987), 1.

5. In Spanish "derechos del hombre" became "derechos humanos." However, the French have continued to use "droits de l'homme" to translate "human rights."

6. Walter J. Landry, "The Ideals and Potential of the American Convention on Human Rights," *Human Rights* 4, no. 3 (Summer 1975):396-97.

7. David P. Forsythe, *Human Rights and World Politics* (Lincoln: University of Nebraska Press, 1983), 3. In practical terms if a subject is in a treaty, it is an issue of human rights.

8. There are two tests for customary international law: the principle or rule must reflect the practice of the great majority of states, and the practice must be seen as an

obligation rather than a courtesy. "Today it is a common view of international lawyers that the Universal Declaration has attained something of the status of customary international law, so that the rights it contains are in some important sense binding on states." Howard and Donnelly, "Introduction," *International Handbook of Human Rights*, 7.

9.   Robert B. McKay, "What Next?", in *Human Dignity: The Internationalization of Human Rights*, ed. Alice Henkin (New York: Aspen Institute for Humanistic Studies, 1979), 67.

10.   Asbjørn Eide, "Dynamics of Human Rights and the Role of the Educator," in *Frontiers of Human Rights Education*, ed. Eide and Marek Thee (New York: Columbia University Press, 1983), 105.

11.   "The Rule of Law and Human Rights—Principles and Definitions," in *International Commission of Human Rights* (Geneva: 1968), 44. Quoted in Fernando Fournier, "The Inter-American Human Rights System," *De Paul Law Review* 21, no. 1 (1971):380.

12.   Louis Henkin, "Rights: American and Human," *Columbia Law Review* 79, no. 3 (April 1979):405.

13.   Abba Hillel Silver, "Prophetic Religion and World Culture," in *Religious Faith and World Culture*, ed. Amandus William Loos (Freeport, N.Y.: Books for Libraries Press, 1951; reprinted 1970), 138.

14.   Erich Weingärtner, *Human Rights on the Ecumenical Agenda: Report and Assessment* (Geneva: Commission of the Churches on International Affairs, World Council of Churches, 1983), 11. See Charles E. Curran, "Religious Freedom and Human Rights in the World and the Church: A Christian Perspective," in *Religious Liberty and Human Rights in Nations and Religions*, ed. Leonard Swidler (Philadelphia: Ecumenical Press, Temple University, 1986), 152-53.

15.   Tertullian, *Liber ad Scapulam*, 2; PL. I, col. 699; quoted in Gabriel Daly, "Church, State, and the Ideal of Freedom," in *Understanding Human Rights: An Interdisciplinary and Interfaith Study*, ed. Alan D. Falconer (Dublin: Irish School of Ecumenics, 1980), 166.

16.   Daly, "Church, State, and the Ideal of Freedom," 167-68.

17.   John Langan, "Human Rights in Roman Catholicism," in *Human Rights in Religious Traditions*, ed. Arlene Swidler (New York: The Pilgrim Press, 1982).

18.   Hersch Lauterpacht, *An International Bill of the Rights of Man* (New York: Columbia University Press, 1945), 4.

19.   Pius IX, *Syllabus of Errors*, in *Church and State through the Centuries*, ed. and trans. Sidney Ehler and John Morrall (London: Burns and Oates, 1954), 284-85. Quoted in John Langan, "Human Rights in Roman Catholicism," in *Human Rights in Religious Traditions*, 31.

20.   John Langan, "Human Rights in Roman Catholicism," in *Human Rights in Religious Traditions*, 32.

21.   J. Robert Nelson, "Human Rights in Creation and Redemption: A Protestant View," in *Human Rights in Religious Traditions*, 1.

22.   These early liberal movements and their descendants—Free Congregations, Liberal Protestant churches, Brethren churches, Mennonites, Unitarians, and others—carry on this tradition today. Many are represented in the International Association for Religious Freedom, which in 1987 pledged its support for "all who are working toward world understanding and peace, and toward promoting the dignity and rights of human beings everywhere." "1987 IARF World Congress Declaration," IARF World Congress: Proceedings (Frankfurt, Federal Republic of Germany: IARF, 1987), 31.

23.   Max L. Stackhouse, "Piety, Polity, and Policy," in *Religious Beliefs, Human Rights, and the Moral Foundation of Western Democracy*, ed. Carl H. Esbeck (Columbia: University of Missouri, 1986), 15. Harlan Cleveland writes: "The kernel of human rights was always there—in the idea that Adam was created in the image of God, and in the practice of a few of

the many—the civil disobedience which brought Daniel to the lions' den, the claim of the early Christians that Rome governed by transgressing the dictates of the divine, the resentment of oppression that brought the Puritans to America, all precedents for Martin Luther King who violated American laws as contrary to the laws of God. Only with the Enlightenment comes the idea that every human being has rights that are to be recognized, even protected, but are not conferred, by society." Quoted in Jonathan Power, *Against Oblivion: Amnesty International's Fight for Human Rights* (Great Britain: Fontana Paperback, 1981), 217.

24.   Max L. Stackhouse, "Piety, Polity, and Policy," in *Religious Beliefs, Human Rights, and the Moral Foundation of Western Democracy*, 16.

25.   Elaine Pagels, "The Roots and Origins of Human Rights," in *Human Dignity: The Internationalization of Human Rights*, ed. Alice Henkin (New York: Aspen Institute for Humanistic Studies, 1979), 4.

26.   Louis Henkin, "Judaism and Human Rights," *Judaism: A Quarterly Journal of Jewish Life and Thought* 25, no. 4 (1976):437.

27.   Louis Henkin, *The Rights of Man Today*, 4.

28.   Stanley S. Harakas, "Human Rights: An Eastern Orthodox Perspective," in *Human Rights in Religious Traditions*, 14.

29.   Carl F. H. Henry, "The Judeo-Christian Heritage and Human Rights," in *Religious Beliefs, Human Rights, and the Moral Foundation of Western Democracy*, 30.

30.   Ibid.

31.   Kana Mitra, "Human Rights in Hinduism," in *Human Rights and Religious Traditions*, 79.

32.   Hersch Lauterpacht, *International Law: Being the Collected Papers of H. Lauterpacht*, ed. E. Lauterpacht, vol. 2 (Cambridge: Cambridge University Press, 1975), 47.

33.   Quoted in J. G. Starke, "Human Rights and International Law," in *Human Rights*, ed. Eugene Kamenka and Alice Erh-Soon Tay (New York: St. Martin's Press, 1978), 118. The "four freedoms" are freedom of speech, freedom of religion, freedom from fear, and freedom from want.

34.   Quoted in Egan Schwelb, *Human Rights and the International Community: The Roots and Growth of the Universal Declaration of Human Rights, 1948-1963* (Chicago: Quadrangle Books, 1964), 25. This book was published for the B'nai B'rith, International Council, Anti-Defamation League of B'nai B'rith, and the U.S. Committee for the United Nations.

35.   Louis Henkin, "Rights: American and Human," *Columbia Law Review* 79, no. 3 (April 1979):410. Rebecca J. Cook writes: "The origin of modern international law in the natural law tradition shows that the recent growth of human rights law is faithful to the moral principles of international legal humanitarianism which developed through both religiously inspired and secular scholarship." Cook, "Human Rights and Infant Survival: A Case for Priorities," *Columbia Human Rights Law Review* 18, no. 1 (Fall-Winter 1986-1987):3.

36.   John Humphrey, "The Revolution in the International Law of Human Rights," *Human Rights* 4, no. 2 (Spring 1975):209. See also Humphrey, "The International Bill of Rights: Part One," in *Philosophical Foundations of Human Rights* (Paris: UNESCO, 1986), 59-72. Allessandra Luini de Russo asserts that until 1948 "it was the consensus of opinion among jurists, diplomats and internationalists in general, that the question of fundamental freedoms was to be solved exclusively on the national level." Allessandra Luini de Russo, *International Protection of Human Rights* (Washington, D.C.: Lerner Law Book Co., 1971), 252. René Cassin, who represented France in the Human Rights Commission that drafted the Universal Declaration, writes: "In the area of human rights, which is linked with the maintenance of peace, we are witnessing a trend towards divesting the State of its traditional *exclusive* domestic competence." Cassin, "Man and the Modern State," in *An Introduction to the Study of Human Rights*, ed. Sir Francis Vallat (London: Europa Publications, 1970), 45. And Jerome Shestack, after noting the dismal record in enforcing human rights law, observes

that nonetheless human rights are embraced by "the masses of the world" and thus "Human right may well turn out to be the true revolutionary movement of our time." Shestack, "The World Had a Dream," *Human Rights* 15, no. 2 (Summer 1988):45.

37.   Egan Schwelb, *Human Rights and the International Community*, 25.

38.   James Frederick Green, "NGOs," in *Human Rights and World Order*, 90. The growing influence of nongovernmental organizations on the development of international human rights law has led to a profusion of organizations. At the UN, over fifty NGO observers are members of the NGO Human Rights Committee. Directories published by Human Rights Internet list over seven hundred organizations in the U.S. and Canada, nearly fourteen hundred in Western Europe, and over six hundred in the Third World. See Lowell W. Livezey, *Nongovernmental Organizations and the Ideas of Human Rights* (Princeton, N.J.: Center of International Studies, Princeton University, 1988).

39.   Helle Kanger, *Human Rights in the United Nations Declaration* (Stockholm: Almquist and Wiksell Int., 1984), 14.

40.   Ibid. Abdullahi Ahmed An-Na'im notes that Egypt supported the amendment to the Dumbarton Oaks proposal to require the UN Charter to include obligations to promote respect for human rights. An-Na'im, "Religious Freedom in Egypt: Under the Shadow of the Islamic *Dhimma* System," in *Religious Liberty and Human Rights in Nations and in Religions*, ed. Leonard Swidler (Philadelphia: Ecumenical Press, Temple University, 1986), 48.

41.   N. Robinson, *The Universal Declaration of Human Rights* (New York: Institute of Jewish Affairs, 1958), 102-05.

42.   Hersch Lauterpacht, *An International Bill of the Rights of Man*, v. In 1943 Jacques Maritain published a scheme of human rights in *The Rights of Man and Natural Law*, trans. Doris C. Anson (New York: Charles Scribner's Sons, 1943), 111-14. This scheme is excerpted as appendix C in *Human Rights: Problems, Perspectives and Texts*, ed. F. E. Dowrick (England: Saxon House, 1979), 148-49.

43.   Hersch Lauterpacht, *An International Bill of the Rights of Man*, 69.

44.   UN GAOR 933, UN Doc. A/777 (1948). Nations abstaining were Byelorussia, Czechoslovakia, Poland, Saudi Arabia, the Ukraine, South Africa, the USSR, and Yugoslavia.

45.   John P. Humphrey, *Human Rights and the United Nations: A Great Adventure* (Dobbs Ferry, N.Y.: Transnational Publishers, 1984), 74.

46.   J. E. S. Fawcett, "Human Rights: The Applicability of International Instruments," in *Human Rights: Problems, Perspectives and Texts*, 78.

47.   G. I. A. D. Draper, "Human Rights and the Law of War," *Virginia Journal of International Law* 12 (1971-72):336. Philip C. Jessup, a former member of the International Court of Justice, argues: "It is already law at least for members of the United Nations, that respect for human dignity and fundamental rights is obligatory. The duty is imposed by the Charter, a treaty to which they are parties." Quoted in Frank C. Newman, "Past Problems and Future Directions," in *International Human Rights Law and Practice: The Roles of the United Nations, the Private Sector, the Government, and Their Lawyers*, ed. James C. Tuttle (Philadelphia: International Printing Co., 1978), 254.

48.   United Nations Document A/CN. 4/245, 23 April 1971, 196: Survey of International Law, a working paper prepared by the Secretary-General of the United Nations for the International Law Commission.

49.   John P. Humphrey, "The Revolution in the International Law of Human Rights," 207. Thomas Buergenthal and Judith V. Torney take the same position in *International Human Rights and International Education*, 49-50. Richard B. Bilder asserts that however one evaluates the arguments, "the Declaration is frequently invoked as if it were legally binding, both by nations and by private individuals and groups." Bilder, "An Overview of International Human Rights Law," in *Guide to International Human Rights Practice*, ed. Hurst Hannum (Philadelphia: University of Pennsylvania Press, 1984), 11.

50.   *Thirty Years of Human Rights at the United Nations: The Record and the Prospects* (New York: Columbia University in the City of New York, 1979), 12. U Thant, as Secretary-General of the UN, later echoed this sentiment. See Schwelb, *Human Rights and the International Community*, 7.

51.   Arthur Holcombe, "Human Rights under the United Nations Charter," *Law and Contemporary Problems* 14, no. 3 (Summer 1949):433. On the occasion of the twentieth anniversary of the Universal Declaration of Human Rights, the President's Commission for the Observance of the Human Rights Year 1968 published a selection of documents and statements updating a similar publication by the Department of State in 1949 entitled *Human Rights, Unfolding of the American Tradition* (Washington, D.C.: U.S. Department of State, 1968). On the page before the foreword, quotes from the 1776 Declaration of Independence and the 1948 Universal Declaration of Human Rights are printed side by side.

52.   J. H. Burns, "The Rights of Man since the Reformation: An Historical Survey," in *An Introduction to the Study of Human Rights*, 29.

53.   Edward Kennedy, "Never Again," *Human Rights* 13, no. 3 (Summer 1986):32. This article is excerpted from remarks made when Senator Kennedy received an award from the International Human Rights Law Group in Washington, D.C., 13 May 1986.

54.   Benjamin B. Ferencz, prosecutor at the Nuremberg war crimes trials, asserts with Ken Keyes, Jr. that "*International concern for human rights and welfare is a great historical force of our time.*" They also proclaim as "the ultimate human right" the right "to live in a peaceful world free from the threat of death by nuclear war," as this right "makes possible all of our other rights and goals." Ferencz and Keyes, *PlanetHood: The Key to Your Survival and Prosperity* (Coos Bay, Ore.: Vision Books, 1988), 87 and 1-2. Italics in the original.

55.   Myers McDougal and Gertrude Leighton, "The Rights of Man in the World Community: Constitutional Illusions versus Rational Action," *Law and Contemporary Problems* 14, no. 3 (Summer 1949):490.

56.   Quoted in Seán MacBride, "The Universal Declaration—Thirty Years After," in *Understanding Human Rights*, 10.

57.   Pierre de Senarclens, "Research and Teaching of Human Rights: Introductory Remarks," in *Frontiers of Human Rights Education*, 9. This language of convergence is criticized for being ambiguous by Timothy Fuller in his "Commentary" on Mark L. Schneider's essay, "Tenets of Official Policy on Human Rights," in *Rights and Responsibilities: International, Social, and Individual Dimensions* (Los Angeles: University of California Press, 1980), 210-11. However, in an essay entitled "A Bedrock Consensus of Human Rights," Thomas W. Wilson, Jr. writes that the issue of human rights "has burst the sacred bounds of national sovereignty." In *Human Dignity: The Internationalization of Human Rights*, 47.

58.   James Nickel, *Making Sense of Human Rights: Philosophical Reflections on the Universal Declaration of Human Rights* (Berkeley: University of California Press, 1987), xi. The reasons for the flourishing of human rights are obviously complex. For instance, Amnesty International, which today provides invaluable advocacy in defense of the human rights of prisoners of conscience, was founded by Peter Benenson. Why did he do it? "We know from things he's said that Eleanor Roosevelt and Martin Luther King were influences, yet in his own chemistry there was his Jewish background, the bell of the Holocaust still tolling, and his Catholic belief, shaped in part by the peasant Pope, John XXIII, who stripped layers off an ossified, even corrupt church and revealed the freshness of the liberating teaching of Jesus of Nazareth beneath." Jonathan Power, *Against Oblivion: Amnesty International's Fight for Human Rights*, 218.

59.   Henkin, *The Rights of Man Today*, 27-28.

60.   Jacques Maritain, *Man and the State* (Chicago: University of Chicago Press, 1951), 111.

PART I

CHRISTIAN SUPPORT FOR HUMAN RIGHTS

Chapter 1

LIBERAL PROTESTANTS

It is not particularly surprising to find liberal Protestants supporting human rights. The liberal Protestant lobby was active among the nongovernmental organizations which were successful in having human rights provisions written into the UN Charter and the Universal Declaration of Human Rights. Moreover, individual leaders of mainstream Protestant churches have long spoken out strongly on human rights issues.

However, the story behind the development of the theology and the international movement which sustains such witness is less well known. In particular, the crucial role played by the World Council of Churches has received little attention. In this chapter I will describe the significant support of liberal Protestants for human rights.

Theological Justification

Methodist theologian J. Robert Nelson offers a fine summary of a liberal Protestant position on human rights. He writes that "Concern for the integrity, worth, and dignity of persons is the basic presupposition of human rights."[1] Such concern requires at least three personal freedoms: "freedom of conscience, freedom from unjust exploitation or oppression, and freedom to live a properly human life."[2] Nelson affirms that "Christian faith, as based upon biblical teaching and expressed in the experience of believers through the centuries, assuredly affirms these freedoms."[3] Furthermore, he asserts: "Of the three main divisions of Christianity, Protestantism enjoys the best, but not an unsullied, reputation for securing, extending, and enhancing human freedoms."[4]

He suggests that within the Protestant tradition Calvinism has served more "as stimulus and tutor to human rights" than Lutheranism, because

Calvinist theology fostered the rise of democratic government based on the notion of a covenant.[5] Therefore: "It is not coincidental that the constitutional document of Woodrow Wilson's League of Nations was called the Covenant, and the covenant concept persists in the United Nations' program to further human rights."[6]

However, often the Protestant view of human rights is flawed in its emphasis that each person is of "infinite value," as "liberal Protestants usually say," in that the claim of one person to a human right cannot in all cases be held to be absolute:

> The right of one member of the community must not be used to override the well-being of the whole, any more than the whole community may annul the right of any one member. The individual always exists in community, and it is within this community that the truly personal character of the individual's life is realized.[7]

Clearly for many Protestants, despite their great emphasis on individual rights, "it is the intimacy and solidarity of members of the community which are the distinctive signs of their concept of the church."[8] However, it is equally clear that Orthodox and Roman Catholic Christians have often defended these communal values more vigorously than Protestants.

Nelson suggests that the concept of the church in the teachings of the apostle Paul provides a check on individualism. Paul argues that the gifts of the Spirit must be used for the good of the church community (1 Cor. 12:26; 14:12). Moreover, "Paul gave an exemplary instance of the application of human rights within a communal context when he instructed the Corinthian Christians about their dispute over eating sacrificed meat."[9] He told the Corinthian Christians, who claimed a right to eat meat used in pagan sacrifices, that for the sake of other Christians who opposed this practice they should waive their right. Nelson concludes: "The right of the individual was here subordinated to the welfare of the community, but it was a freely chosen abstinence in which his right was weighed against a more important responsibility (1 Cor. 8)."[10]

The Protestant tradition embraces this notion that the church consists of the voluntary association of believers. In this "gathered church" the individual precedes, at least theologically, the organization of the church, and thus the members of the church are not inert building blocks in some impersonal edifice but "living stones" in the corporate "temple" (1 Pet. 2:5). Nelson suggests that this type of ecclesiological concept has for the last four centuries "contributed to the most overt and persistent championing of human rights."[11]

World Council of Churches

The World Council of Churches is the Protestant international and ecumenical voluntary association most directly involved in the struggle for human rights.[12] Max Stackhouse asserts that the World Council of Churches "has done more for human rights among the peoples of the world than any other single international body."[13] He also argues that "the principles which were enunciated in the United Nations Declaration on Human Rights after World War II can not be accurately understood" unless the liberal Protestant tradition is "seen as part of the background of its essential shape and content, and the conciliar organizations of ecumenical Protestantism are [seen as] clearly dedicated to those principles."[14]

The involvement of the World Council of Churches in the struggle for human rights dates back to its inception. At the inaugural Assembly in Amsterdam in 1948, the members of the WCC affirmed:

We are profoundly concerned by evidence from many parts of the world of flagrant violations of human rights. Both individuals and groups are subjected to persecution and discrimination on grounds of race, color, religion, culture or political conviction. Against such actions, whether of governments, officials, or the general public, the churches must take a firm and vigorous stand, through local action, in cooperation with churches in other lands, and through international institutions of legal order. They must work for an ever wider and deeper understanding of what are the essential human rights if men are to be free to do the will of God.[15]

In the early years of the WCC its concern with human rights was dominated by the Western emphasis on individual civil and political rights, with a particular concern for religious liberty. However, by the mid 1960s human rights were understood more broadly, and at the Geneva Conference in 1966 a scale of values was developed "with human rights at the top" rather than simply freedom of religion.[16]

Through the years the WCC not only changed its conception of human rights, as international law developed through the United Nations, but also changed its composition to include many independent Third World churches. Today the WCC espouses an ecumenical theological position on human rights which is greatly shaped by the concerns of Third World Christians:

For instance, human beings are seen to possess a transcendental worth not subordinate to any other end, a conception which is incompatible with material conceptions or systems which result in materialistic goals and life-styles. Human dignity is therefore inherent to all individuals. Human rights are not ends in themselves, but the conditions for the realization of human dignity.

Since all dimensions of human dignity are considered, economic, social and cultural rights are stressed to the same extent as civil and political rights. Therefore the church must make a preferential option for the poor, rather than giving primacy to individual freedoms over, or even at the expense of, basic human necessities.[17]

As the task of the church is to enable or assist rather than enact or enforce human rights, "there is less emphasis on the question of legal enforcement than on the creation of conditions conducive to the realization of human rights, including the elimination of root causes of human rights violations."[18]

The World Council of Churches has long involved churches from Eastern Europe as well as the Western hemisphere and Western Europe. Many in the churches of Eastern Europe have supported the construction of socialism in their countries "out of a genuine Christian concern for the collective welfare of the people."[19]

This became clear in 1974 when a working group of Christians from the predominantly Protestant German Democratic Republic (East Germany) submitted a paper on human rights at an ecumenical consultation held at St. Pölten, Austria by the Commission of the Churches on International Affairs (CCIA) of the WCC.[20] They argued that "the inviolability of life, dignity and property are not a constitutive element of the human being," as these rights belong to God alone.[21] Moreover, at the Fifth Assembly of the WCC in 1975 in Nairobi, the churches of Eastern Europe sided with the Russian Orthodox Church in defending the evolution of democratic principles under socialism against those who, in the wake of the Helsinki Declaration, wanted a resolution from the WCC condemning the Soviet Union.

The report of the Nairobi Assembly was "a remarkable milestone in the ecumenical understanding of human rights" for two reasons: the question of religious liberty had become "inseparable from other fundamental human rights" and "for the first time in ecumenical history, the churches arrived at a consensus regarding the *content* of human rights."[22] This consensus is set forth in terms of the six headings developed at St. Pölten:

1. the right to basic guarantees of life,
2. the rights to self-determination and to cultural identity, and the rights of minorities,
3. the right to participate in decision-making within the community,
4. the right to dissent,
5. the right to personal dignity,
6. the right to religious freedom.[23]

Throughout 1976 discussion between church representatives of Eastern and Western Europe focussed on the Helsinki Declaration and the

involvement of the WCC in human rights issues in Europe.

In 1979 the World Council of Churches took the position that the responsibility for human rights work was primarily that of local, national and regional church bodies. In a report to the 1979 meeting of the WCC Central Committee in Jamaica, it also affirmed the notion of *international ecumenical solidarity*:

> This concept rests on the responsibility of churches within the ecumenical community to support each other morally, materially and politically. It implies that many churches live in situations so grave that they cannot cope with the problems using their own resources alone. It also implies, however, that help must be sought by those in need, and must not be imposed however well meant, from the outside. In addition, it takes seriously the fact that in an interdependent world, the causes of human rights violations, or the insufficient realization of human rights, are rarely phenomena limited to any given local situation, but are linked with a variety of international structural dependencies.[24]

As "a switching station among the many member churches," the WCC "stimulates the churches in each region to take seriously the human rights aspects of a variety of church concerns, draws the attention of churches to human rights problems in their own region of which they may not be aware, and assists churches and church agencies to fulfill these responsibilities."[25]

Although the bulk of the WCC's involvement in human rights is administered by the Commission of the Churches on International Affairs, "almost all programs of the WCC, in all subunits and units, have elements of work directly or indirectly relevant to human rights."[26] It is mainly through the CCIA, however, that the WCC engages in monitoring human rights violations, in advocacy to promote human rights, and in the study of human rights issues.

The CCIA in 1979 offered to coordinate an "Interconfessional Study Project on the Theological Basis of Human Rights"; the Christian groups that chose to participate included the World Alliance of Reformed Churches, the Lutheran World Federation, the Preparatory Committee of the Pan-Orthodox Council, the Baptist World Alliance, the Anglican Consultative Council, the World Methodist Council, the Reformed Ecumenical Synod, and the Pontifical Commission *Justitia et Pax*. Although the justification for human rights had long been assumed by those active in the WCC, more conservative elements within the Protestant community were demanding a theological rationale.

The St. Pölten report in 1974 set forth the foundation for Christian support for human rights in very general terms:

> It is our conviction that the emphasis of the Gospel is upon the value of all human beings in the sight of God, on the atoning and redeeming work of Christ that has given to man his true dignity, on love as the motive for action, and on love for one's neighbor as the practical expression of an active faith in Christ.[27]

In 1976, after six years of study, the Lutheran World Federation Consultation on Human Rights published a report containing the following statement:

> Being aware of the unconditional acceptance of man by God in Christ, we affirm that the Church is a community in which Christians accept each other unconditionally and extend the same love to all people. This gift commits the Church to respect and to promote the understanding and the implementation of human rights.[28]

The Lutherans followed Heinz-Eduard Tödt[29] and Wolfgang Huber in structuring human rights around the concepts of freedom, equality and participation, which are said to be biblically justified as the basic elements of all human rights. Nelson observes that the Lutherans did not just "baptize" the Universal Declaration of Human Rights, "but see in its rights the secular analogies to the essential terms of the Gospel by which all persons should be able to live."[30]

The Calvinist theologians involved in consultations sponsored by the World Alliance of Reformed Churches were led by Jürgen Moltmann to identify a different set of three fundamental principles: "liberation by Jesus Christ, creation in the image of God, and hope in the coming Reign of God."[31] "As translated into the language of rights," these dynamic concepts "speak of the activity of God in human history, recreating in Christ the persons who were first created in the divine image, and providing them hope, despite privation and suffering, for liberation of life in society to its fulfillment in God's purpose."[32] However, the Reformed theologians agree with the Lutheran theologians that all human rights are under the sovereignty of God, the Creator and the Redeemer: "Human rights are not, therefore, given in the laws of creation, in natural law."[33]

In his book *On Human Dignity: Political Theology and Ethics*, published seven years after these consultations, Moltmann reflects on this period of intense theological reflection within the Protestant traditions. He notes that the CCIA of the World Council of Churches was involved in human rights advocacy from the time of the Universal Declaration through the development of the international human rights covenants passed by the UN General Assembly in 1966 up through their ratification and coming into force in 1976. At the same time the Roman Catholic Church was clarifying its position, in a "Message Concerning Human Rights and Reconciliation" by the Roman Synod of Bishops and the working paper, "The Church and Human Rights," by the Pontifical Commission *Justitia et Pax*.[34]

Moltmann clearly acknowledges that since the 1974 St. Pölten conference, "socialist concepts of human rights" have been discussed openly in
Protestant circles.[35] More recently, Third World concerns have come to
dominate:

> The history of the ecumenical discussion concerning human rights shows a
> quite striking development from the almost entirely accepted predominance of
> the Western civil-liberal view of human rights and the social rights of the
> human community to the eventual perception of the life interests of the Third
> World.[36]

Moreover, he affirms that Christianity "has trod a common path in the
ecumenical movement" and thus "preserved its solidarity in the three
worlds" in spite of conflicts. Therefore, he asserts that the "advancement
of human rights"

> has become the framework of ecumenical politics and ethics. Liberation,
> development, passive and active resistance, the overcoming of racism,
> economic aid to developing countries, nuclear reactors, and the building up
> of a sustainable society are discussed today within the framework of human
> rights. For church guidelines on political and social matters gain their universal
> significance only through reference to human rights.[37]

By involving itself in the struggle for human rights, Moltmann affirms, "the
church becomes the church for the world."[38]

This ferment of theological activity in the late 1970s was accompanied
in the World Council of Churches by numerous published reports on
human rights by the CCIA concerning violations in specific situations and
strategies for protest and support.[39] In addition, in 1978 an ecumenical
and international Human Rights Advisory Group was established out of
the "conviction that God wills a society in which all can exercise full
human rights."[40] In 1980 the Human Rights Advisory Group unanimously
recommended that "human rights education" be developed at all levels:
"local congregations, national church leaders, grass roots groups, families,
Sunday schools, confirmation classes, theological institutions, as well as
the whole realm of secular schools, trade unions, political parties, social
action groups, etc."[41] Then in 1981 the Human Rights Advisory Group
asserted:

> As the churches and groups of Christians have become more actively engaged
> in the defense of human rights, we have experienced this divisiveness in our
> own midst. We are in need of the mediation of the Spirit to reconcile us and
> to strengthen our unity as we seek to be faithful to the demands of the
> Gospel.[42]

It also affirmed that "work for human rights can forge new bonds of unity within and between the churches, and with people of other faiths or those motivated by secular inspiration whom we encounter in the struggle for justice. . . ."[43]

In the report of the 1980 Melbourne Conference, the kingdom of God and the struggles for human rights are directly related:

> The worldwide church is itself a sign of the kingdom of God because it is the Body of Christ in the world. It is called to be an instrument of the kingdom of God by continuing Christ's mission to the world in a struggle for the growth of all human beings into the fullness of life. This means proclaiming God's judgment upon any authority, power or force, which would openly or by subtle means deny people their full human rights.[44]

Therefore, *"Participation in struggles for human rights is in itself a central element in the total mission of the church to proclaim by word and act the crucified and risen Christ."*[45]

Publications

The publications of the WCC contain numerous statements and articles on human rights concerns and activities all over the world and provide a history of the development of human rights affirmations from earlier liberal concepts to present Third World notions.

In the April 1975 issue of *The Ecumenical Review*, the quarterly of the WCC, we find the following affirmations of human rights. Julio Barreiro writes from Latin America: "We believe that human dignity is the dignity of the children of God. The defense of human rights implies an obstinate struggle against modern dictatorships which deny the possibility of such dignity."[46] The Human Rights Working Group of the Christian Conference of Asia in 1974 affirms that the power of the state is not absolute: "We believe that man has the inherent right to witness to the truth."[47] A human rights paper, prepared by the UN Working Group of the GDR Regional Committee of the Christian Peace Conference, is published.[48] Burgess Carr, Secretary-General of the All Africa Conference of Churches, shares with readers a paper entitled "Biblical and Theological Basis for the Struggle for Human Rights," which he presented at the consultation on human rights held in Khartoum, 16-22 February 1975.[49] David Jenkins supports the thesis that "The struggle for human rights requires no theological justification."[50] Finally, Swedish theologian Gustav Wingren analyzes the human rights responsibility of the churches.[51]

Numerous other articles affirming human rights have appeared in theological journals in the United States.[52] Furthermore, denominational

publications of the member churches of the World Council of Churches carry news stories and appeals, as in the "Soapbox" piece in the weekly publication of the Christian Church,[53] the column in the *Baptist Times* urging President Reagan to sign the UN treaty condemning torture,[54] and the article in the newsletter of the Episcopal Church of New York on its peace and justice network.[55] In addition, various church groups are reported to be carrying out human rights programs of different kinds.[56]

In 1983 Ninan Koshy of the World Council of Churches wrote that

> The struggle for human rights takes place in each situation where our member churches live. The test of the concern of the churches for human rights is in ensuring that involvement in and support for this struggle is part of their witness.[57]

For Sithembiso Nyoni of Zimbabwe, this means: "Christians in the poor nations have to be Christ's ambassadors, encouraging, developing and defending the rights of the poor."[58]

Similarly, Metropolitan Geevarghese Mar Osthathios, Principal of the Orthodox Theological Seminary in Kerala, India, asserts that

> To identify with the poor and fight for their rights is not a theology of combat or a utopian dream of a classless society. Those who pray "Your kingdom come, your will be done on earth . . ." have a duty to work for the goal implied in the prayer.[59]

In the words of theologian F. Ross Kinsler, the mission of the church involves "struggles for human rights" because it "is the mission of God's redemptive kingdom, which transforms human life in all its relationships."[60]

Human Rights: A Challenge to Theology, published by the WCC with IDOC International in 1983, is notable in that it contains only a brief chapter in Part I on the justification of human rights but devotes twenty-five chapters in Part II to ethical issues relating to the struggle for human rights in the Third World. Five of these chapters are written by Roman Catholics, and other chapters are reports from ecumenical conferences involving both Protestants and Roman Catholics.[61] In fact, Part II begins with just such an ecumenical working document, "The Challenge of Reality to Theology," from the Fifth Conference of the Ecumenical Association of Third World Theologians (EATWOT), which met in New Delhi in August of 1981.

Conclusion

Liberal Christian organizations, and in particular the World Council of Churches, have been in the forefront of the human rights movement since its beginning in this century. Moreover, the changes in international human rights law in the last four decades are clearly reflected in the teaching and work of the World Council of Churches today. Law and theology are evolving together.

Liberal Protestant theologians from different denominational backgrounds continue to differ over theological categories. However, they agree on the content of human rights, for they support the Universal Declaration of Human Rights and the international covenants developed to implement it.

Today, in the crucible of the Third World, the religious ethics of human rights is being reformed along with the law of human rights. Here Protestants and Roman Catholics are joining together with others of good will in a common struggle for the conditions of human dignity. They are united by the universality of God's love, which Christians affirm is offered as a gift through Jesus Christ. Christian supporters of human rights are concerned with more than material human sustenance, because they believe that "human rights belong to our redemption, not just to our creation."[62]

Notes

1. J. Robert Nelson, "Human Rights in Creation and Redemption: A Protestant View," in *Human Rights in Religious Traditions*, ed. Arlene Swidler (New York: The Pilgrim Press, 1982), 1.
2. Ibid.
3. Ibid.
4. Ibid.
5. Ibid., 2.
6. Ibid.
7. Ibid., 3.
8. Ibid.
9. Ibid.
10. Ibid., 4.
11. Ibid.
12. For a brief analysis of the WCC's human rights activity, see Marc Lienhard, "Protestantism and Human Rights," in *Human Rights Teaching* 2, no. 1 (1981), 24-37.
13. Max L. Stackhouse, "Public Theology, Human Rights and Mission," in *Human Rights and the Global Mission of the Church* (Cambridge, Mass.: Boston Theological Institute, 1985), 16.
14. Ibid.
15. *Report of the Church and the Disorder of Society*, WCC First Assembly, Amsterdam, 1948. Quoted in Erich Weingärtner, *Human Rights on the Ecumenical Agenda: Report and*

Assessment (Geneva: Commission of the Churches on International Affairs, World Council of Churches, 1983), 8.

16.   David J. Bosch, "The Melbourne Conference: Between Guilt and Hope," *International Review of Mission* 69, nos. 276-77 (October 1980-January 1981):515.

17.   Erich Weingärtner, *Human Rights on the Ecumenical Agenda*, 11.

18.   Ibid.

19.   Ibid., 20.

20.   See Günter Krusche, "Human Rights in a Theological Perspective: A Contribution from the GDR," *Lutheran World* 1 (1977):59-65.

21.   "The Meaning of Human Rights and the Problems They Pose," *The Ecumenical Review* 27 (April 1975):143.

22.   Erich Weingärtner, *Human Rights on the Ecumenical Agenda*, 24.

23.   Ibid.

24.   Ibid., 30.

25.   Ibid.

26.   Ibid., 32.

27.   *Human Rights and Christian Responsibility*, Report of the Consultation, St. Pölten, Austria, 21-26 October 1974 (Geneva: World Council of Churches, 1975).

28.   Report from Working Group III, "The Responsibility of the Church for Promoting Human Rights," *Theological Perspectives on Human Rights*, ed. Jorgen Lissner. Report on an LWF Consultation on Human Rights, 29 June-3 July 1976 (Geneva: Lutheran World Federation, 1977), 27.

29.   See Heinz-Eduard Tödt, "Theological Reflections on the Foundations of Human Rights," *Lutheran World* 1 (1977):45-58.

30.   Robert J. Nelson, "Human Rights in Creation and Redemption," in *Human Rights and Religious Traditions*, 11.

31.   Ibid. See Jan Milic Lochman, "Um eine christliche Perspektive für die Menschenrechte," *Reformatio* 25 (July-August 1976):418; and Jürgen Moltmann, "Christian Faith and Human Rights," in *Understanding Human Rights*, 182-95. See *A Christian Declaration of Human Rights*, ed. Allen O. Miller (Grand Rapids, Mich.: Wm. B. Eerdmans, 1977), for an English translation by Catherine Keller of Lochman's paper and for papers by Moltmann entitled "The Original Study Paper: The Theological Basis of Human Rights and of the Liberation of Human Beings" (1971), translated by M. Douglas Weeks, and "A Definitive Study Paper: A Christian Declaration on Human Rights" (1977), 25-34 and 129-43, respectively, and for other related materials.

32.   Robert J. Nelson, "Human Rights in Creation and Redemption," in *Human Rights in Religious Traditions*, 12.

33.   Ibid.

34.   See *The Gospel of Peace and Justice: Catholic Social Teaching since Pope John*, ed. Joseph Gremillion (Maryknoll, N.Y.: Orbis Books, 1976), 513-629; and "Working Paper No. 1," *The Church and Human Rights* (Vatican City: Pontifical Commission *Justitia et Pax*, 1975).

35.   Jürgen Moltmann, *On Human Dignity: Political Theology and Ethics*, trans. M. Douglas Meeks (Philadelphia: Fortress Press, 1984), 6.

36.   Ibid. Early in the 1970s Latin Americans raised issues about the individualistic orientation of Western concepts of human rights. Warren Lee Holleman reports that in 1973 delegates from Uruguay to the Second General Assembly of the Latin American Council of the Protestant Methodist Church pointed out that one of the first references to human rights, in the writings of Spanish philosopher Alfonso el Sabio, affirms the "right of the peoples (*derecho de gentes*)" rather than individual rights. Holleman, *The Human Rights Movement: Western Values and Theological Perspectives* (New York: Praeger, 1987), 22. See "The

Application of Human Rights in Latin America," in Commission of Churches, *Human Rights and Christian Responsibility*, Dossier 1 (May 1974), 42.

37. Ibid.

38. Ibid.

39. See Erich Weingärtner, *Human Rights on the Ecumenical Agenda*, 57-58, for a partial list of publications.

40. Fifth Assembly 11, in "Minutes: XXXII Meeting of the Commission of the Churches on International Affairs," *Commission of the Churches on International Affairs* (April 1977):19.

41. Erich Weingärtner, *Human Rights on the Ecumenical Agenda*, 63. See "Gearing Education to Human Rights Issues," *Education Newsletter* (Office of Education, Program Unit on Education and Renewal, World Council of Churches, no. 1, 1985).

42. Ibid., 66-67.

43. Ibid., 67.

44. Melbourne Conference Section Reports: Good News to the Poor," *International Review of Mission* 69, nos. 276-77 (October 1980-January 1981):401.

45. Ibid., 402. Emphasis in original.

46. Julio Barreiro, "In Defense of Human Rights," *The Ecumenical Quarterly* 27, no. 2 (April 1975):108.

47. Alice Wimer, "One Step on a Journey," *The Ecumenical Review* 27, no. 2 (April 1975):115.

48. "The Meaning of Human Rights and the Problems They Pose," *The Ecumenical Review* 27, no. 2 (April 1975):139-46.

49. Burgess Carr, "Biblical and Theological Basis for the Struggle for Human Rights," *The Ecumenical Review* 27, no. 2 (April 1975):139-46.

50. David Jenkins, "Theological Inquiry Concerning Human Rights," *The Ecumenical Review* 27, no. 2 (April 1975):99.

51. Gustav Wingren, "Human Rights: A Theological Analysis," *The Ecumenical Review* 27, no. 2 (April 1975):124-27.

52. See Robert McAfee Brown, "Human Rights: A Context," *Christianity and Crisis* (27 December 1976):302-16; Donald M. Fraser, "The U.S. and Human Rights," *Christianity and Crisis* 36 (27 December 1976):314-16; Wes Michaelson, "Human Rights: A Surer Standard," *Sojourners* 6 (April 1977):3-5; Ernst Saunders, "The Bible and Human Rights," *Church and Society* 69 (November-December 1978):48-53; Nancy Bancroft, "Christian Human Rights Thought: Can Marxism Contribute?" *Horizons* 8, no. 2 (1981):247-59; Robert V. Rakestraw, "Human Rights and Liberties in the Political Ethics of John Wesley," *Evangelical Journal* 3, no. 2 (1985):63-78; Robert Traer, "Religious Communities in the Struggle for Human Rights," *The Christian Century* 105, no. 27 (28 September 1988):835-38; and Pablo Martinez, "The Right to be Human," *Evangelical Review of Theology* 10, no. 3 (July 1986):270-76. These examples go beyond the liberal Protestant tradition, but are part of its discourse.

53. Gerald Vandezande, "Follow Justice Alone," *The Banner* (26 May 1981):18.

54. "Baptists Press Reagan on Torture," *Baptist Times* (17 April 1986):5.

55. "Anglican Consultative Council, Family Networks Meet," *Diocesan Press Service* (30 April 1987):4-7.

56. For example, Clergy and Laity Concerned identifies in its flyer "Covenant Against Apartheid at Home and Abroad" that one of the program areas of its 54 chapters located in 28 states is "Human Rights and Racial Justice." And a letter from Habitat for Humanity dated 1 January 1988 affirms: "adequate housing must be a basic human right." In its flyer the California/Nevada Interfaith Committee on Corporate Responsibility lists as a present concern "Pressuring Corporations to Protect Human Rights in Central America." And the Peace with Justice Commission of the Northern California Ecumenical Council administers a "Central

American Human Rights/Refugee Project."

57. Ninan Koshy, "Director's Introduction," in Weingärtner, *Human Rights on the Ecumenical Agenda*, 5.

58. Sithembiso Nyoni, "All Christians Are Called to Witness," *International Review of Mission* 72, no. 288 (October 1983):645.

59. Metropolitan Geevarghese Mar Osthathios, "Kingdom of God and Identification with the Poor," *International Review of Mission* 69, nos. 276-77 (October 1980-January 1981):506.

60. F. Ross Kinsler, "Equipping God's People for Mission," *International Review of Mission* 71, no. 282 (April 1982):135.

61. The WCC also collaborated in publishing a book by Archibald A. Evans entitled *Workers' Rights Are Human Rights* (Rome: IDOC International, 1981), containing both Protestant and Roman Catholic positions on human rights and labor issues.

62. Robert J. Nelson, "Human Rights in Creation and Redemption," in *Human Rights in Religious Traditions*, 12. For an ecumenical position that further develops this theology, see Agnes Cunningham, Donald Miller, and James E. Will, "Toward an Ecumenical Theology for Grounding Human Rights," *Soundings* 67, no. 2 (Summer 1984):209-39.

Chapter 2

ROMAN CATHOLICS

Richard McCormick, S.J., a prominent moral theologian, asks: "What is the Church's proper mission in the sphere of the defense and promotion of human rights?"[1] He answers that we know "human dignity" in "the Christ-event and the Church's commission to spread the good news" and thus: "Unless the Church at all levels is an outstanding promoter of the rights of human beings in word and deed, her proclamation will be literally false."[2]

In the context of recent Roman Catholic social teaching, this answer is not surprising. For at least since the momentous encyclical, *Pacem in Terris*, human rights have been the heart of the social teaching of the Roman Catholic Church. In the words of John XXIII, the entire tradition "is always dominated by one basic theme—an unshakable affirmation and vigorous defense of the dignity and rights of the human person."[3]

In this chapter I will describe the development of the Roman Catholic human rights tradition. I will examine the central documents of the tradition. Then I will illustrate how these teachings are being reaffirmed in the church around the globe.

Roots of the Tradition

While the roots of the Roman Catholic human rights tradition extend back to Thomas Aquinas, Augustine, the Bible, and Aristotle, the modern teaching begins with the pontificate of Leo XIII (1878-1903): "It was with Leo XIII that the Church began to move from a stance of adamant resistance to modern Western developments in political and social life to a stance of critical participation in them."[4] Thus partially in response to liberal and socialist assertions Leo XIII affirmed in the 1891 encyclical

Rerum Novarum that "Man precedes the State."[5] Human dignity is the standard for law.

Leo XIII was particularly concerned to clarify "the relative rights and mutual duties of the rich and of the poor, of capital and labor."[6] The encyclical affirms as conditions of human dignity the right to a just wage, the right to use one's earned wages to purchase and own property, and the rights to adequate food, clothing, and shelter. Each of these rights has a corresponding duty:

> Employers are under an obligation to recognize and protect each of these rights. The encyclical, however, is not content with leaving the recognition of these rights to the good will of employers. Workers have the further right to organize associations or unions to defend their just claims. This is a specific form of the more general right of association which belongs to all human persons as both self-determining and social beings.[7]

The state is obligated to protect the common good, "which consists in the mutual respect of rights and the fulfillment of duties by all citizens," and the state also "has a special obligation to defend the rights of the poor and the powerless."[8]

Pius XI (1922-1939) struggled with the implications of these teachings in the context of the great depression, the development of a communist regime in Russia, and the emergence of fascist dictatorships in Germany and Italy. He developed the notion of social justice as a principle for determining the social conditions of human dignity. In *Quadragesimo Anno* (1931) Pius XI reaffirmed the rights articulated in *Rerum Novarum,* and in *Divini Redemptoris* (1937) he set forth a list of rights: "the right to life, to bodily integrity, to the necessary means of existence; the right to tend toward one's ultimate goal in the path marked out by God; the right of association and the right to possess and use property."[9]

In response to the horrors of World War II, repression in the Soviet Union, and the precarious position of the Roman Catholic Church in Eastern Europe after the war, Pius XII (1939-1958) moved human dignity "from the level of a basic but frequently implicit first principle of Roman Catholic social morality to the level of explicit and formal concern."[10] In his Christmas address of 1942 he affirmed that human dignity requires "respect for and the practical realization of the following fundamental personal rights":

> the right to maintain and develop one's corporal, intellectual and moral life and especially the right to religious formation and education; the right to worship God in private and public and to carry on religious works of charity; the right to marry and to achieve the aim of married life; the right to conjugal and domestic society; the right to work, as the indispensable means toward the

maintenance of family life; the right to free choice of a state of life, and hence, too, of the priesthood or religious life; the right to the use of material goods, in keeping with his duties and social limitations.[11]

In that same address Pius XII also asserted that each person has a right to a government which will protect these rights, and in a later address he specified that

The right to existence, the right to one's good name, the right to one's own culture and national character, the right to develop oneself, the right to demand observance of international treaties, and other like rights, are demanded by the law of nations, dictated by nature itself.[12]

As social justice requires a legal system which protects these rights, the authority of the state "is both based on and limited by these fundamental human rights."[13]

Human dignity, as an expression of the common good, is deeply rooted in the Roman Catholic tradition. The concept of *dignitas humanae substantiae* appeared as early as the Christmas Oration containing the earliest collection of prayers in the Western church, namely those in the *Sacramentarium Leonianum*, and was included in the Oration in the Holy Mass to be spoken after the offering.[14] This Oration begins with the words: "God, who has wondrously created (or established) the dignity of human nature (or existence) and has even more wonderfully transformed it. . . ."[15]

As the separation of church and state developed in the Middle Ages under the influence of the Christian church, the belief that the state was a "sacred community" and each person merely a citizen of it was replaced with the conviction that the individual was a member of the kingdom of God as it was coming into being on earth.[16]

Alfred Verdross asserts that the implications of this shift are enormous, for as a member of the kingdom of God, one

is the owner of certain rights which no earthly community can take. . . . [Thus is] laid the roots of every theory which speaks of unalterable or irrevocable human rights, because such rights can only exist when the authority of the state is limited by a higher order.[17]

Thomas Aquinas agreed with Aristotle that the common good of the state took precedence over the private good of the individual, but affirmed that in matters involving spiritual values the state is without authority. As "the well-being of the soul is not subordinate to the political community entirely in his whole self and with all he possesses,"[18] Aquinas clearly rejected the notion that the state alone determines the rights of its subjects.

During the Christian Middle Ages there was never an all-powerful state, as divine authority was recognized for both the church and the state. However, at the beginning of the modern era Niccoló Machiavelli and Thomas Hobbes denigrated the notion of human dignity and elevated the authority of the state. Hugo Grotius and John Locke were among the major humanist writers who sought to defend the dignity of the individual against the state. Samuel Pufendorf placed the concept of *dignitas naturae humanae* at the center of his theory of natural law, deriving from it "the human rights of freedom and equality."[19] His writings, along with those of Locke and Montesquieu, greatly shaped the early development in America of the concept of separation of church and state, as well as the corresponding notion of the inalienable rights of persons.

The phrase *dignitas humana* first appeared in papal encyclicals in the nineteenth century,[20] but it was not until *Pacem in Terris* that "human dignity" became the foundation for Roman Catholic social teaching.

John Coleman suggests that by itself human dignity may not be an adequate ground for Catholic teaching on human rights, because of its individualistic connotation in the West and because it is rooted in traditional natural law theory which is under attack today.[21] He notes Gregory Baum's similar concern, that a doctrine of human dignity built simply on the notion that the human person has value as created in God's image may not distinguish Catholic social teaching from the liberal political doctrine which only recognizes individual human rights.[22]

However, David Hollenbach argues that the Catholic tradition offers two warrants for the principle of human dignity, as the foundation of all human rights. The first is accessible to all persons, whether they are religious or not: "The imperative arising from human dignity is based on the indicative of the person's transcendence over the world of things."[23] The second is rooted in Christian faith: "The beliefs that all persons are created in the image of God, that they are redeemed by Jesus Christ, and that they are summoned by God to a destiny beyond history serve both to support and to interpret the fundamental significance of human existence."[24] This foundation for human dignity, and thus for human rights, is assumed by the Catholic tradition and developed within it.

John XXIII

John XXIII (1958–1963), in his 1961 encyclical, *Mater et Magistra*, moved toward a notion of human dignity defined more in social and structural terms. Then in *Pacem in Terris* (1961), the most widely acclaimed of modern papal documents, he affirmed that the protection of human rights was the basis for world peace.

Pacem in Terris begins with an affirmation of the central Catholic social teaching of the dignity of the person:

Any human society, if it is to be well ordered and productive, must lay down as a foundation this principle, namely, that every human being is a person, that is, his nature is endowed with intelligence and free will. Indeed, precisely because he is a person he has rights and obligations flowing directly and simultaneously from his very nature. And as these rights are universal and inviolable so they cannot in any way be surrendered.[25]

The encyclical reaffirms Pius XII's assertion that respect for human dignity is possible only within a "community of morally responsible citizens," and *Mater et Magistra's* emphasis on human interdependence in the world:

The rights which protect human dignity, therefore, are the rights of persons in community. They are neither exclusively the rights of individuals against the community nor are they the rights of the community against the individual.[26]

Every right has a corresponding duty to protect that right. Thus both the individual and the state are responsible for the protection of all the rights—social and economic as well as civil and political—which are necessary for human dignity.

Pacem in Terris systematically recapitulates all the rights claims made by the tradition since Leo XIII, including rights asserted by both liberals and socialists. These include:

Rights related to *life* and an adequate *standard of living* are the rights to life, bodily integrity, food, clothing, shelter, rest, medical care, necessary social services, security in case of sickness, unemployment, widowhood, old age or unemployment [*sic*].

As rights concerning *moral and cultural values* the encyclical lists the rights to respect for one's person, to one's good reputation, to freedom of communication, to the pursuit of art, to be informed truthfully; the rights to share in the benefits of culture, to a basic education and to higher education in keeping with the level of development of one's country.

Rights in the area of *religious activity* include the rights to honor God in accord with one's conscience, to practice religion publicly and privately.

In the area of *family* life are the rights to choose one's state of life, that is, to set up a family, with equal rights for men and women, or to choose not to found a family. Also included are the rights to the economic, social, cultural and moral conditions which are necessary for the support of family life, and the prior right of parents to educate their children.

Economic rights include the right to work, the rights to humane working conditions, to appropriate participation in the management of an economic enterprise, to a just wage, to own property within the limits established by social duties.

The encyclical also affirms the rights of *assembly* and *association*, the right to organize societies according to the aim of the members, and the right to organize groups for the purpose of securing goods which the individual cannot attain alone.

All persons have the rights of *freedom of movement* and residence, and to internal and external migration when there is just reason for it.

Political rights include the rights to participate in public affairs and to juridical protection of all one's human rights.[27]

All these human rights are seen in the light of the tradition of Catholic social teaching as the conditions for human dignity.

Among the various "signs of the times" recognized by John XXIII in this encyclical are the advent of the United Nations and the approval of the Universal Declaration of Human Rights. While acknowledging some reservations about the Universal Declaration, John XXIII embraces it "as an important step" on the path toward a world community subject to the rule of law:

> For in it, in most solemn form, the dignity of a human person is acknowledged in all men. And as a consequence there is proclaimed, as a fundamental right, the right of free movement in the search for truth and in the attainment of moral good and of justice, and also the right to a dignified life, while other rights connected with those mentioned are likewise proclaimed.[28]

Thus John XXIII prays for the United Nations: that the day will soon come "when every human being will find therein an effective safeguard for the rights which derive directly from his dignity as a person, and which are therefore universal, inviolable and inalienable rights."[29]

The Second Vatican Council

In 1965 during its last session, the Second Vatican Council approved two significant statements which advance the social teaching of the Roman Catholic Church on human rights. The *Declaration on Religious Liberty (Dignitatis Humanae Personae)*, which is subtitled "On the Right of the Person and of Communities to Social and Civil Freedom in Matters Religious," asserts that religious freedom is fundamental to human dignity:

> This Vatican Synod declares that the human person has a right to religious freedom. . . . The Synod further declares that the right to religious freedom has its foundation in the very dignity of the human person, as this dignity is known through the revealed Word of God and by reason itself.[30]

Furthermore, because people cannot discharge their obligation to seek and do the truth without immunity from coercion, "the right to religious freedom has its foundation, not in the subjective disposition of the person, but in his very nature."[31]

The common welfare of the society requires the social conditions necessary for people to seek to live out their sense of the truth. This welfare consists chiefly

> in the protection of the right, and in the performance of the duties, of the human person. Therefore, the care of the right to religious freedom devolves upon the people as a whole, upon social groups, upon government, and upon the Church and other religious communities, in virtue of the duty of all toward the common welfare, and in the manner proper to each.[32]

Government bears a special responsibility to protect human dignity and to promote "the inviolable rights of man."[33]

Dignitatis Humanae, Hollenbach asserts, provides "an important key to the problem of the foundation, interrelation and institutionalization of human rights":

> Responsible use of freedom defines the very nature of social morality. The definition of the content of this responsibility must occur within the context of changing cultural and social structures. Thus human rights are rights *within society.*[34]

The state may not regulate and order all human interaction but must allow the freedom of persons to act in society.

The *Pastoral Constitution on the Church in the Modern World* (*Gaudium et Spes*) reaffirms that human rights are the necessary conditions for human dignity:

> there is a growing awareness of the exalted dignity proper to the human person, since he stands above all things, and his rights and duties are universal and inviolable. Therefore, there must be made available to all men everything necessary for leading a life truly human, such as food, clothing, and shelter; the right to choose a state of life freely and to found a family, the right to education, to employment, to a good reputation, to respect, to appropriate information, to activity in accord with the upright norm of one's own conscience, to protection of privacy and to rightful freedom in matters religious too.[35]

As God intends that the goods of the earth be used for the common good of all, "The right to have a share of earthly goods sufficient for oneself and one's family belongs to everyone."[36]

Clearly, the Roman Catholic doctrine of human rights differs from the liberal political view "in its distrust of individualism and its emphasis on community."[37] In addition, it is distinct from Protestant affirmations of human rights in that it is presented philosophically rather than in biblical or theological categories. John Langan concludes:

Catholic human-rights doctrine emerges as a comprehensive and generous structure within which religious believers can both share and address the moral dilemmas of a religiously pluralistic and increasingly secular world and which, while not without some internal points of tension and incompleteness, is able to offer shelter to those who are repelled both by the neglect of social and economic rights for the disadvantaged in liberal societies and by the repressiveness of authoritarian and totalitarian regimes.[38]

However, it is not clear in the tradition just what forms of government are best suited to realize the conditions of human dignity.

Hollenbach suggests that this ambiguity is in part the recognition by the Council that human dignity is only realized in particular historical and social circumstances:

Gaudium et Spes thus suggests a fruitful way to combine the traditional view of human rights as rooted in human nature with modern historical consciousness. There are domains of human existence which cannot be suppressed without oppressing human beings. These include respect for the bodily, interpersonal, social-political, economic and cultural dimensions of human existence. Because of the increasing interdependence of persons the means to this respect must be more and more through the organized action of communities and of society as a whole.[39]

Therefore, "social, economic and cultural rights, defined in relation to historical conditions, assume a new place of importance in the Catholic human rights tradition."[40] This allows for diverse forms of human dignity in different cultures.

Paul VI

The encyclicals of Paul VI (1963-1978) on social morality, *Populorum Progressio* (1967) and *Octogesima Adveniens* (1971), refer very little to human rights directly, as they wrestle with the complex questions of economic development in the modern world. Andrew Greeley suggests that this represents a step back from the human rights doctrine of *Pacem in Terris*, but Hollenbach argues it is rather a shift of emphasis reflecting the immediate concerns of the Third World.[41] Furthermore, François

Refoulé asserts, anyone who reviews the writings of Paul VI "cannot but be impressed by the place occupied by the defense of the dignity and rights of man."[42]

In 1972 Paul VI wrote the Secretary-General of the UN: "The Church feels wounded in her own person whenever a man's rights are disregarded or violated, whoever he is and whatever it is about."[43] And his last words at the Synod of Bishops in 1974 were: "We declare our determination to promote the rights of man and reconciliation among men, in the Church and in the world today."[44]

In 1971 the Synod of Bishops created by the Second Vatican Council turned its attention to the problem of justice and human rights in the Third World. The statement of the Synod, *Justice in the World*, explicitly recognizes the right to development as a basic right of participation necessary for human dignity in the modern world: "The right to development must be seen as a dynamic interpenetration of all those fundamental human rights upon which the aspirations of individuals and nations are based."[45]

John Paul II

During the pontificate of John Paul II, human rights have continued to be central to Roman Catholic social teaching. Hollenbach writes:

The central place which human rights have come to hold in Catholic social thought is evident from even a cursory reading of the numerous addresses of Pope John Paul II during his world travels. Whether in Poland or Brazil, the United States or the Philippines, Mexico or Africa, the most consistent and forceful theme of the pope's message has been the appeal for the protection of human rights and the denunciation of patterns of human rights violations.[46]

Similarly, the "Instruction on Certain Aspects of the 'Theology of Liberation'" asserts: "The fight for the rights of man, which the Church does not cease to reaffirm, constitutes the authentic fight for justice."[47] And the 1986 "Instruction on Christian Freedom and Liberation" affirms that the contemporary "formulation of human rights implies a clearer awareness of the dignity of all human beings."[48]

Also in 1986 the final report of the extraordinary synod celebrating the twentieth anniversary of the conclusion of the Second Vatican Council proclaimed

. . . a missionary opening-up for the integral salvation of the world. Through this all truly human values are not only accepted, but fiercely defended: the dignity of the human person; the fundamental rights of man; peace; freedom from oppressions, misery and injustice.[49]

However, it is also clear that "Integral salvation . . . is obtained only if these human realities are purified and further raised by grace and familiarity with God through Jesus Christ in the Holy Spirit."[50]

John Paul II has not only forcefully spoken out against human rights violations, but explicitly identified human rights with the mission of the church.[51] In Singapore in 1986, John Paul II reminded sixty-three thousand people gathered at the national stadium that peace is "possible only where there is a just order than ensures the rights of everyone."[52] He described justice as an "attitude which recognizes the dignity and equality of all men and women and a firm commitment to strive to secure and protect the basic human rights of all."[53] And during his visit to Australia John Paul II "defended the rights" of the aborigines.[54]

When asked on his trip to Chile if he expected to help bring democracy to that country, he replied:

> Yes, yes, [although] I am not the evangelizer of democracy, [for] I am the evangelizer of the Gospel. To the Gospel message, of course, belongs [sic] all the problems of human rights, and if democracy means human rights it also belongs to the message of the church.[55]

Moreover, he affirmed that the church's support for human rights is not political: "This is what we are."[56]

Finally, in the recent encyclical *Sollicitudo Rei Socialis* John Paul II identifies the first positive sign of our time as "the *full awareness* among large numbers of men and women of their own dignity and that of every human being" which is expressed "in the more *lively concern* that *human rights should be respected*, and in the more vigorous rejection of their violation."[57] Moreover, during his trip to the United States in 1987, John Paul II singled out "the concern for human rights" and praised the UN for recognizing in the Universal Declaration of Human Rights, and in the international covenants which seek to implement it, "the basic human rights," including "the inalienable rights of individuals and of the communities of peoples."[58]

The Roman Catholic Church in the United States

The U.S. Conference of Catholic Bishops, in its pastoral letter, *The Challenge of Peace*, reaffirms church statements on human rights and asserts: "In the past twenty years Catholic teaching has become increasingly specific about the content of these international rights and duties."[59] And in a pastoral letter on *Catholic Social Teaching and the U.S. Economy*, the bishops extend

a personal invitation to Catholics to use the resources of our faith, the strength of our economy, and the opportunities of our democracy to shape a society that better protects the dignity and basic rights of our sisters and brothers, both in this land and around the world.[60]

They affirm that economic rights are among the human rights which constitute *"the minimum conditions for life in community"* and that "A renewal of economic life depends on the conscious choices and commitments of individual believers who practice their faith in the world."[61]

In responding to criticism of this pastoral letter, Milwaukee's Archbishop Rembert Weakland, who chaired the drafting committee, reminds readers that "all people have a right to participate in the economic life of a society" and that the society has "a moral responsibility to enhance human dignity and protect human rights for all."[62] And Ted Zuern urges his readers to write to Congress to protest the "human rights violations" of "hunger, poor housing, serious unemployment, the denial of equal opportunities for education and health care in this nation of remarkable wealth."[63]

This same concern for social and economic rights is reiterated frequently in the publications of Catholic Charities, U.S.A.[64] In summarizing Catholic social teaching for the California Catholic Conference, William J. Wood argues for "a theory of justice that is both biblical and spelled out in systematic terms of rights and duties," and which asserts "a preferential option for the poor" and "democratic participation in decision-making."[65] Moreover, this Catholic social teaching appears even in local publications like the occasional newsletter of the Pikes Peak Justice and Peace Commission in Colorado.[66]

Other articles in Catholic publications take up the right to life,[67] issues concerning human rights and liberation theology,[68] and the rights of members of the Roman Catholic Church.[69] Henri Nouwen reminds us that the struggle for human dignity "to which the God of the Bible calls His people is much larger than a struggle for political or economic rights . . . [for it] is a struggle for life in the fullest sense."[70]

Human rights concerns are also included in the prayers of Catholics in North America:

Help us never to forget those whom you keep under your special care—the poor, the sick, the oppressed.
We pray for the life of the world:
that every nation may seek the way that leads to peace;
that human rights and freedom may everywhere be respected,
and that the world's resources may be ungrudgingly shared.[71]

Protestant and Orthodox Christians, too, can join in this prayer, for it reflects a faith common to Christians around the globe.

Priorities

David Hollenbach notes that in the Catholic rights tradition human dignity is an indicative rather than an imperative:

> Human persons *have* dignity. They *are* sacred and precious. In this sense, dignity is not granted to persons by the ethical activity of others. Dignity is not bestowed on persons by other persons, by the family or society or the state. Rather the reality of human dignity makes claims on others that it be recognized and respected. The moral imperatives set forth as human rights express the more specific content of these claims. Human dignity, however, is more fundamental than any specific human right.[72]

As "a transcendental characteristic of persons" human dignity is the source of all moral principles, and thus is "the foundation of human rights."[73]

"As the cause of human rights is inescapable and compelling," Stephan Pfürtner argues, human rights are "a call to reform and a chance for the further development of Christian ethics."[74] Hollenbach carries forward this development by asserting that Christian love requires in "an affluent society especially," that "claims based on need deserve to be granted priority status in a human rights policy."[75] Thus Christian love requires the primacy of social rights, which Hollenbach suggests can be formulated in "three strategic moral priorities":

1) The needs of the poor take priority over the wants of the rich.
2) The freedom of the dominated takes priority over the liberty of the powerful.
3) The participation of marginalized groups takes priority over the preservation of an order which excludes them.[76]

He concludes that the "strategic morality expressed in these three principles is both an expression and a renewal of the Catholic human rights tradition" and, when manifested in action, is "an expression of Christian love."[77]

Therefore, in the Roman Catholic tradition one finds today that the discussion of human rights is central to ethical reflection. For human rights are understood in faith as the necessary social conditions for the human dignity which is God's gift to all the peoples of the earth.

Notes

1. Quoted in Robert A. Evans and Alice Frazer Evans, *Human Rights: A Dialogue between the First and Third Worlds* (Maryknoll: Orbis Books, 1983), 245.
2. Ibid.
3. "A Preview of *Mater et Magistra*," in *The Encyclicals and Other Messages of John XXIII*, editorial staff of *The Pope Speaks Magazine* (Washington, D.C.: TPS Press, 1964), 233. Quoted in David Hollenbach, S.J., *Claims in Conflict: Retrieving and Renewing the Catholic Human Rights Tradition* (New York: Paulist Press, 1979), 42.
4. David Hollenbach, *Claims in Conflict*, 43. See "Church and Human Rights in History," *Convergence*, no. 2 (1979):5-9.
5. *Rerum Novarum*, 1891 Encyclical of Leo XIII on the Rights and Duties of Capital and Labor, no. 7. In *The Church Speaks to the Modern World: The Social Teachings of Leo XIII*, ed. Etienne Gilson (Garden City, N.Y.: Doubleday, Image, 1954).
6. Ibid., no. 2.
7. David Hollenbach, *Claims in Conflict*, 48.
8. Ibid., 49.
9. David Hollenbach, *Claims in Conflict*, 56.
10. Ibid.
11. Christmas Address, 1942, in *Claims in Conflict*, 60.
12. Address of 6 December 1953, in *Claims in Conflict*, 60.
13. David Hollenbach, *Claims in Conflict*, 61.
14. Alfred Verdross, "Fundamental Human Rights: The Journey of an Idea," trans. John D. Gorby, *Human Rights* 8, no. 3 (Fall 1979):22. See Jungmann, *Missarum Sollemnia* II (1949), 74 and Durig, *Imago* (1952), 126 and 167.
15. Ibid., translator assisted by Dr. William Carroll of the John Marshall Law School faculty.
16. Alfred Verdross, "Fundamental Human Rights: The Journey of an Idea," trans. John D. Gorby, *Human Rights* 8, no. 3 (Fall 1979):22.
17. Ibid.
18. Thomas Aquinas, *Summa Theologica*, 1, II, 21, 4, reply 3, trans. Thomas Gilby, quoted in Verdross, "Fundamental Human Rights: The Journey of an Idea," trans. John D. Gorby, *Human Rights* 8, no. 3 (Fall 1979):23.
19. Alfred Verdross, "Fundamental Human Rights: The Journey of an Idea," trans. John D. Gorby, *Human Rights* 8, no. 3 (Fall 1979):23. Mohammed Allal Sinaceur writes: "Even if it is true that Christianity raises man to divine estate, the new feature as the modern era dawns is the substitution of the rule of statute law and the empire of man for the legal order of ancient societies, the unique encounter between Christian doctrine and a renascent jurisprudence, the transformation of the *jus suum cuique tribuere* of Roman tradition into *jus suum cuique reddere*. From this point on Europe is attuned to the notion of human rights." Sinaceur, "Islamic Tradition and Human Rights," in *Philosophical Foundations of Human Rights*, 201.
20. Herbert Spiegelberg, "Human Dignity: A Challenge to Contemporary Philosophy," in *Human Dignity: This Century and the Next*, 42.
21. John A. Coleman, S.J., "Catholic Human Rights Theory: Four Challenges to an Intellectual Tradition," *Journal of Law and Religion*, 2, no. 2 (1984):349-55. He suggests that the positions of David Hollenbach and Bryan Hehir, the two major Catholic writers on human rights, are basically derived from Jacques Maritain's assertion: "The dignity of the human person? The expression means nothing if it does not signify that, by virtue of the natural law, the human person has the right to be respected, is the subject of rights, possesses rights." Maritain, *The Rights of Man and Natural Law*, trans. D. Anson (1951), 65;

quoted in Coleman, "Catholic Human Rights Theory," 350. Hollenbach indicates that modern Catholic social teaching has shifted from natural law to human dignity, as a basis for human rights, which allows for development of a more realistic and universal doctrine of human rights. See *Claims in Conflict,* 131-33.

22. See Gregory Baum, "The Catholic Foundation of Human Rights," *The Ecumenist* 18, no. 1 (November-December 1979):10.

23. David Hollenbach, S.J., *Justice, Peace, and Human Rights: American Catholic Social Ethics in a Pluralistic Context* (New York: The Crossroad Publishing Company, 1988), 95.

24. Ibid., 96.

25. *Pacem in Terris,* 1963 Encyclical of John XXIII on World Peace, in Joseph Gremillion, ed., *The Gospel of Peace and Justice: Catholic Social Teaching since Pope John* (Maryknoll, N.Y.: Orbis, 1976), no. 9.

26. David Hollenbach, *Claims in Conflict,* 65.

27. Ibid., 66-67. All these rights are listed in *Pacem in Terris,* nos. 11-27. Philibert Secretan asserts: "The only right which must resolutely be refused to man is that of acting as though he were himself the source of his rights." Secretan, "Thoughts on Respect for Human Rights," *Convergence,* no. 2 (1979):15.

28. *Pacem in Terris,* no. 144. In Gremillion, *The Gospel of Peace and Justice,* 232.

29. Ibid., no. 145.

30. *Dignitatis Humanae,* no. 2, in Gremillion, *The Gospel of Peace and Justice,* 339.

31. Ibid.

32. Ibid., 342, no. 6.

33. Ibid.

34. David Hollenbach, *Claims in Conflict,* 77.

35. *Gaudium et Spes,* no. 26, in Gremillion, *The Gospel of Peace and Justice,* 264.

36. Ibid., 305, no. 69.

37. John Langan, "Human Rights in Roman Catholicism," in *Human Rights in Religious Traditions,* 31. François Refoulé claims that section 30 of *Gaudium et Spes,* which is entitled "The need to go beyond an individualistic ethic," was drafted to alert readers to the danger in the Universal Declaration of Human Rights and the French declaration of 1789, although the former includes social and economic rights as well. See Refoulé, "Efforts made on behalf of Human Rights by the Supreme Authority of the Church," trans. John Maxwell, in *The Church and the Rights of Man,* ed. Alois Müller and Norbert Greinacher (New York: The Seabury Press, 1979), 79; and David Hollenbach, *Justice, Peace, and Human Rights,* 19. J. Bryan Hehir distinguishes both the classical and Christian natural law positions from the "Liberal-Christian" position developed by John Locke. Hehir, "Human Rights from a Theological and Ethical Perspective," in *The Moral Imperatives of Human Rights: A World Survey,* ed. Kenneth W. Thompson (Washington, D.C.: University Press of America, 1980), 1-24.

38. Ibid. See John Langan, "Introduction," in *Human Rights in the Americas: The Struggle for Consensus,* 2. Raymond F. Collins asserts: "It is the consideration of human rights which forms the context within which today's ethical decision-making takes place." Collins, *Christian Morality: Biblical Foundations* (Notre Dame, Ind.: University of Notre Dame Press, 1986), 51.

39. David Hollenbach, *Claims in Conflict,* 75. "This move amounts to a shift from a social ethic that proposed a concrete model of the structure of society as a necessary exigency of natural law to a social ethic in which all social models and structures are held accountable to the standards of human rights. The difference between the two perspectives is the acceptance of social, political, and ideological pluralism as an inescapable fact in the contemporary world." Hollenbach, *Justice, Peace, and Human Rights,* 90.

40.   Ibid. Michael Novak argues that the primary responsibility of government is to protect public order. Novak, "Economic Rights: The Servile State," *Catholicism and Crisis* 3, no. 10 (October 1985):10. In response, David Hollenbach asserts the Catholic ethical principle of subsidiarity. Economic necessities are not, in the first instance, the responsibility of government; however, when the problem exceeds the power of mediating individuals and institutions, "government can and should intervene in ways guided by political prudence." Hollenbach, *Justice, Peace, and Human Rights*, 104-06. Novak agrees with Hollenbach that both the society and the state have obligations for the "general welfare" of people, although basic needs are in the first instance the responsibility of the individual person; however, he disagrees that these responsibilities constitute "economic rights" equivalent to civil and political rights. Novak, "The Rights and Wrongs of 'Economic Rights': A Debate Continued," *This World* no. 17 (Spring 1987):43-52.

41.   See Andrew Greeley, *No Bigger than Necessary: An Alternative to Socialism, Capitalism and Anarchism* (New York: Meridian, 1977), 12; and David Hollenbach, *Claims in Conflict*, 78-84.

42.   François Refoulé, "Efforts made on behalf of Human Rights by the Supreme Authority of the Church," in *The Church and the Rights of Man*, 77.

43.   Ibid.

44.   Ibid. See Claude Geffre, O.P., "Theological Reflections on a New Age of Mission," *International Review of Mission* 71, no. 284 (October 1982):478-92.

45.   *Justice in the World*, no. 15, in Gremillion, *The Gospel of Peace and Justice*, 516.

46.   David Hollenbach, "Both Bread and Freedom: The Interconnection of Economic and Political Rights in Recent Catholic Thought," in *Human Rights and the Global Mission of the Church*, 31.

47.   "Instruction on Certain Aspects of the 'Theology of Liberation'" (Vatican City: Sacred Congregation for the Doctrine of the Faith, 1984), 31.

48.   "Instruction on Christian Freedom and Liberation," *Origins: NC Documentary Service* 15, no. 44 (17 April 1986):716.

49.   "The Church Subject to the Word of God Celebrating the Mysteries of Christ for the Salvation of the World," *Convergence*, no. 2 (1986):32.

50.   Ibid.

51.   Roberto Suro, "Pope, on Latin Trip, Attacks Pinochet Regime," *The New York Times*, 1 April 1987, 1.

52.   "Justice and Peace Challenge in Singapore," *Asia Focus* 2, no. 45 (25 November 1986):7.

53.   Ibid.

54.   "Aborigines Welcome Pope," *The Oakland Tribune*, 30 November 1986, A-6.

55.   Roberto Suro, "Pope, on Latin Trip, Attacks Pinochet Regime," *The New York Times*, 1 April 1987, 7.

56.   Ibid.

57.   "Encyclical Letter of the Supreme Pontiff John Paul II: *Sollicitudo Rei Socialis*," *L'Osservatore Romano*, English edition, 29 February 1988, 6.

58.   "Building an Authentic World Community," *The Pope Speaks: The Church Documents Quarterly* 33, no. 1 (1988):27.

59.   National Conference of Catholic Bishops, *The Challenge of Peace: God's Promise and Our Response* (Washington, D.C.: United States Catholic Conference, 1983), 74.

60.   National Conference of Catholic Bishops, *Economic Justice for All* (Washington, D.C.: United States Catholic Conference, 1986), v.

61.   Ibid., xi and xiv. See John Langan, S.J., "Defining Human Rights: A Revision of the Liberal Tradition," in *Human Rights in the Americas: The Struggle for Consensus*, 69-101.

62.   Rembert Weakland, O.S.B., "Dear Reader," *Catholic Trends* (15 November 1986):3.

63. Ted Zuern, S.J., "Bread and Freedom . . . Justice and Faith," *Newsletter: Bureau of Catholic-Indian Missions* 7, no. 10 (January/February 1987):3.

64. The right to health care is asserted in "1985 Issues of Concern," *Charities USA* 13, no. 2 (February 1986):29. The Catholic bishops' statement, "The Right to a Decent Home," is discussed in "Background Paper on Housing" in the same issue. The president of Catholic Charities affirms the organization will defend "the right of the poor to struggle against injustice" and "the right of each person to self-determination." Mary Ann Quaranta, "Catholic Charities: Service and Action," *Charities* 13, no. 7 (12 April 1986):7 and 9.

65. William J. Wood, S.J., "Who in the World Is the Church?" *Commentary* 7, no. 7 (November 1986):2. Original italicized.

66. See Joan Brown, "Human Dignity: Have We Failed Ourselves?" *Active for Justice* 11, no. 7 (July 1987):5; Shawn Crawford, "Human Rights: The Mentally Disabled—What About Their Treatment?" *Active for Justice* 15, no. 11 (December 1987):1 and 4; and Robert Traer, "The Struggle for Human Rights in China," *Active for Justice* 9, no. 6 (July/August 1989):5.

67. See Archbishop Daniel E. Pilarczyk, "Taking It on the Chin—For Life: Reflections on a Vatican Instruction," *America* 156, no. 14 (11 April 1987):295-96; and Virgil C. Blum, S.J., "America's Shameful Apartheid," *Catholic League Newsletter* 14, no. 2 (February 1987):8.

68. See John C. Cort, "Christians and the Class Struggle," *Commonweal* (11 July 1986):400-04.

69. See Sidney Callahan, "Association for the Rights of Catholics in the Church," *America* 155, no. 1 (19-26 July 1986):22-23; and articles in the newsletter *Light* published by the Association for the Rights of Catholics in the Church. Gregory Baum asks, it would seem, rhetorically: "Is the Church's defense of human rights authentic and credible if it fails to recognize human rights in its own organizational life?" Baum, "Catholic Foundation of Human Rights," *The Ecumenist* 18, no. 1 (November-December 1979):12.

70. Henri J. M. Nouwen, "We Drink from Our Own Wells," *America* 149, no. 11 (15 October 1983):206.

71. Thursday morning prayer in *A Christian's Prayer Book: Poems, Psalms and Prayers for the Church's Year*, ed. Peter Coughlon, Ronald C. D. Jasper, Teresa Rodrigues, O.S.B. (Chicago: Franciscan Herald Press, 4th printing, 1972?), 132.

72. David Hollenbach, *Claims in Conflict*, 90.

73. Ibid. See R. J. Henle, S.J., "A Catholic View of Human Rights: A Thomistic Reflection," in *The Philosophy of Human Rights*, 87-92.

74. Stephan H. P. Pfürtner, "Human Rights in Christian Ethics," in *The Church and the Rights of Man*, 57; the phrase is used as the heading of a section on page 59.

75. David Hollenbach, *Claims in Conflict*, 175.

76. Ibid., 204.

77. Ibid., 207.

Chapter 3

CONSERVATIVE PROTESTANTS

Among conservative Christians one also finds support for human rights. Involvement by conservative Protestants in human rights advocacy is justified on the basis of biblical texts.

This is true despite the warning by Lutheran scholars Foster McCurley and John Reumann that, viewed historically, human rights "are rooted in the assumptions of deism" which, "in its concept of God and its view of human autonomy, was far removed from any notion of God who acts in history or of people in bondage to sin or self, redeemed by Jesus Christ."[1] Thus the preacher who wants to use lessons from the Bible "to rouse a congregation to greater sensitivity for the oppressed and for justice in a repressive world will have to do some careful exegesis."[2]

However, McCurley and Reumann acknowledge that human rights are an important ethical concern in the modern world. Furthermore, they affirm that there are ways "to connect this ethical concern with the Scriptures," for there are "a whole series of areas where biblical thought relates to the modern concern for human dignity and rights."[3]

Two Christian theologians who have rigorously pursued this task are Jacques Ellul and John Warwick Montgomery. Each sets forth a biblical argument justifying support for human rights as an expression of Christian faith.

Jacques Ellul

The French lawyer and theologian Jacques Ellul was one of the first to attempt such a justification. In 1946 he published a book under the title *Le Fondement Théologique de Droit*, which in 1960 was republished as *The Theological Foundation of Law*.

Ellul argues that in the judicial relativism of the modern era "established human rights are in no way protected against arbitrary power," as "the discernment of right and wrong" is simply "given over to an all-powerful state charged with making its own criteria."[4] Attempts to revive the doctrine of natural law are understandable. However, he believes they are doomed to fail, as natural law cannot satisfy "the common thinking of contemporary man and the modern concept of law. . . ."[5] For Ellul the task is rather "to see clearly the significance of law within, and in relationship to, biblical revelation."[6]

He argues that in the Bible, law is justice and Jesus Christ is God's justice:

> There can be no justice whatsoever, even relative, outside Jesus Christ. This is clearly demonstrated by the fact that he who rejects Jesus Christ immediately condemns himself, because justice is no longer possible for him (John 3:18). He can indeed no longer invoke his just works before God, since there is no justice outside of him who is righteousness. Works, whatever they may be, cannot be separated from the person of Jesus Christ. Conversely, he who believes is already justified by his believing, without being judged, for he who judges is also he who justifies (John 3:18 and 5:24). This is another way to show that there can be no study of law outside Jesus Christ; there can't even be human law, however relative, if it is not founded in Jesus Christ.[7]

Ellul asserts that in the Bible there are no natural rights: "'My right is in the Lord' (Isaiah 49:4). Man has no other right but that which is in the Lord and given by the Lord."[8] Thus Jesus Christ "alone has rights before God. From him alone men receive rights before God."[9]

Human rights are given to humanity through God's covenants which recognize human worth and thus include "the idea of human dignity."[10] In these covenants God both establishes law and grants rights: "The notion of human rights depends on man's God-given status as party to a contract. To put it differently, God gives man certain rights, placing him in a juridical situation in order to make his covenant genuine."[11] Thus it is here that human rights "receive their absolutely firm foundation," for:

> While Jesus Christ radically abolishes human justice and divests man of all his conquests, his powers and his rights, he is also the foundation of man's new rights. For he, Jesus Christ, acquires these rights for man. In the new covenant Christ is not only the victim in whose blood the covenant is concluded. He is also the one who concludes the covenant with God in behalf of all men. He is the only man with whom God is well pleased. Through him God views all mankind. This is the miracle of substitution wherein Jesus Christ asserts human rights.[12]

As Christ died for all, and not only Christians, all persons can claim these rights.

The first of these rights before God is the "privilege of belonging to Christ," for:

> Because of Christ man is no longer at the mercy of events in history, nor of juridical despotisms. Because of Christ human rights are now established which no one may dispute, neither God who eternally founded them, nor men who cannot blot out the historic fact of Christ's death and resurrection. This even objectively establishes man's rights in the covenant.[13]

For Ellul all law, and thus every human right, is grounded in the saving event of Jesus Christ.

The church has the responsibility of watching the legal affairs of a society, to affirm the limits of law, to judge the legal system, and if necessary, to rectify the law. For:

> Precisely because the Church is commissioned to be a witness of Jesus Christ's love for all men, because its ministry is to suffer with and for men, it is bound to know man's true right. It will not be deceived, inasmuch as to it alone has been revealed the true nature of man, his true situation before God, and his true misery. Consequently, the Church is summoned in the course of human history to speak a discerning word to each concrete situation, "These are the rights of man, here and now. This is what man may demand. This is what he needs to be protected from." This discerning word is part of the Church's proclamation.[14]

Moreover, this proclamation cannot be simply stated by some administrative body, for when "it comes to speaking up and taking a stand for human rights, it must be done by the entire Christian community. . . ."[15] The church has a duty to educate its members about human rights so that they, as the church, can address the society and the state on behalf of peole's God-given human rights.

John Warwick Montgomery

John Warwick Montgomery, lawyer and philosopher as well as theologian, also argues that Christians should affirm human rights. He acknowledges with John A. Whitehead that "from a biblical perspective, 'rights' as such do not exist."[16] And he agrees with Marc Lienhard of the University of Strasbourg that

> The Christian theologian, and particularly the Protestant theologian, will have a number of reservations to make about this vision of things. He will contrast

the optimistic conception, which sees man endowed with reason and capable of fulfilling his potentialities and achieving a just social order, with the biblical message of the subjection of man and the reality of sin. He will question an over-individualistic interpretation of the traditional conception of human rights. . . . It will also be pointed out that the Bible contains no irrefutable evidence of the idea that man, by the mere fact of his existence, is entitled to make a number of fundamental demands or claims on other members of society. There are admittedly commandments which tie in with human rights (e.g., Matthew 7:12; Romans 13:7), though rather than rights or demands written into man's nature as such, what is involved is an attitude towards one's neighbor, not of inherent rights but of responsibility and service due to him. The Christian ethic is, on principle, directed towards others because it reposes on love.[17]

However, Montgomery finds it impossible to end the discussion here. For since World War II human rights affirmations have been "a battleground in which human dignity is at stake and the enemy is no less than barbarism."[18]

Montgomery asserts that the philosophical attempt to define human rights "leads inexorably to the deeper question of justifying the rights one is at pains to define."[19] He agrees with Belgian philosopher Ch. Perelman that legal positivism, the theory that law is whatever the state legislates, is incapable of justifying any standard of human dignity:

This conception of juridical positivism collapses before the abuses of Hitlerism, like any scientific theory irreconcilable with the facts. The universal reaction to the Nazi crimes forced the Allied chiefs of state to institute the Nuremberg trials and to interpret the adage *nullum crime sine lege* [no crime without law] in a nonpositivistic sense because the law violated in the case did not derive from a system of positive law but from the conscience of all civilized men. The conviction that it was impossible to leave these horrible crimes unpunished, although they fell outside a system of positive law, has prevailed over the positivistic conception of the grounding of the law.[20]

However, if positive law is not adequate for such a standard, Montgomery believes that reassertions of natural law simply flounder on the naturalistic fallacy of deriving what ought to be from what is.[21] After reviewing the philosophical debate on human rights, he concurs with Alan White's analysis that

None of the answers commonly suggested to the question "what gives one the right to so and so?", that is, none of the grounds suggested for any of the rights which it is maintained we either have or ought to have, shows . . . any strictly logical connection between the right in question and the basis suggested for it. All that it is possible to argue is that the suggested basis gives a non-deductive, evaluative reason for possession of the right, a reason which is, of course, often supported by common sense, our shared moral values, the

apparatus of the law, some institutionalized system of regulations or conventions, etc.[22]

Montgomery concludes: "A survey of the most challenging philosophies of human rights has left us with no adequate foundation for human dignity."[23]

Montgomery argues that if legal rules of evidence are applied, the witnesses of the New Testament to Jesus Christ as the risen Son of God will be found credible; thus the teachings of Jesus Christ may be seen to reveal God's will and to establish a foundation for human rights.[24] The epistemological problem is resolved by demonstrated divine revelation. "Once you have met God incarnate you have no choice but to trust Him: as to the way of salvation, as to the reliability of the entire Bible, and as to human rights."[25]

Human rights are therefore to be derived from the Bible and, with it, are sanctioned by God through his Son Jesus Christ. Montgomery's list of human rights includes the following procedural due process rights: impartiality of tribunal (Mal. 2:9; 1 Tim. 5:21); fair hearing (Exod. 22:9); prompt trial (Ezra 7:26); confrontation of witnesses (Isa. 43:9); no double jeopardy (Nah. 1:9). Under substantive due process rights he lists nondiscrimination in general (Acts 10:34; Deut. 16:19; Prov. 24:23); equality before the law (Matt. 5:45); racial, sexual and social equality (Gal. 3:28; Amos 9:7; Ex. 21:2); equality of rich and poor (James 2:1-7; Amos 5:12; Isa. 1:16-17); equality of citizens and foreigners (Exod. 12:47; Lev. 23:22, 24:22; Num. 9:14, 15:15-16); even the sovereign is subordinate to the law (2 Sam. 11-12).

Rights encompassing all three generations of human rights include: right to life (Exod. 20:13; Ps. 51:5; Matt. 5:21-22; Luke 1:15, 41; right to family life (1 Tim. 5:8); humane treatment and punishment (Luke 6:45); freedom of thought, conscience, religion, expression, assembly, association, movement (John 7:17); social and economic rights in general (1 Cor. 6:19-20); right to universal education (Deut. 6:7, 11:19); right to work, fair remuneration and good working conditions (Luke 10:7; 1 Tim. 5:18; Deut. 23:25-26, 24:6, 10, 12-13, 15); right to protection of honor and reputation (Exod. 20:16); right to leisure time (Exod. 20:8-11); right to asylum (Exod. 21:13; Josh. 20; 1 Chron. 6:67; passages concerning cities of refuge); and right to equitable distribution of land (Num. 33:54; Lev. 25:14-18, 25-34).

Montgomery even suggests, quoting Herbert Brichto, that notions of environmental rights may be found in Scripture.

The modern concern with preventing the extinction of various species of animal life is in resonance with the biblical prescription not to collect the dam with her chicks but to release her to hatch another generation. Cruelty to animals is proscribed in such prescriptions as not to yoke animals of different

strengths (ox and ass) to the plough or not to muzzle the ox which treads the grain. Ecological considerations are exemplified in the prohibition of sowing the vineyard's aisles with a second crop or the destruction of defenseless fruit trees while waging war in enemy territory.[26]

Thus Montgomery claims that these "biblically supported human rights" provide as much protection for men and women as the rights elaborated through the actions of the United Nations:

> Our tabular summary of the Revelational Foundations for Specific Human Rights should leave no doubt that the Bible, though appealed to again and again as the source and justification of first-generation rights, by no means limits itself to the category of civil and political liberties. What today are termed economic, social, education, and solidarity rights are likewise woven into the very fabric of biblical revelation.[27]

Montgomery even finds the redistribution of wealth, envisioned in UN resolutions proposing a New International Economic Order, to be supported by the biblical perspective, so long as the recipient nations "institute and observe civil and political liberties and use the donated resources to increase distributive justice and aid the poor in their territories" and so long as this redistribution is voluntary.[28]

In answer to the assertion that the Bible sets forth moral ideals, rather than rights, he quotes Jerome Shestack:

> There is a positivist aspect to divine orders since obedience derives from one's duty to God, not from one's inherent nature. Still, the fact remains that once the duties are ordered by God, those duties accrue to the individual's benefit and may be inviolate from denigration by the State, which is an important objective of any human rights system.[29]

As the teachings of the Bible may be accurately stated in human rights language, Montgomery affirms Roland de Pury's rendition of the Last Judgment:

> We can only welcome the Kingdom in engaging body and soul in the struggle for human rights. Otherwise, how could we be among those to whom the Shepherd, Judge, and Lamb will say on the Last Day, "Come my sheep, for I was hungry, I was cold, I was a prisoner, and you did something about it—you respected my right to be fed, clothed, healed, liberated, treated with dignity."[30]

Similarly, traditional theological statements can be translated into human rights affirmations. Again Montgomery quotes de Pury: "In Jesus Christ divine and human rights are conjoined and become inseparable. To violate the rights of a creature of God in the name of divine right is thus to serve

another god—to commit idolatry."[31] Or as René Coste asserts: "The more one believes in the mystery of the Incarnation, the more one's commitment to human rights becomes a matter of motivational urgency."[32]

Other Witnesses

In 1968 General Frederick Coutts wrote of the "Salvation Army commitment in the field of human rights" and claimed that "Salvationists are identified with the high ideals of social justice and acceptance as the unchallenged right of *every* man as stated in the Universal Declaration of Human Rights."[33] However, Lieutenant-Commissioner Francis A. Evans, who represented the Salvation Army at the UN and the World Council of Churches from 1966-68, asserted that the Salvationist, "with his affirmation of belief in the year of Human Rights, [will] proclaim his still stronger belief in the year of Divine Grace."[34]

In the *Christian Science Sentinel* Mary Baker Eddy is reported to have observed: "Mankind will be God-governed in proportion as God's government becomes apparent, the Golden Rule utilized, and the rights of man and the liberty of conscience held sacred."[35] Even a recent publication of the Adventist Church contains an affirmation of human rights.[36]

In 1984 the *Quarterly* of the conservative Christian Legal Society published a special issue on human rights including a human rights bibliography, a list of human rights organizations, an article by Samuel Rabinove entitled "Religious Freedom for All: A Jewish Perspective," and an article by H. Victor Conde entitled "The Theological Basis for Human Rights."[37] Also in this issue Carl F. H. Henry criticized humanists, who "champion human rights," on the grounds that

> humanism as a philosophy provides no metaphysical basis adequate to preserve human rights in distinction from other principles that it reduces to a socio-cultural byproduct of a particular period in history. Universal and permanent human rights are logically inconsistent with the humanist theses that personality is an accident in the universe and that human nature is evolving.[38]

However, Henry commended "humanists who promote human rights" and extended a hand to them "and others who, even if their alien and contrabiblical philosophies seem to many of us unpromising, nonetheless would share in the defense and promotion of authentic human rights in a bleak age of totalitarian tyranny."[39]

The National Association of Evangelicals (NAE) represents over thirty-six thousand churches from seventy-four denominations as well as colleges and other organizations in addressing issues of public policy. In 1983 it helped

launch a Peace, Freedom, and Security Studies program to promote "the linkage between peace among the nations and the advancement of international human rights."[40] The highest priority of the NAE is religious freedom; however, it also protests the violation of other civil and political rights, as contrary to biblical teaching. For instance, racial discrimination is condemned on the grounds that Jesus emphasized "the inherent worth and instrinsic value of every man, regardless of race, class, creed, or color. . . ."[41]

Words of Caution

For Carl Henry, the contrast between the biblical view and the modern notion of human rights is decisive:

> The Universal Declaration of Human Rights (1948) presents a panorama of human rights while it says very little about human duties and nothing at all about duties to God. Only Article 29, which limits the exercise of rights by reciprocal rights and a regard for morality, public order and general welfare, refers to human duty, and even here the context is anthropological. Although the stipulated rights are considered the generally acknowledged norms of modern civilization, none is legally enforcible [sic] since the Declaration wholly ignores the subject of the ultimate source and sanction of rights and does not even obligate states to enact the stipulated rights.[42]

Only the revealed truth of the Bible, Henry asserts, can provide a justification for human rights. It is God, as Creator, who gives us rights. Thus it is important to be clear: "In the Christian view, inalienable rights are creational rights governing the community and individual, rights implicit in the social commandments of the Decalogue."[43]

For Edward Norman, however, there can be no "Christian view" of human rights. Therefore, he strenuously defends Christian faith against its secularization by advocates of human rights. In a chapter entitled "A New Commandment: Human Rights," he argues that Church leaders have identified "the Church with the moral sanctions claimed as the justification for the goals of western liberalism," with the result that "the Churches now see Human Rights as the essence of the Christian message."[44] For Norman, both liberal Protestants and Roman Catholics are guilty of this reduction of the Gospel to contemporary ideology.

> "The Church", according to one of the documents uttered by the Second Vatican Council, "by virtue of the Gospel entrusted to her, proclaims man's rights and acknowledges and esteems the modern movement to promote these rights everywhere." The World Council of Churches, a decade later, in the more precise language which represents the escalation of Human Rights ideology,

has declared: "The struggle of Christians for human rights is a fundamental response to Jesus Christ. That Gospel leads us to become ever more active in identifying and rectifying violations of human rights in our societies.[45]

Norman argues that in rhetoric and content, as well as chronology, "the Christian passion for Human Rights exactly corresponds to the development of ideas within the western intelligentsia as a whole."[46]

He suggests that this accommodation by Christians to prevailing social and political values is well advanced not only in Western Europe and North America, but also in Latin America.

> In the 1930's and '40's, the Church leadership adopted the ideals of the European corporate state; in the 1950's they were attracted to "developments" social reform; in the 1960's they reflected the radical critique of capitalist society then common within the western intelligentsia; in the 1970's they have moved on to identify Christianity with the ideology of Human Rights.[47]

For Norman, this represents not progress but decay. What is needed is separation of the absolute concern of the Christian message from the relative concerns of culture. Thus he pleads: "The most urgent task of Christianity in our day is to rediscover that sense of historical relativism, before the faith itself is absorbed by a single historical interpretation."[48]

Max Stackhouse sounds a similar note of warning. He argues that in the last century a new "piety . . . centered on the Great god Freedom" has developed in the United States:

> It is rooted in the conviction that the most important and ultimate forces of the universe are on the side of those who advocate the reduction of religious influence in all public things. Freedom has become the core of our national creed, as confessed by both major parties; of our national liturgies, such as the recent celebration of Lady Liberty; and of our life-styles, as documented by astute social analysts.[49]

He is not only critical of the liberal church, but suggests that liberals, conservatives, and liberationists who contest with each other do so within the general doctrine of this new piety, as "three sects" all of which affirm "that the end, the goal, the highest standard and noblest vision for humanity, for society, and for civilization, is Freedom."[50]

Stackhouse asserts that in this respect this "new piety" is in "conflict with the great traditional religions and philosophies of human history," for these "great ecumenical faiths have always held that freedom is not enough."[51]

> Liberty, true liberty, is not Freedom alone. *Moksha* and *Nibbana*, say the Eastern traditions, requires attentiveness to *Dharma* (*dhamma*). Freedom

begins in submission, says Islam. Freedom finds its fulfillment in obedience, says Judaism. Liberty finds its foundation, its root, its base and its end in higher principles of righteousness, deeper visions of the good and wider principles of love than the Great god Freedom can provide, says Christianity.[52]

Liberty may be necessary for civilization and religion, but it cannot create or sustain itself.

This critique of the U.S. wing of the human rights tradition is telling. However, the human rights tradition includes equality and fraternity, or solidarity, as well as liberty. Stackhouse sees the problem here somewhat differently. He argues that human rights are "essentially a matter of religious ethics":

> each view of human rights entails an ultimate metaphysical-moral vision about what is meaningful, about what relationships or memberships are sacrosanct, and what social ethic should be followed in order to prevent chaos, social alienation, and tyranny from destroying essential humanity. Because human rights claims and movements are religious in this sense, and exist both within and without the major world faiths, it is important for the world's religions to come to terms with human rights.[53]

Human rights claims involve a "vision of what is sacred, inviolable, and absolute in human affairs."[54] For this reason, Stackhouse argues, in the current debate about human rights "the Judeo-Christian traditions of the West confront one of the greatest challenges of the modern age."[55]

For Stackhouse, the issue is not whether human rights doctrine is akin to religious doctrine, for clearly it is: "human rights implies, above all, there is a universal moral order under which all peoples and societies live. Here is a doctrine of a very high order."[56] The question is whether or not this doctrine should become a creed: "A *doctrine* is a teaching, claim, or assertion; a *creed* is a doctrine held to be true, embraced with commitment, celebrated in concert with others, and used as a fundamental guide for action."[57] Stackhouse analyzes human rights doctrines in three different cultural contexts and finds both the Indian and the Marxist contexts wanting. Thus he concludes that human rights may be "a proper credo," but only if it is conceived in the Judeo-Christian traditions of the West.[58]

Conclusion

Support for human rights among conservative Christians is not unanimous. The deist roots of the human rights tradition are worrisome to many. Norman is not alone in expressing a concern that human rights

advocacy is mired in a secularized view of the world. Stackhouse clearly gives support to human rights advocacy only if it is grounded in biblical faith.

Yet major theologians within this wing of the Protestant church do support human rights on the basis of biblical authority. Jacques Ellul argues that human rights are part of God's covenant and thus are central to the witness of the church. John Warwick Montgomery asserts that there are clear biblical warrants for human rights. Carl Henry urges other evangelicals to work for the protection and realization of human rights law, even if it means cooperating with secular humanists. For all of them, as for many Christians, human rights may be understood as the gift of grace.

Thus human hope lies in trusting in the Creator of these rights, who revealed the divine purpose of life through the life, death and resurrection of Jesus Christ. The foundation for human rights is the revelation of God: "No other foundation can a man lay than that which is laid, even Jesus Christ."[59]

Notes

1.   Foster R. McCurley and John H. Reumann, "Human Rights in the Law and Romans (Series A)," in *Human Rights: Rhetoric or Reality*, ed. George W. Forell and William H. Lazareth (Philadelphia: Fortress Press, Justice Books, 1978).

2.   Ibid.

3.   Ibid., 18.

4.   Jacques Ellul, *The Theological Foundation of Law*, trans. Marguerite Wieser (London: SCM Press, 1960), 9.

5.   Ibid., 35.

6.   Ibid.

7.   Ibid., 42.

8.   Ibid., 48-49.

9.   Ibid., 49.

10.   Ibid., 53.

11.   Ibid., 55.

12.   Ibid., 56-57.

13.   Ibid.

14.   Ibid., 135.

15.   Ibid., 137.

16.   John A. Whitehead, *The Second American Revolution* (Elgin, Ill.: David C. Cook, 1982), 116.

17.   Marc Lienhard, "Protestantism and Human Rights," in *Human Rights Teaching* 2, no. 1 (Paris: UNESCO, 1981), 31.

18.   John Warwick Montgomery, *Human Rights and Human Dignity* (Grand Rapids, Mich.: Zondervan, 1986), 23.

19.   Ibid., 78.

20.   Ch. Perelman, "Can the Rights of Man Be Founded?" in *The Philosophy of Human Rights*, ed. Alan Rosenbaum (Westport, Conn.: Greenwood Press, 1980), 47.

21. John Warwick Montgomery, *Human Rights and Human Dignity*, 90. Ethicist G. E. Moore coined the phrase "the naturalistic fallacy," in *Principia Ethica* (Cambridge: Cambridge University Press, 1903), chap. i.

22. Alan R. White, *Rights* (Oxford: Clarendon, 1984), 172-73.

23. John Warwick Montgomery, *Human Rights and Human Dignity*, 106.

24. Montgomery argues that the New Testament is competent evidence as a historical document because it meets the historian's requirements of transmissional reliability, internal reliability, and external reliability, as well as the ancient documents rule that texts "be fair on their face" (show no internal evidence of tampering) and have been maintained in reasonable custody (their preservation has been consistent with their content). Moreover, he argues that the testimony of the witnesses within the New Testament is sufficiently credible evidence to withstand even the hearsay objection.

25. Ibid., 160.

26. Herbert Chanan Brichto, "The Hebrew Bible on Human Rights," in *Essays on Human Rights: Contemporary Rights and Jewish Perspectives*, ed. David Sidorsky (Philadelphia: The Jewish Publication Society of America, 1979), 229-30. Quoted in Montgomery, *Human Rights and Human Dignity*, 169.

27. John Warwick Montgomery, *Human Rights and Human Dignity*, 173.

28. Ibid., 175.

29. Jerome Shestack, "The Jurisprudence of Human Rights," in Theodor Meron, *Human Rights in International Law: Legal and Policy Issues*, ed. Meron (New York: Oxford University Press, 1984), 76, note 24. Quoted in Montgomery, *Human Rights and Human Dignity*, 179.

30. Roland de Pury, *Evangile et Droits de l'Homme* (Geneva: Labor et Fides, 1981), 266. He is paraphrasing Matthew 25:31-46. Quoted in Montgomery, *Human Rights and Human Dignity*, 182.

31. Roland de Pury, *Evangile et Droits de l'Homme*, 261. Quoted in Montgomery, *Human Rights and Human Dignity*, 215.

32. René Coste, *L'Eglise et les Droits de l'Homme*, 79. Quoted in Montgomery, *Human Rights and Human Dignity*, 215.

33. *Human Rights and the Salvation Army* (London: The Campfield Press, 1968), 5.

34. Ibid., 11.

35. In *The First Church of Christ Scientist, and Miscellany*, 222, quoted in "The Freedom in Choosing What is Right," *Christian Science Sentinel* 89, no. 27 (6 July 1987):30.

36. George Colvin, "Social Conscience at the General Conference," *Adventist Currents* (September 1986):36.

37. In *Christian Legal Society Quarterly* 5, no. 3 (1984).

38. Carl F. H. Henry, "Religious Freedom: Cornerstone of Human Rights," *Christian Legal Society Quarterly* 5, no. 3 (1984):7.

39. Ibid., 8, 9.

40. Lowell W. Livezey, "US Religious Organizations and the International Human Rights Movement," *Human Rights Quarterly* 11, no. 1 (February 1989):33.

41. National Association of Evangelicals Resolution B, "Human Rights" (1956). Quoted in Livezey, "US Religious Organizations and the International Human Rights Movement," *Human Rights Quarterly* 11, no. 1 (February 1989):34.

42. Carl F. H. Henry, "The Judeo-Christian Heritage and Human Rights," in *Religious Beliefs, Human Rights, and the Moral Foundation of Western Democracy*, ed. Carl H. Esbeck (Columbia: University of Missouri, 1986), 30.

43. Ibid., 38.

44. Edward Norman, *Christianity and the World Order* (Oxford: Oxford University Press, 1979), 32-33.

45. Ibid., 32. He is quoting from *Gaudium et Spes: Pastoral Constitution on the Church in the World Today* (London: Catholic Truth Society, 1966), 41; and Report of Section V of the Fifth Assembly (Nairobi, 1971) on "Structures of Injustice and Struggles for Liberation—Human Rights." In *Religious Freedom: Main Statements by the World Council of Churches*, 73.

46. Ibid., 31.

47. Ibid., 44.

48. Ibid., 83.

49. Max L. Stackhouse, "Piety, Polity, and Policy," in *Religious Beliefs, Human Rights, and the Moral Foundation of Western Democracy*, 21. In a note he refers to Robert Bellah et al., *Habits of the Heart: Individualism and Commitment in American Life* (Berkeley: University of California Press, 1984).

50. Ibid., 22.

51. Ibid.

52. Ibid., 23.

53. Ibid., 6.

54. Max L. Stackhouse, *Creeds, Society, and Human Rights: A Study in Three Cultures* (Grand Rapids, Mich.: William B. Eerdmans Publishing Company, 1984), 1.

55. Ibid.

56. Ibid., 2.

57. Ibid.

58. Ibid., 23 and 277.

59. 1 Corinthians 3:11. Quoted in Montgomery, *Human Rights and Human Dignity*, 218.

Chapter 4

THE WORLD CHURCH

Support for human rights within the church is not limited to statements by theologians or world church leaders. Nor do Western Christians dominate this witness. All around the globe the cry for human rights resounds in the churches. In the last few years Protestants and Roman Catholics have joined in the struggle for human rights, and today Christians everywhere are providing leadership for the human rights movement.

In this chapter I will describe the human rights advocacy in the churches around the world. I will begin with activity in the churches in Europe, then discuss the struggle in the churches of Africa and Asia, and finally conclude with a description of the Latin American human rights movement. I will not discuss human rights activities by Christians in North America, as these are well documented elsewhere.[1]

Europe

In 1971 Theo C. van Boven, who was then the only person in Holland teaching a human rights course, observed "that the churches are becoming more and more interested in human rights in the 'wider sense'; i.e., that they are no longer interested only in their 'own folk' but in human rights in a universal sense."[2] In the next several years Christian advocacy of human rights in Europe would grow substantially.

Seven years later IDOC International published a collection of documents reprinted from Eastern and Western Europe on religious involvement in the human rights movement. Among the documents are statements by Protestant, Roman Catholic and Orthodox leaders. For example, Renate Riemeck of the Evangelical Church in Germany wrote in 1977: "Jesus Christ vested us with human dignity. So deep are the roots of human rights."[3]

That same year Monsignor Roger Etchegaray, president of the Roman Catholic Bishops' Conference of France, Pasteur Jacques Maury for the French Protestant Federation, and His Excellency Monsignor Meletios, the Orthodox Metropolitan of France, released a common declaration containing the following statement:

> We are ready to act with increasing determination to promote respect for human rights, in cooperation with all men of good will. Many organizations are already at work, within and outside of the churches. We ask Christians to consider this to be one of the forms of their obedience to God who calls on all people to recognize and treat each other as brothers.[4]

Similarly, the Federation of Evangelical Churches of the German Democratic Republic affirmed that "in the light of the Gospel, the churches' task in the field of human rights is a comprehensive one and cannot be limited to the aspects of freedom of belief and freedom of conscience."[5]

In Hungary the Evangelical Lutheran Church asserted that the older individualistic view of human rights is inconsistent with the Gospel, and that the churches need to come to terms with socialism: "By the grace of God, we are in the privileged position to have already undergone that epochal change which the appearance of socialism has meant in the history of the world."[6] Socialism is not seen as a form of oppression, but as "a call to daily service and witness."[7] However, too often

> The ideologizing of individuality inhibits Christian assent to possible measures taken in order to limit individual interests which are pressed at the cost of public interest. This is one of the reasons why, in the case of human rights, Christian reaction is usually more lively to individual injuries than to injuries which harm the public interests and common human rights.[8]

This ideology of individualism "may hinder Christians in their cooperation with non-Christians on an honest human basis, and acting out of their faith for common human goals, whereas such a cooperation today is vital to the survival of mankind."[9]

In the Soviet Union church groups involved in human rights advocacy include: Adventist Group for Legal Struggle and Investigation of Facts concerning the Persecution of Believers in the USSR, Christian Seminar on the Problems of Religious Renaissance, Council of Relatives of Prisoners of Evangelical Christian-Baptists, Fraternal Council of Christians of Evangelical-Pentecostal Faith, Fund to Aid the Evangelical Christian-Pentecostals of Russia, and the Group for the Defense of the Rights of Evangelical Christian-Pentecostals.[10]

In a letter to its more than one hundred member churches including Orthodox, Protestant and Anglican expressions of Christian faith in every

European country except Albania, the Conference of European Churches (CEC) noted that as early as 1967 the CEC had worked for a conference of European governments which was finally accomplished at Helsinki. It urged its members to avoid using human rights "as a propaganda weapon" but asserted: "The member churches of CEC recognize their obligation to inform their respective governments in appropriate fashion of shortcomings in the implementation of social or individual rights."[11]

Both on the continent and in Britain, Christians have been involved in the human rights campaign against torture. In 1978 Christians in France organized Action des Chrétiens pour l'Abolition de la Torture (Action of Christians for the Abolition of Torture) through religious orders and church congregations. ACAT uses the same methods of letter writing and adoption of prisoners as Amnesty International, but its members also pray for both the perpetrators and victims of torture. The organization now has about three hundred groups in eleven countries, with over thirteen thousand members in France alone.[12]

In 1984 the Ministers responsible for cultural affairs in the member countries of the Council of Europe, including the Holy See, issued a statement entitled "European Declaration on Cultural Objectives" which was reprinted in *Church and Culture*, the bulletin of the Pontifical Council for Culture. This declaration affirms that "The main aim of our societies is to enable everyone to achieve personal fulfillment, in an atmosphere of freedom and respect for human rights. . . ."[13]

Monsignor Paul Poupard, as president and chief officer of the Pontifical Council for Culture, led the delegation from the Holy See which helped to draft this declaration. He argued that

The Declaration rightly assigns to the spiritual and religious values their proper place in the cultural dynamism of Europe. The European concept of the human being, or his rights, or his fundamental institutions, finds its deepest roots in the Judaeo-Christian tradition, which strongly emphasizes the unique dignity of the person. . . .[14]

Similarly, Fr. Hervé Carrier, secretary of the Pontifical Council for Culture, stressed the need to guarantee *"the cultural rights of believers"* in today's pluralistic societies.[15]

In addition to statements in support of human rights, the churches of Europe provide space for organizations working on human rights issues and incorporate human rights issues into worship. The International Human Rights Conference held in Krakow, Poland 25-28 April 1988, "could not have been organized or convened without the help of the Church" and its many parishes.[16] In the Church of Saint Maximilian Kolbe, where the conference was held, and in surrounding churches, "images of

the Pope, Lech Walesa, the Black Madonna of Czestochowa, Popielusko (the priest slain in 1984), the recently beatified Edith Stein, and *Solidarnosc* mementoes" were surrounded by constantly lit candles giving "evidence of the tight links between the Church—some parishes more than others, inevitably—and the human rights movement represented by Solidarity."[17]

Africa

In Africa the Christian churches are part of a "new consciousness" which the Diocese of Nampula described as follows in a report in 1977 to the Mozambican National Pastoral Assembly: "There is no doubt that the event of independence and the revolutionary process have deeply affected our way of life and, consequently, our way of being Christians and expressing our faith."[18]

Yet this new consciousness is in some ways a return to an older way of thinking. A communique of the Pan African Conference of Third World Theologians, which was held in Ghana in 1977, asserts that resistance to "the suppression of human rights and the violation of human dignity" is to be understood with a renewed appreciation of the traditional setting where there is "no dichotomy between the sacred and the secular."[19] The values of religion belong in politics and are to be derived from the African experience: "The God of History speaks to all peoples in particular ways. In Africa the traditional religions are a major source for the study of the African experience of God."[20] Thus in 1975 the thirty participants from Protestant, Orthodox and Roman Catholic traditions in the "first church-sponsored consultation on violations of human rights in the independent countries of black Africa" called for "a recovery of our own political, economic and cultural styles and [means of] applying them to the task of development."[21]

In Africa today it is argued that the "entire teaching ministry of the churches—from literacy programs to theological education—should place emphasis on human rights."[22] The 1975 consultation called for a Human Rights Commission for Africa, commended the Christian Council of Lesotho for its legal assistance program, and recommended "that churches become actively involved in promoting human rights throughout Africa through awareness-building and support for those whose rights are abused."[23]

Burgess Carr, as secretary-general of the All Africa Conference of Churches, presented a "Biblical and Theological Basis for the Struggle for Human Rights" to this consultation on human rights. He affirmed that

The struggle for justice and human rights is essentially a power struggle. On the one hand, it involves the politically powerful and the economically secure. On the other hand, it involves the poor, the powerless outcasts, and the marginal multitudes groaning under grinding oppression. Where does *our* God stand? Where does He require the churches—the local congregations and the hierarchies—to stand? Ultimately it is the response to these questions that is determinative both of the character as well as of the content of the Christian's faith, hope and love.[24]

Similarly, Canaan Banana, a Zimbabwe Methodist minister, has argued that because God cares for them, "the oppressed have the right to stand up and fight for their freedom with every means at their disposal."[25]

The Associated Members of the Episcopal Conferences of Eastern Africa (AMECEA), made up of the Catholic bishops of Kenya, Malawi, Tanzania, Uganda and Zambia, published in 1979 a "Declaration on Human Rights and Social Justice," affirming that

This belief in God as our common Father is the basis for the brotherhood of man which recognizes that all men are equal members of the one human family and share in the same human dignity. All men have the same God-given rights and an equal claim to social justice.[26]

In a pastoral letter the Catholic bishops of Angola asserted that all believers "should be aware of their rights" and, quoting *Gaudium et Spes*, that the church wants "to be able to develop freely for the welfare of all, in any political regime which acknowledges the fundamental rights of the individual and his family for a common well-being."[27]

Numerous human rights articles have appeared in the *African Christian*, a pan-African and interdenominational newsletter published fortnightly in Nairobi, Kenya. Human rights issues are also discussed in other African church periodicals.[28] The Catholic bishops of the seven Eastern African countries, in the ninth AMECEA plenary in Tanzania, appealed "to all people in Eastern Africa to respect the human person" and "to all leaders to develop institutions which protect these human rights of all."[29]

The All Africa Conference of Churches, the most representative ecumenical organization in Africa,[30] discussed among other agenda items at its Fourth Assembly "The Gospel—Good News to the Poor (Human Rights)."[31] Moreover, it affirmed that "all men are created equal before God, and ought therefore to enjoy equal rights to life, health, information and freedom of choice."[32]

In a 1986 issue of *African Christian Studies*, Rev. Joseph Kariuki argued from Roman Catholic social teaching that because "every human being has an in-born or natural right to life" the primary "or inalienable right to life carries with it the secondary or consequent right to the means

necessary to sustain life with human dignity."[33] In the same issue Rev. J. M. Waliggo put human rights concerns into a prayer. At the second station of the cross the people pray: "May they [the African people] build a new future on the blood and suffering of all who have witnessed your ideals of human rights, justice and love for all."[34] At the fifth station of the cross the people pray:

> Lord God, we thank you for those churches and organizations and individuals who assist the suffering and the deprived. . . . May their brotherly and sisterly concern lead to the elimination of suffering in the world and strengthen people in the defense of their God-given rights.[35]

And at the eleventh station of the cross the people pray for all innocent prisoners and to "Strengthen all organizations, especially Amnesty International, and those individuals who give hope to such people."[36]

In South Africa Anglican Bishop Desmond Tutu has written of "A Prophetic Church and Human Rights in the Third World," and Trevor Huddleston has argued that Bishop Tutu expresses the essential truth about Christian faith: "that it is based on an infinite respect for human dignity and human rights because of the fact that God himself has taken human nature and therefore endowed it with an infinite purpose and meaning which transcend the barriers of color, race and creed."[37] Moreover, in a letter to the South African Minister of Justice, pastor Allan Boesak asserted: "Your policy is unjust, it denies people their basic human rights and it undermines their humanity."[38]

T. Simon Gqubule, principal of John Wesley College of the Federal Theological Seminary in Alice, has written that: "Apartheid stands for the separation of races whereas the Universal Declaration of Human Rights and the Christian gospel stress the essential *unity of the human race.* . . ."[39] And C. M. Ramusi, Minister of the Interior of Lebowa Legislative Assembly, has asserted:

> I am concerned with human beings living in South Africa who have rights endowed upon them by the Almighty God. I am concerned with human rights, the rights which must recognize inherent dignity in South Africa as members of the human family in a free, just and peaceful world.[40]

John Rees, general secretary of the South African Council of Churches, has argued for a Bill of Human Rights in South Africa because: "The Gospel constrains us and demands of us to recognize the dignity of all men."[41]

Asia

The Seventh Assembly of the Christian Conference of Asia (CCA) in 1981 asserted that Asians "are increasingly becoming conscious of their rights . . . even as these rights are being denied on every side."[42] In 1986 Chinese theologian C. S. Song wrote: "Struggles for human rights are taking place not just in remote lands, but right here in Asian lands. Aspiration for freedom and democracy is not merely the political right of the so-called democratic West; it is also a political right in Asia."[43]

The human rights struggle in the churches began at least fifteen years earlier when the Human Rights Working Group of the Christian Conference of Asia, with participants from most Asian countries, issued a statement affirming that

> As Christians, our convictions on human rights rise out of faith in God, as expressed in the biblical heritage and historical traditions of the Christian community. At the same time, we recognize the question of human rights as being the concern of all humanity, of all traditions and of all ages.[44]

The statement asserts that the "Christian witness in the history of Asian peoples is intertwined with the struggle of the people for liberty and justice" and that one of "the basic facts of the Asian people's experience" is the violation of human rights: "It is in this Asian historical context that we express our theological convictions on human rights."[45]

By 1986 the Christian Conference of Asia had grown to include over one hundred churches and national councils from sixteen countries. On "Asia Sunday," the Sunday before Pentecost, the theme of the special observance was "Fulfilling the Servant Ministry of the Church," and prayers offered for the peoples of Asia in its represented countries included numerous references to concerns for justice and four specific references to "human rights."[46] A year later, the following prayer of thanksgiving was suggested for observance of Asia Sunday:

> For the freedom and unity to which He calls us.
> For all those who proclaim the right to be free.
> For those who work hard to secure it for all.
> For those whose lives are a symbol of unity.
> For the Gift of faith which will not let us rest till we are free and united.[47]

The liturgy, prepared by the Seminari Theologi Malaysia and edited by the CCA, concludes with a prayer of petition: "Enable us by your Holy Spirit to struggle for justice and human rights, and to be agents of mercy and reconciliation."[48]

In addition to caste, many other human rights problems are being addressed within the Indian churches.[49] In his study of the philosophy and history of human rights in India, K. K. Kuriakose notes that by 1980

> The Christian community throughout the country had raised its voice for its religious rights. Moreover, many Christian groups which originally had been formed for church activities were transformed into units to struggle for human rights.[50]

He concludes: "It is a Christian duty to preach, teach, and fight to liberate the millions of economically and socially oppressed people and thereby secure their human rights and dignity."[51]

The quarterly bulletin of the Christian Institute for the Study of Religion and Society devoted a whole issue in 1977 to the controversy in India over Indira Gandhi's emergency decree in 1975 suspending many constitutional rights. The editorial board justified this coverage on the grounds that "the mission of the churches is not merely or primarily to safeguard Christian 'communal' interests but to work for the human dignity and rights of all citizens of this country."[52]

In this issue it was reported that clergy representing the various churches of Kerala[53] had formed a "Clergy Fellowship Concerned with Human Rights" and had jointly affirmed: "We believe the struggle of Christians for Human Rights is a fundamental response to Jesus Christ."[54] Their statement concludes:

> Finally, we affirm that wherever human rights are suppressed or violated by the Government, churches have a duty to work for the defense of human rights, especially of the oppressed. We believe the whole question of THE MISSION OF THE CHURCH is involved in this issue.[55]

They ground their "concerns for human rights" on the "conviction that God wills a society in which all can exercise full human rights."[56]

An editorial in *The Examiner* quotes the document on "The Church and Human Rights" issued by the Pontifical Commission *Justitia et Pax* to argue that private property is a conditional right which derives "from the law of the communal purpose of earthly goods as ordained by the Creator," whereas fundamental rights "are human because they belong to the very nature of man":

> All these rights the Christian can defend as human, together with followers of all religions and none. Those who believe in God, naturally, draw their conclusions about the sacredness of human rights from the fact that God in creating man has called him to an eternal destiny and fashioned him to his own image and likeness. At the basis of their belief in human rights is human dignity and

the infinite worth of every human person, the fact that every man is not an object but a subject. For the Christian, however, human dignity has been essentially transformed ever since God became man in order that sharing in this humanity man might share in God's divinity. That is the mystery we celebrate at Christmas, when we see in the crib a child, that is bone of our bone and flesh of our flesh, born of a woman, born under the law but in order to redeem those who are under the law and bring them true liberation.[57]

Therefore, "Christ's solidarity with all men is the reason for the Church's strong defense of human rights wherever they are trampled underfoot, as indeed they are in so many countries."[58]

In 1986 in India participants in a National Conference on "The Emerging Church of the Poor" affirmed that "the marginalized" have begun "to assert their inalienable right to participate in decision-making processes" because there is

a new awakening of thought and sensitivity in the Churches, as evidenced in the struggles of the marginalized who have become conscious of their dignity and destiny, and in the committed lives of individuals and groups of Christians and others who have opted to be with the poor.[59]

Moreover, they asserted, "This view of human life is what faith affirms."[60]

Examples of personal witness abound. At a "Symposium on Asian Spirituality" held in Indonesia in 1983, the Rev. Donald Kanagarataam of Sri Lanka reported that he had left teaching at Lanka College "to enter an experimental ministry to work on human rights" and "had twice been arrested for 'doing Christian ministry'."[61] For similar acts of witness the Indonesian Legal Aid Foundation on Human Rights Day in 1986 gave awards to "Father Josef Baliarta Mangunwijaya [a lecturer at Gadjab Mada State University who lives with landless poor people] and village chief Willi Prasetya, a Catholic, who together led poor people living on the bank of Yogyakarta's Code River in a successful fight against relocation."[62]

That same year, at a conference on the Vocation of the Laity in the Life and Mission of the Church in Oceania, Lucy Keino, a diocesan development education officer from Papua New Guinea with only a primary school education, described her responsibilities:

to give seminars at grass-roots level on an understanding of what true development of the persons really means (that is: The promotion of the good of the whole person and every person); also to give justice awareness seminars (that is: To point out that persons have rights and duties which flow from their dignity as human persons).[63]

Of course, she knew that church educators have been murdered for carrying out these responsibilities.

In the Philippines Bert Cacayan describes the changes in his mother, a devout Filipino Catholic, which occurred in the 1970s when the church "took to heart the teachings of Vatican II and popularized subsequent documents like Populorum, Justice in the World and other social documents":

> Now my mother still goes to Church every day. She is a prayer leader and still sings in the Church choir. But more than that, she attends conscientizing seminars, she joins mass demonstrations and rallies protesting violations of human rights. She visits detainees and leads the Apostleship of Prayer group in taking radical options on certain political issues like boycotting sham elections. She teaches her children that the struggle for freedom and justice is an imperative of the Christian faith.[64]

He concludes: "The testimony and witness of persecuted Christians will deepen the Church's involvement in human rights . . . , will purify its proclamation of the liberating Gospel, and will make her a sacrament and an instrument for the realization of the 'new heaven and the new earth'."[65]

Jack Clancey, of the Hong Kong Center for the Progress of Peoples, has written:

> I know of several parishes in Hong Kong with a human rights group. These groups regularly ask for prayers, write letters, or have signature campaigns for people whose human rights have been abused. I think there should be such groups in all parishes.[66]

He has argued that as "human rights are necessary to help people live a more fully human life" and "Christ came to help all people live a fuller life . . . one role, or mission, of a Christian is to help people in their struggles to attain and protect their human rights."[67]

In 1986 a pastoral letter of the Presbyterian Church in Taiwan urged the government "to guarantee the people's freedom and rights as prescribed in the Constitution" and to respect "human rights and rectify past deficiencies in the verdicts of the civil courts by immediately setting free all prisoners of conscience, through due process of law."[68] Moreover, on 11 March 1987 eighty pastors, laity and students from the Taiwan (Presbyterian) Theological College protested the seizure of the Presbyterian *Taiwan Church News,* which was reporting a statement of the Taiwan Association for the Promotion of Human Rights.[69]

Korean Cardinal Kim has long been outspoken in support of human rights. In 1986, at a mass celebrating human rights, he declared that "if the Government of South Korea continues to violate human rights, it has

no competence to govern and it should resign."[70] In February of 1987 Cardinal Kim called "for nine days of nationwide prayer for human rights" to coincide with the Korean Independence Day and Ash Wednesday, and the forty-ninth day after the death of police torture victim Park Chung-chul, the day Buddhists believe his soul would leave the earth.[71]

In 1987 the Catholic Justice and Peace Commission at its annual meeting gave the Korean Bar Association's campaign against torture its full support and over $1,000 from the Christian Human Rights Memorial subcommittee.[72] Catholics in Korea also support economic rights. In the words of Columban missionary Fr. Noel Mackey, who works in the slums of Seoul, "I think the Church should become involved in the three basic rights for people: right to eat, right to be clothed, and right to have a house."[73]

Protestant churches in Korea have also been in the forefront of the human rights movement. The Sixty-ninth General Assembly of the Presbyterian Church in South Korea protested the harassment of Rev. Park Hyung Kyu, minister of Chei Church in Seoul,[74] who wrote from his hospital bed that

> [the church's] evangelization movement must stand at the side of the workers and farmers, and protect and support their human rights and interests. Although I am dishonored and denounced as a pro-communist pastor because of my vocation, which is commanded by God, I will continue to devote myself to this task which I believe is the real mission of the church.[75]

That same year, members of the Korea Association of Accredited Theological Schools and the Korea Association of Christian Studies, who participated in the Centennial Theologians Conference, affirmed their "resistance against an ideology of totalitarian dictatorial powers that oppress human rights or dignity."[76]

In 1986 the National Council of Churches in Korea formed the Pan-Christian Committee to Promote a Democratic Constitution, released the names of one thousand clergy who supported constitutional revision, and affirmed:

> The people's desire for the direct election of the president must be respected and we must establish a democratic constitution that protects the people's basic rights and freedoms, and guarantees the people's right to secure their livelihood.[77]

Furthermore, they asserted: "We devoutly believe that it is God's will for democracy to be established at this moment in our nation's history."[78] That same year *Activity News*, published by the National Council of Churches in Korea, reported under a regular section entitled "Human

Rights News" the arrests, protests, and self-immolations of human rights advocates.[79]

Latin America

In 1969 the Sixth Annual Catholic Inter-American Cooperation Program (CICOP) Conference attempted to address the concern Paul VI expressed in his letter to the International Conference on Human Rights in Teheran in 1968, on the twentieth anniversary of the Universal Declaration of Human Rights:

> How can the fundamental rights of man be assured, when they are flouted? How, in a word, can we intervene to save the human person wherever it is threatened? How to make the leaders aware that this concerns an essential heritage of mankind which no one may harm with impunity, under any pretext, without attacking what is most sacred in a human being and without thereby ruining the very foundations of life in society?[80]

Among those at the conference addressing this question were Hector Borrat of Uruguay, Archbishop Helder Pessoa Camara of Brazil, Paulo Freire of Chile, Jorge Mejia, S.J. of Argentina, Luis Alberto Meyer of Paraguay, and René de León Scholotter of Guatemala. This conference represents the beginning of the Christian human rights movement in Latin America.

Carolyn Cook Dipboye provides a good summary of the church-state struggle "which dominated the decade separating the Latin American Episcopal Conference at Medellín in 1968 (CELAM II) and the conference at Puebla in 1979 (CELAM III).[81] With Dom Helder Camara in the lead, the Brazilian hierarchy became "a massive force for advancing human rights."[82] In 1973 the hierarchies in the central west, the northeast, and the northern areas of Brazil all published statements on human rights,[83] as the Brazilian Bishops Conference issued its own "Universal Declaration of Human Rights" and initiated an ecumenical Campaign for Human Rights and Dignity.[84] And in 1974 the Brazilian hierarchy "adopted a worldwide plan" to disseminate information on human rights violations and ways to respond, which grew to include some fifteen hundred small groups all over the world.[85]

The hierarchy of the Roman Catholic Church in Chile also used episcopal declarations to resist human rights violations and supported the ecumenical Committee of Cooperation for Peace which processed some thirty thousand human rights appeals during its two years of operation. When because of pressure Cardinal Silva Henríquez dismantled the Committee, he replaced

it with the Vicariate for Solidarity, which as "an indispensable disseminator of accurate information on the status of human rights in Chile" has assisted in the human rights protests of Amnesty International and the Organization of American States.[86]

In Nicaragua in 1978 a letter from the Episcopal Conference calling upon Somoza to resign was endorsed by every major business organization in the country.[87] And the Priests' Council and the Board of Catholic Religious Orders sent a letter to President Carter two months before Somoza stepped down, asking for an end to aid because of the human rights violations of the regime.[88] In El Salvador Archbishop Oscar Romero also asked for an end to U.S. aid and by 1980 was denouncing specific human rights violations every Sunday from the pulpit, until his assassination on March 24th.[89]

The Roman Catholic Church has denounced retaliatory measures taken against it[90] "for raising its voice in support of human rights as an obvious infringement of its ministry."[91] It asserts that: "The Church's defense of human rights is the completion of the preaching of the gospel, the concretizing of the good news of salvation."[92] Thus many of the "basic Christian communities" created to evangelize the masses of the people of Latin America became involved not only in "meeting for biblical reflection," but also in "sharing common concerns and struggling for human rights and human dignity."[93]

Writing in preparation for the third conference of bishops at Puebla, Ricardo Antoncich asserted that violations of human rights, "which are so loudly denounced by world public opinion, cannot be ignored by the conscience of the Church in its reflections on faith."[94] He argued that the Brazilian bishops make clear that "Jesus Christ is the concrete model of respect for human rights," for in their "Pastoral Communication to the people of God" in 1976 they "point to concrete imitation of Jesus Christ as the way of promoting human rights" by asserting that "Christ was the great defender of human rights."[95]

At Puebla in 1979 the denunciations of human rights violations contained in the first draft of the final document failed by eight votes to receive the necessary two-thirds approval; however, forty cardinals and bishops representing eleven Latin American countries later signed a letter of support denouncing the human rights abuses in Nicaragua and El Salvador and supporting the witness of the churches there.[96] Carolyn Cook Dipboye concludes: "Despite the weaknesses in the Final Document, Puebla did not represent a retreat from the Church's work for human rights."[97]

Diego Irarrazaval, a Roman Catholic deacon in the Peruvian church, wrote after Puebla of a "pastoral ministry of human rights," suggesting "that the main elements of popular religiosity—prayer, the fiesta, the practice of believers—are integrated in the ministry of human rights, in a

context of oppression where the poor are taking steps toward liberation."[98] As "prayer affirms the justice of God and, consequently, the rights of the poor," the "ministry of people's rights" is, "among other things, a ministry of prayer."[99] Just as in the Bible:

> The fiesta of faith celebrates the liberation from oppression, the alliance that God makes with the poor, the right to a new land, and then, the death and resurrection of Christ and the brotherhood of believers. . . . All this celebration of the faith expresses and strengthens the right of the people to laugh and struggle, that is, to look for a new and dignified life.[100]

Irarrazaval argues that the Latin American church has a "long and rich tradition of defending and promoting people's rights.[101] Moreover, he concludes: "the ministry of the rights of the people has to take place in all the life of the church," is rooted in "the religiosity of the oppressed and of those who struggle," and "encourages the evangelizing potential of the poor."[102]

Julio de Santa Ana of Uruguay has suggested that the churches "are contributing to an understanding that human rights cannot be reduced to civil rights" but are basically the rights of peoples:

> The defense of human rights, understood from this perspective, assumes a lot more than defending the rights of the persecuted, of the prisoners, of the tortured ones. It must deal with the causes by which many are unjustly persecuted, put in prison and subjected to torture and with the recovery of the right to work, the right to a life of dignity, the right of native communities to their lands, the right to a just salary, the right to the [sic] participation in the social and political life, the right to peace.[103]

He believes that this "new element in the mission of the Church," which has been discovered in the Third World, should not be overlooked by churches in more affluent and secure societies.[104]

Former Methodist Bolivian Bishop Mortimer Arias has written that "Human rights in Latin America is not just a matter for foreign policy; it is a matter of life and death, a matter of our confessing life":

> As the German church had to come to that confessing point before Nazism, so the church in Latin America has had to stand on the matter of human rights. Human rights are God-given rights to every human creature; as I said to my interrogators who asked again and again, "Why are you defending human rights?"[105]

Arias believes that in the churches' defense of life, "Human rights assumed the character of a *status confessionis*, the dividing line between

what was Christian or un-Christian."[106] He notes that Christian organizations, often working with non-Christian groups, used "all non-violent means available" in this defense, including "Assemblies for Human Rights, Commissions for Justice and Peace, advocacy for prisoners of conscience, public denunciations and publications, low-profile intercessions with authorities, monitoring of 'missing persons,' legal assistance to the victims and their families, demonstrations, hunger strikes and fastings."[107]

Bishop Helmut Frenz of the Evangelical Lutheran Church in Chile has also been imprisoned for his human rights advocacy. He affirms that "The Kingdom of God . . . begins where persons take the divine rights so seriously that they start to put them into practice as human rights."[108] Thus it became "clear in Chile that defending human rights and commitment to human dignity were an unabandonable part of the preaching of the Gospel."[109]

The Latin American Protestant Commission on Christian Education (CELADEC) has developed since 1962 into a major ecumenical organization involving both Protestant and Roman Catholic leaders at regional, national and local levels in the struggle for human rights. By 1981 it had published over one hundred and seventy booklets, including a sixty-page study entitled *Human Rights: With Blood and Fire* and a manual entitled *Manual de Derechos Humanos*, which explains how to file complaints about human rights violations with intergovernmental organizations and lists the nongovernmental organizations which can assist. This manual also presents all the relevant human rights texts of the UN, the International Labor Organization, and the Inter-American Commission on Human Rights.

Finally, since 1976 the Human Rights Resources Office for Latin America of the World Council of Churches has worked with the Latin American Council of Churches and the Caribbean Conference of Churches to help victims of torture and police brutality and to support human rights education and action. In 1985 the Human Rights Resources Office for Latin America funded the publication of *Nuncia Mais* ("Never Again"), which presents seven years of research conducted by Sao Paulo's Roman Catholic archdiocese into the torture used by the Brazilian government. And in 1987 alone it channeled about $1.7 million to churches and church-related human rights groups in Latin America.[110]

Conclusion

One might well conclude then that the leadership of the human rights movement in Latin America, and around the globe, is in its churches, rather than in its law schools or political parties.[111] For the churches worldwide have made human rights a central part of their Christian

witness in societies where brutal violations of human rights and the basic conditions of human dignity are tragically commonplace.

Notes

1.   Lowell W. Livezey argues that religious organizations have played an increasingly important role in the "nongovernmental human rights movement in the United States since the Vietnam War." Livezey, "US Religious Organizations and the International Human Rights Movement," *Human Rights Quarterly* 11, no. 1 (February 1989):14. This article is excerpted from his monograph, *Nongovernmental Organizations and the Ideas of Human Rights* (Princeton, N.J.: Center of International Studies, Princeton University, 1988).

2.   Jeffrey S. Brand, "Memorandum to Professor Frank C. Newman," in the Human Rights Collection of the Boalt Hall Library, 23 January 1971, 7.

3.   "The Human Rights Debate and Its Historical Background," in *Human Rights Is More than Human Rights: A Primer for Churches on Security and Cooperation in Europe,* ed. Erich and Marilyn Weingärtner (Rome: IDOC International, 1977), 7.

4.   "Declaration," in *Human Rights Is More than Human Rights,* 19.

5.   "Helsinki Today," in *Human Rights Is More than Human Rights,* 37.

6.   "In Jesus Christ—A New Community," in *Human Rights Is More than Human Rights,* 13-14. For a historical analysis of human rights in Hungary, see Lázló Makkai, "The Development of Human Rights in Hungary from the Reformation to the Present," *Soundings* 67, no. 2 (Summer 1984):154-64.

7.   Ibid.

8.   Ibid., 14.

9.   Ibid., 15. For human rights recommendations developed at Taizé, see "Contacts with the United Nations," *Letter from Taizé* (February-March 1987):7, and "Youth Suggestions for the UN," *Letter from Taizé* (February-March):6.

10.   David Kowalewski, "The Union of Soviet Socialist Republics," *International Handbook of Human Rights,* ed. Jack Donnelly and Rhoda E. Howard (Westport, Conn.: Greenwood Press, 1987), 414-15.

11.   "The Helsinki Followup Conference in Belgrade: A Letter to Member Churches," in *Human Rights Is More than Human Rights,* 38-39.

12.   Gretchen Ellis, informal talk to International Seminar in Theology and Law, 27 July 1987, Strasbourg, France.

13.   "European Declaration on Cultural Objectives," *Church and Cultures,* no. 2 (1984):9.

14.   Monsignor Paul Poupard, "Intervention of the Holy See," *Church and Cultures,* no. 2 (1984):10.

15.   Fr. Hervé Carrier, "Cultural Forum, Budapest Intervention of the Holy See," *Church and Cultures,* no. 4 (1985):6, printed in *L'Osservatore Romano,* English ed., 25 November 1985.

16.   Rita Maran, "How Should We Promote Human Rights Today?" in *Report on the International Human Rights Conference,* an insert in *Human Rights Advocates,* no. 12 (December 1988).

17.   Ibid. Stefania Szlek Miller argues that the church in Poland both provides a justifying theory for human rights and "is the leading conservative body in opposing, on human rights principles, the norms and patterns of behavior of modern industrial society." Miller, "Poland," *International Handbook of Human Rights,* 304.

18.   "A New Consciousness Is Emerging," in *Human Rights: A Challenge to Theology*, ed. Marc Reuver (Rome: CCIA and IDOC International, 1983), 151. This report is published in full in *IDOC International Bulletin*, nos. 2-3 (1978):15-16.

19.   "A Relevant Theology," in *Human Rights: A Challenge to Theology*, 130-31.

20.   Ibid., 132. S. Amos Wako, a Christian theologian, also supports this position. See Wako, "Human Rights in Africa Today," in *Political Trends in Africa: Development, Arms Race, Human Rights* (Geneva: Commission of the Churches on International Affairs, World Council of Churches, 1981/2), 26-34.

21.   "Ecumenical Diary," *The Ecumenical Review* 27, no. 2 (April 1975):159-60.

22.   Ibid., 160.

23.   Ibid.

24.   Burgess Carr, "Biblical and Theological Basis for the Struggle for Human Rights," *The Ecumenical Review* 27 (April 1975):123.

25.   Canaan Banana, "The Biblical Basis for Liberation Struggles," *International Review of Mission* 68, no. 272 (October 1979):418. Former Presiding Bishop of the Lutheran World Federation Josiah Kibira of Tanzania has "urged the Churches to emphasize missionary work, peace efforts and human rights." "Special Issue on the Lutheran World Federation's Seventh Assembly," *Asia Lutheran News* (July-August 1984):13.

26.   "Declaration on Human Rights and Social Justice," *Exchange: Bulletin of Third World Christian Literature* 15, no. 45 (December 1986):26.

27.   "The Catholic Bishops' Pastoral Letter (Angola)," *Exchange* 15, no. 45 (December 1986):45 and 47.

28.   For example, in 1986 the *Baptist Times* reported that Reverend Clive Calver, General Secretary of the Evangelical Alliance, protested the imprisonment of members of the Coptic Evangelical Church in Egypt: "The family's detention is a flagrant breach of their constitutional rights and Egypt's stated policy on religious freedom under the International Covenant on Civil and Political Rights. I urge people to protest against this open violation of human rights." See "In Prison for Sake of the Faith," *Baptist Times* (1 May 1986):21.

29.   "Solidarity with the Suffering," *African Christian Studies* 2, no. 1 (July 1986):114. The "Message of the Synod to the People of God," which reaffirms "the dignity of the human person" and "the fundamental rights of men," was reprinted in the African periodical *AFER*. See "Documents of the Extraordinary Synod: The Final Report," *AFER* 2, no. 2 (December 1986):59. An analysis of Roman Catholic social teaching on the right to private property was published in an earlier issue. See G. Lobo, S.J., "Towards a Theology of Development," *AFER* 13, no. 1 (1971):21-23.

30.   P. Hoogeveen, "Introducing the Declarations," *Exchange* 15, no. 45 (December 1986):7.

31.   A. C. Fiaferana, "Know the AACC: Assemblies and Pre-Assemblies," *The African Challenge* 1, no. 3 (August 1986):27.

32.   "Human Rights: A Choice between Good and Evil," *The African Challenge* 1, no. 3 (August 1986):9.

33.   Joseph Kariuki, "Social Justice and the Option for the Church in Eastern Africa: The Ethical Perspective," *African Christian Studies* 2, no. 2 (December 1986):67. Cardinal Jaime Sin of the Philippines, speaking in Nairobi, apparently agrees, as he "challenged the clergy to fight for peoples' rights" because their primary duty "was to protect people and fight for their noble rights in society." See "Fight for Peoples' Rights," *African Christian* 5, Congress Special (18 August 1985):7.

34.   Rev. J. M. Waliggo, "A Prayer of Solidarity with the Suffering and the Oppressed of the World," *African Christian Studies* 2, no. 2 (December 1986):59.

35.   Ibid., 61.

36.   Ibid., 63.

37. Desmond Tutu, *Crying in the Wilderness: The Struggle for Justice in South Africa*, foreword by Trevor Huddleston (Grand Rapids, Mich.: William B. Eerdmans Publishing Company, 1982), 113 and 7.

38. Allan Boesak, "Mission to Those in Authority," *International Review of Mission* 69, no. 273 (January 1980):73. In a fund-raising letter for Amnesty International, black African minister Tshenuwani Simon Farisani of the Evangelical Lutheran Church of Southern Africa reported that he was imprisoned four times in South Africa without charges, "Because of beliefs I share with you—like the freedom of speech and assembly, and support of human rights." He affirms: "While I don't know what life has in store for me after I regain my strength, one thing is certain—I will continue to be a human rights activist and I hope you will too." See Letter to "Amnesty International Supporter," 11 May 1987.

39. T. Simon Gqubule, "Black Experience," in *Human Rights in South Africa*, ed. Brian Johanson (Johannesburg: South Africa Council of Churches, 1974), 6.

40. C. M. Ramusi, "Hope from a Black Homeland," in *Human Rights in South Africa*, 9.

41. John Rees, "The Christian Community Looks to the Future," in *Human Rights in South Africa*, 41. Joshua Lobelo has written: "As a pastor, my duty is to educate people about their rights and responsibilities." See Rev. Joshua Lobelo, "The Minister as Pastor to the Oppressed," *The Drew Gateway* 53, no. 3 (Spring 1983):17.

42. Extract from *Living in Christ with People: Introducing the Theme*, "The Asian Context," in *Human Rights: A Challenge to Theology*, 89.

43. Choan-Seng Song, "Open Frontiers of Theology in Asia: Ten Theological Proposals," in *Human Rights: A Challenge to Theology*, 107. In 1986 Hindu, Muslim, Christian, and Ayya Vazhi leaders joined in a common statement of belief. See "Kanyakumari Declaration: On Inter-Religious Social Action towards Justice and Peace," *Christian Conference of Asia News* 21, no. 8 (15 August 1986):10.

44. "Human Rights in Asia," *Exchange* 15, no. 45 (December 1986):70.

45. Ibid.

46. "Christian Conference of Asia: Asia Sunday," *Asia Focus* 2, no. 17 (2 May 1986):3.

47. "Realizing the Freedom and the Unity of the Church," a Liturgy for Asia Sunday, 31 May 1987 (Singapore: Christian Conference of Asia, 1987). Distributed in *Asia Focus* 9, no. 3 (May 1987).

48. Ibid.

49. See George Mathew, "Structures for Institutionalizing Human Rights and Moral Values," *Religion and Society* 28, no. 1 (March 1981): 3-13; *Religious Freedom*, ed. J. R. Chandran and M. M. Thomas (Bangalore City: The Bangalore Press, 1956); and Aruna Gnanadason, "Human Rights and Women's Concerns," *Religion and Society* 28, no. 1 (March 1981):14-24.

50. K. K. Kuriakose, *Human Rights and Christians in India (1947-1980)* (M.A. thesis, Graduate Theological Union, December 1982), 114. See Felix N. Sugirtharaj, "A Case Study on Organizing Agricultural Laborers for Human Rights, Self-Dependence and People's Organization," *Religion and Society* 28, no. 1 (March 1981):48-63.

51. Ibid., 118.

52. Editorial, *Religion and Society* 24, nos. 2 and 3 (June and September 1977):2. M. M. Thomas writes of the human rights struggle in India in "Preston's Approach to the 'Fourth World'," *Religion and Society* 28, no. 1 (March 1981):64-75.

53. The Church of South India, the Mar Thoma Church, the Orthodox Syrian Church, the Jacobite Syrian Church, the Chaldean Syrian Church, and the Roman Catholic Church.

54. "Fellowship of the Clergy Concerned with Human Rights Formed in Kerala, India," *Religion and Society* 24, nos. 2 and 3 (June and September 1977):65.

55. Ibid., 68. Emphasis in original.

56. Ibid., 67. The Human Rights Forum of Tamilnada Theological College released a similar statement entitled "Let Us as Christians Raise Our Voice to Protect Human Rights." In *Religion and Society* 24, nos. 2 and 3 (June and September 1977):84-85.

57. Editorial, *The Examiner*, 18 December 1976, in *Religion and Society* 24, nos. 2 and 3 (June and September 1977):186-87.

58. Ibid., 187.

59. "Report: Statement of the National Conference on 'The Emerging Church of the Poor'," *East Asia Journal of Theology* 4, no. 2 (October 1986):24 and 27.

60. Ibid., 28.

61. Grover F. Tyner, Jr., "Symposium on Asian Spirituality," *East Asia Journal of Theology* 3, no. 1 (April 1985):8. This comment was reported as part of a discussion on "Confucianist-Buddhist-Taoist Religious Culture and Spirituality." The journal was renamed *Asia Journal of Theology* in 1987 and is published by the Association for Theological Education in South East Asia and the North East Asia Association of Theological Schools.

62. "Honors for River Bank Priest," *Asia Focus* 2, no. 45 (28 November 1986):2.

63. Quoted in *The Vocation of the Laity in the Life and Mission of the Church in Oceania* (Vatican City: Documentation Service, 1986), 41-43.

64. Bert Cacayan, "The Humanizing Breeze of Vatican II," *Asia Link* 8, no. 2 (March 1986):5. Marianni Dimaranan, C.F.I.C., one "of the more outspoken nuns and well-known in the country and abroad as a human rights advocate," asserts: "The Church must play a role in the protection of human rights. This is central to the Gospel. Defense of human rights is defense of the image of God in the individual." Ruth Ocera Cortez, "Church Women in the Struggle," *Branches* 2, no. 1 (Fall-Winter 1986):74-85.

65. Ibid. However, Peter G. Gowing argues that Christians and Muslims in the Philippines differ significantly over human rights. Gowing, "Of Different Minds: Christian and Muslim Ways of Looking at Their Relations in the Philippines," *International Review of Mission* 67, no. 265 (January 1978):74-85.

66. Jack Clancey, "Human Rights in Asia," *Asia Link* 8, no. 14 (July 1986):8.

67. Ibid., 7.

68. "A Call for Increased Democracy," *CCA News* 21, no. 12 (15 December 1986):5.

69. "Taiwan Observes 'February 28 Incident'," *Asia Focus* 3, no. 11 (20 March 1987):1-3.

70. "Cardinal Kim: 'Government Should Resign if Human Rights Abuses Continue'," *Asia Focus* 2, no. 47 (12 December 1986):1. It was reported three pages later that the Korean National Council of Churches' Human Rights Commission "had planned prayer meetings at 33 different places throughout the country."

71. "Cardinal Sets Nationwide Prayer for Human Rights," *Asia Focus* 3, no. 8 (27 February 1987):1. Cardinal Kim wrote: "Let us intercede collectively with our merciful Father and Mother Mary, especially on March 1 and 4, for individual conversion, Church reform, democratization and the recovery of human rights here."

72. "Cardinal Sets Nationwide Prayer for Human Rights," *Asia Focus* 3, no. 8 (27 February 1987):4.

73. Noel Mackey, "My View of Social Justice," *Asia Link* 7, no. 4 (July 1985):4.

74. "The 69th General Assembly of the Presbyterian Church in South Korea," *Asia Link* 7, no. 3 (May 1985):8.

75. Park Hyung Kyu, "A Letter from a Korean Church Minister," *Asia Link* 7, no. 3 (May 1985):12.

76. "Declaration of Korean Theologians," *East Asian Journal of Theology* 3, no. 2 (October 1985):290-92.

77. "Churches Throw Their Weight Behind Campaign for Constitutional Revision in Korea," *CCA News* 21, no. 4 (15 April 1986):9.

78.   Ibid.

79.   See *Activity News*, no. 8 (March 1986), no. 9 (April 1986), no. 10 (May 1986), and no. 11 (June 1986). A conservative congregation of a pastor "sentenced to a prison term because of his stand on human rights" initially responded by planning a worship service to pray for his repentance as a sinner; however, when the pastor was finally released, the congregation "had experienced a change of heart" for the pastor "was given a hero's welcome and the theme was: 'The Suffering Servant'." "The Word of God—Astir in Asia: 'Sinner or Servant'?" *Asia Link* 6, no. 4 (July 1987):10.

80.   Quoted in Louis M. Colonnese, "Forward: The Remaining Daylight," in *Human Rights and the Liberation of Man in the Americas*, ed. Colonnese (Notre Dame: University of Notre Dame Press, 1970), xxv.

81.   Carolyn Cook Dipboye, "The Roman Catholic Church and the Political Struggle for Human Rights in Latin America, 1968-1980," *Journal of Church and State* 24 (1982):497. Penny Lernoux describes almost the same period of history in more detail in *Cry of the People: United States Involvement in the Rise of Fascism, Torture and Murder and the Persecution of the Catholic Church in Latin America* (Garden City, N.Y.: Doubleday, 1980).

82.   Ibid., 501.

83.   See Thomas Quigley, "Latin America's Church: No Turning Back," *Cross Currents* 28 (Spring 1978):83.

84.   See Ecumenical Service Commission, *The Universal Declaration of Human Rights* (Washington, D.C.: Latin American Documentation, n.d.) and Brazilian National Bishops Conference, "A Universal Declaration of Human Rights," *LADOC* 4 (October 1973):1-7.

85.   Carolyn Cook Dipboye, "The Roman Catholic Church and the Political Struggle for Human Rights in Latin America, 1968-1980," *Journal of Church and State* 24 (1982):501-02.

86.   Ibid., 504. See "Notes of Church-State Affairs," *Journal of Church and State* 18 (Autumn 1976): 596-97 and 19 (Winter, Spring 1977):146-48, 378-79. Jinny Arancibia, Marcelo Charlin, and Peter Landstreet report that in 1980, "repression mounted against the Catholic Church, which was assuming great visibility on the human rights front. Methods included threats to priests and other church members; the placing of bombs in poor neighborhoods; and a media campaign to discredit the Church hierarchy, especially Cardinal Silva Henríquez, who more than any other single public figure in Chile at this time symbolized in his person opposition to the military regime's human rights violations." Arancibia, Charlin, and Landstreet, "Chile," in *International Handbook of Human Rights*, 60.

87.   See "Notes on Church-State Affairs," *Journal of Church and State* 20 (Autumn 1978):620-21.

88.   "Statement to President Jimmy Carter from Nicaraguan Clergy and Religious," *LADOC* 9 (January-February 1979):12-14.

89.   See "Communiqué from the Archbishop of San Salvador," *LADOC* 9 (November-December 1978):42-45; "Salvadoran Archbishop Asks Carter to End Military Aid," *LADOC* 10 (July-August 1980):44-45; "A Pastor's Last Homily," *Sojourners* 9 (May 1980):16 and 60. Three of the four human rights documentation offices operating in San Salvador at that time were church related: the *Oficina de tutela del Arzobispado* (the Archdiocese Office for Legal Protection), *Socorro Jurídica Cristiano* (Christian Legal Aid Office), and the Documentation and Information Center of the (Catholic) Central American University. Liisa Lukkari North, "El Salvador," in *International Handbook of Human Rights*, 118.

90.   A study conducted in 1979 by the National Conference of Brazilian Bishops revealed that 30 bishops had been threatened with death or imprisonment; 9 bishops, 113 religious, and 273 lay leaders had been arrested; 34 priests had been tortured; and 7 priests had been killed. "News Cue," *National Catholic Reporter* 15 (16 February 1979):7. In El Salvador between 1977 and 1979, six priests were murdered by rightist forces. Thomas Quigley, "Latin America's Church: No Turning Back," *Cross Currents* 28 (Spring 1978):88.

91.   Carolyn Cook Dipboye, "Catholic Church and Human Rights," *Journal of Church and State* 24 (1982):512. Penny Lernoux writes: "The central issue in the ongoing religious war between Church and State in Latin America is human rights." Lernoux, *Cry of the People*, xiii.

92.   Ibid., 513. See Nicaraguan Bishops Conference, "Renewing Christian Hope," in *Latin American Bishops Discuss Human Rights*, LADOC Keyhole Series, no. 15 (Washington, D.C.: Latin-American Documentation, 1977), 36.

93.   F. Ross Kinsler, "Mission by the People," *International Review of Mission* 68, no. 271 (July 179):237. See Dipboye, "Catholic Church and Human Rights," 518.

94.   Ricardo Antoncich, S.J., "Evangelization and Human Rights," in *Human Rights: A Challenge to Theology*, 47. This article originally appeared in Portuguese in the March 1978 special issue of the *Revista Eclesiástica Brasileira*.

95.   Ibid., 56-57.

96.   See Penny Lernoux, "Latin Bishops Reaffirm Church Alliance to Poor," *National Catholic Reporter* 15 (23 February 1979):1, 4, 7, and 9.

97.   Carolyn Cook Dipboye, "Catholic Church and Human Rights," *Journal of Church and State* 24 (1982):522. See Héctor Borrat, "Human Rights at Puebla," *Human Rights Concerns* (July 1979):8-10.

98.   Diego Irarrazaval, "The Rights of Oppressed People and Their Religiosity," in *Human Rights: A Challenge to Theology*, 67 and 71.

99.   Ibid., 69.

100.   Ibid., 70.

101.   Ibid., 71. An International Conference at the Pontifical University of St. Thomas Aquinas in Rome, 4-6 March 1985, commemorated the fifth centenary of the birth of Francisco de Victoria and Bartolomé de las Casas, "two Dominicans whose names remain linked to the defense of the rights of Indians in America at the time of the discovery." "Congresses and Meetings," *Church and Culture*, no. 3 (1985):16.

102.   Ibid. Similarly, José Míguez Bonino argues that the pastoral concern for the life of the people "drives the church to denounce the violation of human rights." Bonino, *Toward a Christian Political Ethics* (Philadelphia: Fortress Press, 1983), 73.

103.   Julio de Santa Ana, "New Frontiers of Christian Mission in Areas of Political Tension," *International Review of Mission* 68, no. 272 (October 1979):428. See also his "Theology and Human Rights," *Convergence*, no. 1 (1982):25-29.

104.   Ibid. See Ismael E. Amaya, "Latin American Critique of Western Theology," *Asia Theological News* (January-March 1986):14-15, and 18.

105.   Mortimer Arias, "Ministries of Hope in Latin America," *International Review of Mission* 71, no. 281 (January 1982):6-7.

106.   Mortimer Arias, "The Emerging Theology of Life in Latin America," *Apuntes* 6, no. 2 (1986):30. However, François H. Lepargneur argues that many Pentecostal groups in Latin America "favor human rights teaching in theory but impede their exercise for lack of attention to the socio-structural dimensions of human life." Lepargneur, "The Church's Role as It Affects Human Rights," in *Human Rights and the Liberation of Man in the Americas*, 42.

107.   Ibid., 32-33.

108.   Helmut Frenz, "Human Rights: A Christian Viewpoint," *Christianity and Crisis* 36, no. 11 (21 June 1976):150. See also Frenz, "Divine Rights and Human Rights," *Church and Society* 69 (November-December 1978):54-55.

109.   Ibid., 151. In "An Open Letter to North American Christians" thirteen Latin American Christian leaders pleaded for help, because "human rights, the grand guidelines of the gospel, are becoming a dead letter without force." In *Mission Trends*, 4, ed. G. H. Anderson and T. F. Stronsky (New York: Paulist Press, 1979), 74.

110.   "Human Rights Resources Office for Latin America (HRROLA)," *One World*, no. 132 (January-February 1988):32-33.

111.   Most of those cited by educator Loretta Carey, as models of devotion to furthering human rights, are, in fact, Christians: "Gandhi, King, Eleanor Roosevelt, Dag Hammarskjöld, Bishop Tutu, Steve Biko, Oscar Romero, the four churchwomen of El Salvador, Lech Walesa and others in the news daily can motivate [us] to understanding and action." Carey, "Human Dignity: Basis for Human Rights Education," *Breakthrough* 10, nos. 2-3 (Winter/Spring 1989):77.

Chapter 5

A CHRISTIAN CONSENSUS

Jürgen Moltmann asserts that despite the tensions in the ecumenical movement "the common faith" lives.[1] In this chapter I will argue that despite the differences among Christians over matters of doctrine, there is a growing consensus today in support of human rights.

It is striking that this consensus on human rights among Christians not only bridges historic divisions in the church, between Roman Catholics and Eastern Orthodox and Protestants and between different Protestant denominations. It also bridges the new conflicts among Christians, which divide those who believe the Bible is the inspired word of God from those who believe it is the inerrant word of God.

By a growing consensus on human rights I mean much more than agreement that violations of human rights are bad and tragic. Christians agree substantially about the justification for human rights advocacy, the content of that advocacy, and its importance for the mission of the church.

Justifying Human Rights

All Christians agree that human rights laws are not authoritative merely because they are laws passed by the state. The Nazi regime is a vivid example of the injustice that can be done through the lawful edicts of a state. Moreover, the death of Jesus, though unjust, was lawful.[2] The law is to be obeyed because it is right, not simply because it is the law. The standard for the law must be sought outside the law.

While this may seem obvious, many lawyers today do not agree. Those who embrace legal positivism hold that human rights are simply what the law says they are and are therefore justified by agreement among law-makers and jurists. However, as John Warwick Montgomery has reminded

us, this is merely to fall victim to the naturalistic fallacy. The "ought" cannot be derived from the "is." The fact that people agree does not mean that they are right.

In addition to rejecting law per se, as authority for human rights, Christians reject arguments which claim that humans have rights because of their intrinsic worth or attributes, if these arguments fail to acknowledge the God who created these persons and the universe in which they live. Christians agree that all affirmations of human rights are grounded in the transcendent reality of God.

Thus Christians do not speak of human rights as "natural rights," for this phrase suggests that human rights are merely self-evident characteristics of the natural order. Christians affirm that human beings have rights not simply because they are part of the natural order, but because they are loved by God.

This is not only the position of conservative Christian theologians Jacques Ellul and John Warwick Montgomery, but also of Christian historian of religion, Wilfred Cantwell Smith, who argues that "no one has any reasonable grounds—has any 'right'—to talk about human rights who rejects metaphysics."[3] Human rights involve what is supernatural, as well as what is natural.

Finally, for much the same reason, most Christians no longer argue for human rights on the basis of a theory of natural law. Protestants have long been wary of this language. Today Roman Catholics, who used it to identify a foundation for values in the created order, speak of human dignity rather than of natural law. Thus the old controversy between Protestants and Roman Catholics over the authority of natural law is now moot among Christian human rights advocates.

Christians then are in substantial agreement that human rights cannot be justified on the basis of law alone, nor simply by invoking the notions of "natural rights" or "natural law." For Christians, human rights are grounded in God. Thus, for Christians, all affirmations about human rights begin with faith in God, who transcends the world and yet is present in it. Human rights are fundamentally a matter of living out Christian faith in God, the creator and redeemer of a moral order with transcendent values which can be known and realized in the world.

Human rights are known both through reason and revelation. Catholic social teaching speaks of "reason enlightened by revelation," and Christopher Mooney says this teaching claims

that all reasonable people should be able to discern a human right to minimum levels of food, clothing, and shelter, the values of work and family, the binding nature of contracts, as well as the need for both freedom and interdependence. At the same time there was also a claim, quite consistent with natural theory,

that Christian faith can make a significant contribution to social morality, because in fact these moral insights of reasonable people correspond with traditional Christian values and teaching.[4]

Protestants often emphasize revelation over reason, but most do not deny the possibility of knowing the good through reason. As scholar and lay theologian C. S. Lewis asserts, it would be disastrous "to present our practical reason as radically unsound."[5]

Thus, although Protestants argue that human rights are grounded in revelation, they agree that they may be known through reason. Carl F. H. Henry writes:

On the basis of God's scripturally revealed purpose, evangelical Christians affirm values that transcend all human cultures, societies, and human rights constituting the norms of civilization. Objectively grounded human rights are logically defensible on this foundation of the supernatural creation of man with a unique universal dignity.[6]

However, Henry resists the argument that Christians ought to avoid human rights advocacy involving humanists, who reject God's revelation in Christ but nonetheless affirm human rights; instead he urges Christians to work with all persons of goodwill in the struggle for a more just world order.

Christians also agree that all human rights are based on the divine right of God. Bishop Helmut Frenz of the Evangelical Lutheran Church in Chile asserts that "Human rights are the social execution of the divine rights."[7] Moltmann says: "The human rights to life, freedom, community, and self-determination mirror God's right to the human being because the human being is destined to be God's image in all conditions and relationships of life."[8] Jacques Ellul argues that, because all human rights are divine rights, Jesus Christ "alone has rights before God."[9] Christians from East Germany affirm that "the inviolability of life, dignity and property are not a constitutive element of the human being," as these rights belong to God alone.[10]

Thus Christians agree that human rights are rooted in the created order of the world:

There is only the divine right. From the idea of creation Christians understand the whole world as a sacred order, dominated by the idea that God is bound to rights as a just God and stipulates rights.[11]

In the words of James M. Childs, Jr., "the basic freedoms and protections of human rights doctrine are divinely revealed in and through the natural order of creation."[12]

Of course, Christians differ in their particular way of describing their positions. Agnes Cunningham, Donald Miller, and James E. Will identify Roman Catholic, Lutheran and Reformed positions in their essay, "Toward an Ecumenical Theology for Grounding Human Rights."[13] These differences show up in ecumenical gatherings, such as the consultation sponsored in 1980 by the World Council of Churches with the Lutheran World Federation, the World Alliance of Reformed Churches, and the Pontifical Commission *Justitia et Pax*, which identified three theological approaches to the justification of human rights:

> The first approach proceeds from the creation and considers the source for human rights to be implicit in natural law. A second approach insists upon the experience of God's covenant with his people. The New Covenant in Christ is the criterion for dealing with historically developed natural and human rights. A third approach takes the event of the justification of sinners through the grace of God to be the basis of freedom and from there proceeds to the responsibility of persons for their neighbors.[14]

However, the consultation affirmed that "a common understanding does exist in the basic doctrine that all theological statements on human rights derive from the Christian anthropology of the human person created in the image of God."[15] This is the basis of the inviolable dignity of the human person.

Christians also agree that human rights are justified because of God's redemptive acts. Ellul and Montgomery make this point sharply, but Moltmann makes the same assertion on behalf of the Reformed Protestant tradition and the statement of the Lutheran World Federation concurs.[16] Roman Catholics, too, assert that human dignity is not merely known in the created order but in "the Christ-event,"[17] for "it is in the meeting of God in the man Jesus Christ that man fully discovers his dignity and the dignity of all others whom he must love as his neighbors (Luke 10:36, Matt. 5:43-48)."[18]

Similarly, the *Handbook of Doctrine* of the Salvation Army asserts that "man is more than a natural being . . . [in that] his spiritual endowments and the revelation given by the gospel of redemption concerning his place in the divine purpose, invest him with a dignity and value of his own."[19] Salvationists believe with Archbishop William Temple:

> There can be no Rights of Man except on the basis of faith in God. But if God is real, and all men are His sons, that is the true worth of everyone of them. My worth is what I am worth to God; and that is a marvelous great deal, for Christ died for me.[20]

Because Salvationists believe in the doctrines of creation and redemption, they support human rights, for they know "what God thinks of man, what He has done for man, [and] what with God is possible for man."[21]

Pablo Martínez provides a succinct summary of the Christian position developed thus far. He notes that human rights are not based on any notion of intrinsic goodness in human beings, or on any human attribute, or on any human act of government. For human rights are based on the right of God alone. They are grounded in the creation of God and the redemptive acts of God: "God has a 'right' over us for a double reason: because he made us and because he ransomed or redeemed us. This act, moreover, increased the value and the worth of every person before God."[22] Thus Christians defend human rights on the basis of eternal principles: "There is no way that we can present our rights independently of God, seeing that all we are and have comes from him and his grace (Ps. 24:1; 1 Cor. 4:7; 2 Cor. 5:18)."[23] Christians affirm human dignity by supporting human rights, because God has created and redeemed the human person.

Max Stackhouse argues that logically all talk of human rights involves at least the following two presuppositions:

members of a society must believe that there is a universal moral law transcending their own culture, society, or period of history about which they can know something with relative clarity . . . [and this] universal moral law must involve an affirmation of the dignity of each person as a *member*, a participant, in relationship with others, in a community that extends to all humankind.[24]

Similarly, Methodist theologian J. Robert Nelson asserts that "Concern for the integrity, worth, and dignity of persons is the basic presupposition of human rights."[25] The shift in emphasis in Roman Catholic social teaching since *Pacem in Terris*, from natural law to human dignity as a basis for human rights, supports the same conclusion.[26]

However, it is important that human dignity be understood, as Nelson suggests, in the context of Paul's vision of the corporate church. Only then will it express the notion of the common good. Robert Bellah makes the same point in arguing that human rights must be "grounded not merely in the self-preservation of the individual" but in the broader "religious context" of divine justice.[27] In the words of Richard Neuhaus, Christians affirm that only "a transcendent understanding of the dignity of the person" will provide a foundation for a Christian doctrine of human rights.[28]

The Content of Human Rights Advocacy

Neither the Bible nor traditional doctrines refer to human rights directly, but Christians derive human rights from both. Whether the emphasis is on grace, covenant, creation, or redemption, God's action calls for human response. Christians accept the commandments to love God and to love their neighbors and to keep the Golden Rule. For many Christians today, this means supporting human rights.

Thus, for Christians, human rights are derived from faith and involve duties to God and one's neighbor. Rights are relational. The human person does not have rights as an individual, but in relation to others in community and ultimately in relation to God. The right to life is derived from the value God gives to life, by creating and redeeming it.

Human rights are not only derived from divine rights but also constitute duties toward others. Christians affirm that because God loves all people, all people have rights and the corresponding duties to respect the rights of all others.[29] This view of human rights is at odds with the notion of individual rights which is central to the development of Western political and philosophical thought. Christians are concerned not with the autonomous individual, and with his or her rights, but with the rights of persons in community and thus with their duties as well as their rights.[30]

Thus, for Christians, the content of human rights transcends political ideologies and includes what have been described in international law as the three generations of human rights.[31] In the words of John Paul II, in his address to the United Nations General Assembly:

> *All* these human rights *taken together* are in keeping with the substance of the dignity of the human being, understood in his entirety, not as reduced to one dimension only. These rights concern the satisfaction of man's essential *needs*, the exercise of his *freedoms, and his relationships with others.*[32]

These human rights may be listed, as in the recapitulation of Catholic social teaching in *Pacem in Terris*, or they may be described more generally as the conditions for human dignity.

Montgomery derives a lengthy list of human rights from the teachings of the Bible, which include most of the rights associated with the three generations of human rights law. Moreover, he affirms that the Bible in some instances sets standards even higher than international law. He also argues that the Bible supports the notion of a new international economic order, so long as freedom of conscience and expression are also protected.[33]

Both Roman Catholic and Protestant leaders point out that the human rights supported by Christians are largely catalogued in the Universal

Declaration of Human Rights.[34] John XXIII embraced the Universal Declaration in *Pacem in Terris*,[35] Paul VI made it the cornerstone of his work, and John Paul II celebrated it in *Sollicitudo Rei Socialis*. Moltmann and Stackhouse support the Universal Declaration,[36] Walter Harrelson suggests it offers "a marvelous set of guidelines,"[37] and Orthodox Christians also endorse it.[38]

Carl Henry sharply criticizes the Universal Declaration, because it "does not identify the transcendent source of rights."[39] However, he does not take issue with its content.[40] Moreover, Bishop Frenz of the Evangelical Lutheran Church goes so far as to affirm that:

Through the Universal Declaration of Human Rights Christ speaks much more clearly than through some synodal proclamations. This proclamation is of Christ's spirit, because it puts the concern for persons, the concern for their dignity, in the center.[41]

Erich Weingärtner suggests the Universal Declaration is a modern "Ten Commandments."[42]

Thus Christians are in substantial agreement today as to the content of human rights advocacy that is justified. Christians affirm the Universal Declaration of Human Rights and covenants incorporating its basic principles into international law.

Importance of Human Rights Advocacy

The statement by Bishop Frenz suggests the importance of human rights advocacy for Christians. At the heart of the Gospel is a concern for persons. The church

is called to be an instrument of the kingdom of God by continuing Christ's mission to the world in a struggle for the growth of all human beings into the fullness of life. This means proclaiming God's judgment upon any authority, power or force, which would openly or by subtle means deny people their full human rights.[43]

Neuhaus warns us not to place our trust in the current enthusiasm for human rights, but to recall that as Christians our commitment to human rights depends "on a promise that bestows dignity upon every person and demands of every person a respect—no, a reverence—for the dignity of all others."[44]

Faith in human rights cuts across the Christian community, uniting those that are divided on other issues of doctrine and practice. Liberal and conservative Protestants, Roman Catholics, Orthodox, and Evangelicals are

remarkably unified on their understanding of the importance of human rights advocacy in our modern world.

To be sure, there is dissent within the Christian community. For instance, Edward Norman argues vociferously that Christians in their human rights advocacy are merely endorsing the political values of their own societies.[45] Moreover, Christians differ in their particular involvements, the degree of their commitment to human rights, and so forth.

Nonetheless, the agreement among Christians about human rights is striking. For instance, statements by the World Council of Churches are clearly in agreement with the assertion, by conservative theologian Jacques Ellul, that Christians must be educated about human rights; for when "it comes to speaking up and taking a stand for human rights, it must be done by the entire Christian community. . . ."[46] Furthermore, Roman Catholic social teaching concurs with the assertion, by evangelical John Warwick Montgomery, that the Christian doctrines of creation and redemption "provide the common denominators for all the sound human rights teaching which we have met in the classical theologians of Christendom."[47]

Clearly for many, if not for all Christians, human rights are central to understanding both the gifts and the demands of the gospel. God has given human beings dignity and thus calls all peoples to the responsibility of protecting human rights, which are the social conditions necessary for human dignity. For many Christians today, human rights are as clear as God's creative and redemptive presence and as compelling as life itself. Human rights are at the heart of what they believe and affirm to be their common faith.

Notes

1. Jürgen Moltmann, *On Human Dignity: Political Theology and Ethics*, trans. M. Douglas Meeks (Philadelphia: Fortress Press, 1984), 7.
2. As Muslim Ali A. Mazrui observes, "The cross was a statement on human rights." Mazrui, "Human Rights and World Culture," in *Philosophical Foundations of Human Rights* (Paris: UNESCO, 1986), 247.
3. Wilfred Cantwell Smith, "Philosophia, as One of the Religious Traditions of Humankind: The Greek Legacy in Western Civilization, Viewed by a Comparativist," in *Différences, Valuers, Hierarchie: Textes Offerts á Louis Dumont et Réunis par Jean-Claude Galey* (Paris: École des Sautes Études en Sciences Sociales, 1984), 269.
4. Christopher F. Mooney, S.J., *Public Virtue: Law and the Social Character of Religion* (Notre Dame, Ind.: University of Notre Dame Press, 1986), 145.
5. C. S. Lewis, "The Poison of Subjectivism," in *Christian Reflections*, ed. Walter Hooper (Grand Rapids, Mich.: William B. Eerdmans Publishing Company, 1967), 79.
6. Carl F. H. Henry, "Religious Freedom: Cornerstone of Human Rights," *Quarterly of the Christian Legal Society* 5, no. 3 (1984):7.

7. Helmut Frenz, "Human Rights: A Christian Viewpoint," *Christianity and Crisis* 36, no. 11 (21 June 1976):149.

8. Jürgen Moltmann, *On Human Dignity*, 17.

9. Jacques Ellul, *The Theological Foundation of Law*, trans. Marguerite Wieser (London: SCM Press, 1960), 49.

10. "The Meaning of Human Rights and the Problems They Pose," *The Ecumenical Review* 27 (April 1975):143.

11. Helmut Frenz, "Human Rights: A Christian Viewpoint," *Christianity and Crisis* 36, no. 11 (21 June 1976):149.

12. James M. Childs, Jr., "The Church and Human Rights: Reflections on Morality and Mission," *Currents in Theology and Mission* 7 (February 1980):15.

13. In *Soundings* 67, no. 2 (Summer 1984):209-39.

14. "Introduction," *Human Rights: A Challenge to Theology* (Rome: CCIA and IDOC International, 1983), 10-11.

15. Ibid. Trutz Rendtorff describes the role of the Christian tradition in "the development of human rights in the modern age" in "Christian Concepts of the Responsible Self," in *Human Rights in the World's Religions*, ed. Leroy S. Rouner (Notre Dame, Ind.: University of Notre Dame Press, 1988), 33-45.

16. Jacques Ellul, *The Theological Foundation of Law*, 42; John Warwick Montgomery, "A Revelational Solution," *Human Rights and Human Dignity* (Grand Rapids, Mich.: Zondervan, 1986), 131-60; Jürgen Moltmann, *On Human Dignity*, 13; *Theological Perspectives on Human Rights* (Geneva: Lutheran World Federation, 1977), 14.

17. Richard McCormick, S.J., quoted in Robert A. Evans, "From Reflection to Action," in *Human Rights: A Dialogue Between the First and Third Worlds* (Maryknoll, N.Y.: Orbis Books, 1983), 245.

18. Jean Giblet, "Human Rights and the Dignity of Man," *Convergence*, no. 2 (1979):2.

19. *Human Rights and the Salvation Army*, 5.

20. Quoted from *Citizen and Churchman* (Eyre and Spottiswoode), 2. In Francis A. Evans, "Human Rights and Divine Grace," in *Human Rights and the Salvation Army* (London: The Campfield Press, 1968), 9.

21. Francis A. Evans, "Human Rights and Divine Grace," in *Human Rights and the Salvation Army* (London: The Campfield Press, 1968), 9.

22. Pablo Martínez, "The Right To Be Human," *Evangelical Review of Theology* 10, no. 3 (July 1986):271-72.

23. Ibid., 272.

24. Max L. Stackhouse, "Public Theology, Human Rights, and Missions," in *Human Rights and the Global Mission of the Church* (Cambridge, Mass.:Boston Theological Institute, 1985), 13.

25. J. Robert Nelson, "Human Rights in Creation and Redemption: A Protestant View," in *Human Rights in Religious Traditions*, ed. Arlene Swidler (New York: The Pilgrim Press, 1982), 1.

26. David Hollenbach, *Claims in Conflict: Retrieving and Renewing the Catholic Human Rights Tradition* (New York: Paulist Press, 1979), 131-33.

27. Robert Bellah, "Faith Communities Challenge—and Are Challenged by—the Changing World Order," in *World Faiths and the New World Order: A Muslim-Jewish-Christian Search Begins*, ed. Joseph Gremillion and William Ryan (Washington, D.C.: Inter-religious Peace Colloquium, 1978), 166.

28. Richard John Neuhaus, "What We Mean by Human Rights, and Why," *Christian Century* 95 (6 December 1978):1180.

29. Dietrich Bonhoeffer argues that duties come from rights, as the gift of God creates a natural right for all creatures: "To idealistic thinkers it may seem out of place for a

Christian ethic to speak first of rights and only later of duties. But our authority is not Kant; it is the Holy Scripture, and it is precisely for that reason that we must speak first of the rights of natural life, in other words of what is given to life, and only later of what is demanded of life. God gives before He demands. And indeed in the rights of natural life it is not to the creature that honor is given, but to the creator. It is the abundance of His gifts that is acknowledged. There is no right before God, but the natural, purely as what is given, becomes the right in relation to man. The rights of natural life are in the midst of the fallen world the reflected splendor of the glory of God's creation. They are not primarily something that man can sue for in his own interest, but they are something which is guaranteed by God Himself. The duties, on the other hand, derive from the rights themselves, as tasks are implied by gifts. They are implicit in the rights. Within the framework of the natural life, therefore, we in every case speak first of the rights and then of the duties, for by so doing, in the natural life too, we are allowing the gospel to have its way." Bonhoeffer, *Ethics*, ed. Eberhard Bethge, trans. N. H. Smith (SCM Press, 1971), 127. Quoted in Andrew Linzey, *Christianity and the Rights of Animals* (New York: The Crossroad Publishing Company, 1987), 70.

30. See Lisa Sowle Cahill, "Towards a Christian Theory of Human Rights," *The Journal of Religious Ethics* 8, no. 1 (Fall 1980):285.

31. Erich Weingärtner, *Human Rights on the Ecumenical Agenda: Report and Assessment* (Geneva: CCIA, World Council of Churches, 1983), 11. Warren Holleman develops the arguments between Christian idealists and realists, as exemplified by the thought of Jacques Maritain and Reinhold Neibuhr. This is basically the old controversy over the extent to which sin has impaired human nature. See Holleman, *The Human Rights Movement: Western Values and Theological Perspectives* (New York: Praeger Publishers, 1987), chapters 6 and 7. Despite this continuing theological debate, there is substantial agreement on human rights, as I have shown.

32. Quoted in David Hollenbach, "Both Bread and Freedom: The Interconnection of Economic and Political Rights in Recent Catholic Thought," in *Human Rights and the Global Mission of the Church*, 31. See *Speeches of John Paul II*, 1980, 74. However, the religious organizations which support economic, social, and cultural rights do very little to realize them. See Lowell W. Livezey, "U.S. Religious Organizations and the International Human Rights Movement," *Human Rights Quarterly* 11, no. 1 (February 1989):81.

33. John Warwick Montgomery, *Human Rights and Human Dignity*, 169-75.

34. Bernard Quelquejeu concludes that the Universal Declaration of Human Rights "is not, and would not claim to be, the establishment of a genuinely universal morality, but it is an irreplaceable formulation, of course open to improvement, of the general criteria which must be satisfied at present by the moral systems in force, in their geographical, national, ethnic and other diversity and according to their economic, juridical, social, civic, political and cultural solidity, if they are not to be destructive of the human dignity which it is their vocation to protect and promote." Quelquejeu, "Diversity in Historical Moral Systems and a Criterion for Universality in Moral Judgment," trans. Francis McDonagh, in *Christian Ethics: Uniformity, Universality, Pluralism*, ed. Jacques Pohier and Dietmar Mieth, English ed. Marcus Lefébure (New York: The Seabury Press, 1981), 52.

35. David Hollenbach sees the consensus achieved at the UN on human rights to be very similar to the global consensus achieved at Vatican II. Hollenbach, *Justice, Peace, and Human Rights* (New York: The Crossroad Publishing Company, 1988), 91.

36. Jürgen Moltmann, *On Human Dignity*, 30; Max L. Stackhouse, "Theology, History, and Human Rights," *Soundings* 67, no. 2 (Summer 1984):195.

37. Walter Harrelson, *The Ten Commandments and Human Rights* (Philadelphia: Fortress Press, 1980), 192-93.

38. Stanley Harakas, "Human Rights: An Eastern Orthodox Perspective," in *Human Rights in Religious Traditions*, 24.

39. Carl F. H. Henry, "Religious Freedom: Cornerstone of Human Rights," *Christian Legal Society Quarterly* 5, no. 3 (1984):7.

40. However, the National Association of Evangelicals does not endorse the Universal Declaration or the international human rights covenants developed to realize it. Lowell W. Livezey, "U.S. Religious Organizations and the International Human Rights Movement," *Human Rights Quarterly* 11, no. 1 (February 1989):34.

41. Helmut Frenz, "Human Rights: A Christian Viewpoint," *Christianity and Crisis* 36, no. 11 (November-December 1978):146.

42. Erich Weingärtner, *Human Rights on the Ecumenical Agenda*, 10.

43. "Melbourne Conference Section Reports," *International Review of Mission* 69, nos. 276-77 (October 1980-January 1981):401.

44. Richard John Neuhaus, "What We Mean by Human Rights, and Why," *Christian Century* 95 (6 December 1978):1177.

45. See Edward Norman, *Christianity and the World Order* (Oxford: Oxford University Press, 1979).

46. Jacques Ellul, *The Theological Foundation of Law*, 137. See Erich Weingärtner, *Human Rights on the Ecumenical Agenda*, 63.

47. John Warwick Montgomery, *Human Rights and Human Dignity*, 206.

PART II

SUPPORT IN OTHER RELIGIOUS TRADITIONS

Chapter 6

JEWS

Christians are not the only religious people to advocate human rights. Jews joined with Christians after World War II in lobbying for the United Nations Charter and for the Universal Declaration of Human Rights. And they continue to play an important part in human rights advocacy. Jews, too, affirm that human rights are an expression of their faith.[1]

Rabbi Daniel Polish acknowledges that the phrase "human rights" is a modern juridical notion. However, he argues that "the system of values and ideas" which constitutes human rights

> are among the beliefs which constitute the very core of Jewish sacred scripture and the tradition of ideas and practices which flows from it. The idea-set which is represented by the phrase "human rights" derives in the Jewish tradition from the basic theological affirmation of Jewish faith.[2]

The "core theological affirmations of the Jewish faith," which require recognition of the sanctity of the individual and the equality of all as children of God, "serve as the undergirding for the Jewish commitment to the idea-set we call 'human rights'."[3] Clearly, Polish asserts, the history of the Jewish people has demonstrated the necessity of the freedoms and protections which the phrase "human rights" connotes.

Traditional Rights

David Daube finds numerous instances of the roots of human rights in rabbinic literature.[4] Moreover, S. D. Goitein asserts that "human rights, and relations among men in general, had been fully established in the Bible and the Talmud, and these formed the very substance of medieval Jewish beliefs and practices."[5] The consequences of this tradition may be

seen in the active involvement of Jews in Europe in the eighteenth and nineteenth centuries, when "the support for universally valid laws and human rights became almost a self-understood Jewish concern."[6]

Polish argues that *human* concerns have always been central in the Jewish tradition: "The recognition of the importance of human life is at the same time both integral to the Jewish faith system and the first and necessary precondition for a belief in human rights."[7] Michael Fishbane makes a similar affirmation of faith:

> The fundamental presupposition of the rights of the person in Judaism is a belief in the absolute and uncompromisable worth of human life. This belief is grounded in the unique value of the individual in the divine scheme of creation and is variously articulated in both biblical literature and rabbinic tradition.[8]

Polish adds that: "The notion of human rights flows as a natural extension of the Genesis account of the creation of humanity."[9] The Genesis story affirms both the sovereignty of God and the sacredness of the individual, for it is a single person that is first made in the image of God. Thus the rabbis teach that killing a person "is tantamount to diminishing the reality of God's own self."

Polish notes that the three major festivals in the Jewish year—*Pesach* (Passover), *Succot* (Tabernacles), and *Shavuot* (Pentecost)—commemorate aspects of the Exodus from Egypt, which is the basis for Jewish affirmations of the human right to political liberty. *Purim*, the commemoration of the events of the Book of Esther, clearly affirms the rights of minority peoples, as does the Torah in its demand that the rights of the stranger be protected. Moreover, on the afternoon of every Yom Kippur (Day of Atonement),

> Jews read a recounting of those who died "for the sanctification of God's Name" to live a life of fidelity to Torah, even when that was proscribed by the Roman occupiers. Martyrdom for acting on higher values has been considered a positive virtue through our history.[10]

In these ways Jews affirm that "the right of conscience cannot be abrogated by law—indeed, that one is entitled to violate the law in order to remain true to one's conscientious beliefs."[11] Similarly, the festival of *Chanukah* (the Feast of Lights) is a "celebration of a human right" for it "celebrates the specific freedom of religion."[12]

In addition to political rights, the Jewish tradition affirms economic and social rights. Polish writes: "There can be little doubt that the Torah and subsequent Jewish teaching argue for the defense of the poor."[13] He argues that the Jewish community has actively sought to alleviate the

deprivations of poor people. Moreover, this is a matter of recognizing a right and not merely of engaging in charitable acts:

> Remarkably, Jewish religious literature and Jewish communal practice reflect an attitude that attending to such needs of the poor is an act not of beneficence but of concern, to which the poor are rightfully entitled by virtue of their circumstances. [14]

Meeting the needs of the poor is a matter of justice, because it is only through such practices that the poor can gain access to that which God has "provided for . . . all."[15]

William Irwin suggests that biblical stories in which prophets confront kings for "their highhanded indifference to human rights"—Nathan confronting King David for taking Bathsheba and killing her husband Uriah, and Elijah confronting King Ahab for taking Naboth's vineyard and having him killed—are highly important "as steps in the rise of Israel's sense of a higher law; for, in both, a prophet intercedes to rebuke the monarch in the name of the Lord."[16] Irwin says of the prophet Amos: "His enlarged concept of the nature and authority of God evidently was rooted in a feeling of common human rights, pervasive beyond the political and religious boundaries of the time. This principle was for him embodied in the person of the God of Israel."[17]

Democratic Rights

Lord Acton agrees that these prophetic examples strengthened "the doctrine of the higher law" which was a part of the covenant relationship between God and the Hebrew people.[18] Similarly, Milton Konvitz writes: "In the Biblical conception, no one is above the law."[19] As Rabbi Phineas said: "All are equal before the law. The duty of observance is for all."[20] Emanuel Rackman acknowledges that "Biblical Hebrew has no word for 'equality'," but he affirms that in Leviticus 24:22 God extends the right to be treated equally under the law even to include those who are strangers within Israel.[21]

The notion of equality is also grounded in the fatherhood of God, which means that all persons are brothers and sisters. Konvitz comments that "wherever one turns in the writings of the Jews this motif of equality, the fatherhood of God and the brotherhood of man, appears irresistibly":

> Thus, at the Passover *seder* a drop of wine is to be spilled from the cup at the mention of each of the ten plagues with which the Egyptians were afflicted, the reason being, say the Rabbis, that one's cup of joy cannot be full as long as there is suffering somewhere in the world. . . . Again, at the *seder* the head

of the household reads of the drowning of the Egyptian hosts in the Red Sea; and the Rabbis comment on the passage by relating that when the drowning was taking place, angels in heaven commenced to sing the praises of the Lord, but He rebuked them, saying, "My children are drowning, and you would sing!"[22]

Therefore Konvitz concludes: "the spirit, the inner values, the energies of democracy are right at the very heart of Judaism."[23]

The notion that democratic values are rooted in the Jewish tradition is reflected in Thomas Paine's argument, in *Rights of Man*, that all persons are equal because they are all descended from Adam.[24] Robert Gordis makes a similar claim: "The classic thesis of the Declaration of Independence is deeply suffused by the spirit of biblical faith, refracted by the rationalist liberalism of John Locke."[25] However, Lenn Evan Goodman argues that in this refraction by Locke there was a shift from the Jewish affirmation of equal dignity before God to an emphasis on enlightened self-interest:

> Judaism founds human right [*sic*] upon the assumption that, ideally, all human beings are of equal merit (*i.e.*, all are, at least at the outset, equal in their moral potential), equal before God and, therefore, equal in desert before the law and their fellow human beings. . . . Locke, following Hobbes, Machiavelli, and, ultimately, the Sophist equation of right with power, founds human equality on the presumed natural equality of power, not to create but to destroy.[26]

Goodman asserts that Locke's "assumption of the virtual equality of the power of all individuals" is a fiction, because it ignores "the plight of the helpless and dependent classes in society."[27] By contrast, the Torah demands "that individuals be treated as equals, regardless of actual differences in their station, wealth or position."[28] Thus the Jewish notion of equality, which requires positive acts by government for the welfare of the people, when refracted by Locke, results in the liberal orthodox doctrine of civil and political rights limited to the noninterference of government in the lives of its supposedly equal citizens.

Even as Jewish law recognizes the fundamental right to equality of treatment as well as equality of opportunity, Emanuel Rackman argues that the Talmud "is a veritable mine of materials pertaining to human rights," in that it recognizes many other rights generally traced back through the liberal philosophical tradition, including the doctrine of judicial review, the right of civil disobedience, the right against self-incrimination, the right of the accused to an adequate defense, the right to dissent, and immunity from being compelled to support an established religion.[29]

Similarly, Herbert Brichto argues that "the biblical ethos has provided the sole ideological base for democracy" in that:

Whatever its political form or organization, society is required by Scripture to uphold the standards of minimum human dignity. These standards include, for example, the right of any Israelite to satisfy his hunger at his fellow's expense but not to harvest his fellow's labors. Among the provisions for the administration of justice are many examples of social legislation such as those permitting the poor and the alien access to harvest gleanings, unreaped borders, and the forgotten sheaf. Another illustration of these egalitarian standards is the protest against the creation of landed estates.[30]

Milton Konvitz suggests that fundamentally, "the democratic faith is a moral affirmation" that no one is to be used merely as a means to an end, for

no matter how lowly his origin, a man is here only by the grace of God—he owes his life to no one but God. He has an equal right to pursue happiness: life, liberty and the pursuit of happiness are his simply by virtue of the fact that he is a live human being.[31]

This faith finds its essence in what Henry Michel calls the "eminent dignity of human personality,"[32] and Konvitz asserts that: "One of the chief sources of this faith is in the wellsprings of Judaism."[33]

In the words of Michael Fishbane, because of the "principled standards of moral choice based on a clear notion of the person," the Jewish legal tradition may provide "a powerful resource for contemporary reflections on human rights and duties in our time."[34]

The Universal Declaration of Human Rights

Israeli jurist Haim H. Cohn has written an extensive commentary on the Universal Declaration of Human Rights from the Jewish perspective. He discusses most but not all of the rights set forth in the Declaration because "Jewish law does not take cognizance of all 'human rights' therein provided for," including "rights to social security and rights to participate in government."[35] By "Jewish Law" he means both "the system of religious law which comprises Scriptural or Written Law, said to emanate from direct or indirect divine revelation, and Oral Law, first expounded in the talmudical sources and later developed by the rabbis."[36] He notes that, because of the divinity of the law, it is "well nigh self-evident that there is not 'any nation so great that hath statutes and judgments so righteous as all this law' (Deut. 4:8)."[37]

In order to discern "human rights" in Jewish law, he looks at commandments (*mitzvot*), including both positive and negative injunctions, with "the premise that the purpose of imposing duties toward your fellowmen was but the recognition and implementation of rights of which these fellowmen stand possessed," which is the same thing as "the fulfillment of their legitimate expectations and legally recognized needs."[38] Thus "from the duty to assist and maintain the poor a fundamental human right of every human being to his livelihood may reasonably be inferred, as the fundamental right to life may justifiably be inferred from the prohibition of homicide."[39]

He notes that all commands of the Jewish law are addressed to individual persons. In this sense Jewish law has much in common with the Universal Declaration of Human Rights, which declares rights but provides no social mechanism of enforcement:

> in the same way that the rights enumerated in the Universal Declaration reflect ethical standards postulated by the founding fathers of the United Nations as the aspirations of a new world sick of war and lawlessness, of inhuman atrocities and human sufferings, so do the duties imposed by Jewish lawgivers reflect their ethical standards, which were postulated by a legal order conditioned by, and wholly dedicated to, the service and worship of God.[40]

Often duties in Jewish law are supported by a threat of divine wrath if they are ignored, as in the obligation to care for widows and orphans:

> if thou afflict them in any wise, and they cry at all unto Me, I will surely hear their cry. And My wrath shall wax hot, and I will kill you with the sword; and your wives shall be widows and your children fatherless (Exodus 22:22- 23).[41]

Cohn observes that this divine threat "shows just to what lengths a wrathful God may go to vindicate human rights."[42]

The human rights of life, liberty, and the pursuit of happiness which Cohn derives from the duties of Jewish law include: the right to life, the right to liberty and security of person, the right to privacy, the right to reputation, freedom of movement and residence, the right to asylum, the right to marry and found a family, the right to property, the right to work and remuneration, the right to leisure, freedom of thought, speech, and conscience, freedom of information, and the right to education and participation in culture.[43]

Jewish law, like Islamic law, does not allow the kind of religious freedom which is declared a human right in the Universal Declaration. Cohn writes: "The premise from which all Jewish law flows, that there is no true and right faith other than the Jewish, necessarily implies an intolerance of contradictory and incompatible religions."[44] However, after

lengthy debate within the tradition, adherents of monotheistic religions—such as Christianity and Islam—were classified as "strangers" and therefore were acknowledged to have rights as being among the strangers "thou shalt love as thyself" (Lev. 19:34, Deut. 10:19).[45]

Talmudic law, developed over centuries in rabbinical schools, distinguishes between a stranger who has converted to Judaism and a stranger who has not, and thus while it achieved "an almost perfect equality between indigenous and converted Jews, it practically obliterated the provisions of biblical law which had been intended and expressed to apply particularly to unconverted aliens."[46] Whatever the theological motivation for this change, Cohn asserts that biblical law stands out among the legal systems of all times as a model of nondiscrimination against strangers: "God Himself loves them (Deut. 10:18) and protects them (Ps. 146:9), and their oppression is a grave offense and abominable sin (Exod. 22:20, 23:9; Lev. 19:33; Jer. 7:6, 22:3; Zech. 7:10)."[47]

The general rule in Jewish law is that the laws "which thou shalt set before them" (Exod. 21:1) apply to women as well as men, with the numerous exceptions to this rule resulting from either physiological or assumed psychological peculiarities of women.[48] Often these distinctions result in discriminations which favor women. However, in marriage law the husband alone consecrates the marriage and only he has the right to write a bill of divorce, even though both husband and wife have a right to sexual intercourse.[49]

Finally, Cohn argues that Jewish law provides for equality in the administration of justice: "Ye shall have one manner of law" (Lev. 24:22).[50] He notes that Jewish law sets judicial standards and elaborates procedural safeguards, and that in the Talmud severe biblical punishments were replaced by monetary compensation and capital punishment was moderated.[51]

Cohn concludes his study by asserting the recognition in both the Universal Declaration of Human Rights and Jewish law that the paramount duty upon every person who claims any right or freedom is to secure "due recognition and respect for the rights and freedoms of others."[52] He writes that Hillel once said, "Do not do to another what you would not like another to do to you: that is the whole of the law—and everything else is but comment and elaboration."[53] And he observes that Jesus, a contemporary of Hillel, echoed this thought in positive terms in the Sermon on the Mount: "Therefore all things whatsoever ye would that men should do to you, do ye even so to them, for this is the law and the prophets" (Matt. 7:12).[54] It is clear then that

All of the law is self-restraint, is practical recognition and implementation of the rights of others; though both the motivation and the justification of such

self-restraint may be the ultimate recognition of and respect for your own rights.[55]

That is, Jewish law concerning human relations is basically altruistic: "If 'human rights' can be said to provide a basis or starting point, or perhaps also the ultimate goal, of the norm-creating process, it is the duties, the do and the do-not, the care and respect for the other man, that make for true law."[56]

Human Rights Advocacy

Despite the lack of protection of their human rights over the centuries, Louis Henkin asserts that "Jews will remain dedicated to human rights in principle and in program; they cannot do otherwise."[57] Jews will continue to advocate the rights of freedom of religion and emigration, because their faith demands it. As Isaac Lewin put it, quoting Exodus 12:37-39 to the UN Sub-Commission on Prevention of Discrimination and Protection of Minorities, "Either we let the people go or, at least, give them the right to bake Matzoth and to practice their religion freely. This is the least justice demands. . . ."[58]

It is interesting that "The right to emigrate, which was formulated by the exodus movement as the right of Jews to return to the land of their ancestors, has now been adopted by the Russian human-rights movement as one of their [sic] basic demands."[59] Thus a Jewish imperative, which now through the development of international law has been recognized by the Soviet regime, has become a rallying cry even for non-Jewish Soviet citizens. Michael Meerson-Aksenov argues that "the Jewish liberation movement has become a social force for spreading awareness of rights" in the Soviet Union:

> Taking up the struggle for the right of Jews to emigrate to Israel, the exodus has caused the entire rights movement to expand into the hearts of the Soviet people. Never before had they realized that, according to their own Constitution, these are rights to which they are entitled *de jure*.[60]

As the exodus movement has attracted Jews from all strata of Soviet society, it has spread to remote parts of the country and even its minimal successes have been inspiring for many.[61]

The Zionist cause has also been formulated in terms of human rights. Theodor Herzl, the founder of political Zionism, was hailed as a champion of the "human rights of the Jewish people."[62] Leslie Green writes:

Zionism advanced a new direction for the achievement of Jewish emancipation and human rights: national self-determination through the founding of a Jewish state. For Herzl, as for many early Zionists, the establishment of a Jewish state represented a continuing expression of the effort to guarantee universal human rights for Jews.[63]

In international human rights law, the issue was to be framed as the right of self-determination.

Because the Palestinians argue for the same right to the same land, and have the support of socialist and many Third World nations, Israel is frequently condemned as a violator of human rights. Jacob Talmon writes: "So, at the very hour and from the very forum of the apparent enshrinement of the universal principle of human rights we have heard the latest version of the denial of the legitimacy and rights to the Jewish people."[64] Walter Laqueur argues that because of the obviously political attacks on Israel, the UN Human Rights Commission is "a farce" and "a totally irrelevant institution."[65] Jews are particularly outraged by the resolution adopted 17 October 1975 by the Social, Humanitarian, and Cultural Committee of the UN General Assembly, for it contains the sentence: "Zionism is a form of racism and racial discrimination."[66]

Daniel Moynihan asserts that the very nature of human rights, as a standard above politics to protect the small and weak of the world, is threatened by such an obviously political attack on Israel.[67] Moreover, Sidney Liskofsky warns, in the battle over international human rights between authoritarian and democratic ideologies and forms of government, it is imperative to struggle so that "the moral and political forces generated by the ideal of human rights" are not lost.[68]

Conclusion

Because of their faith Jews are urged to be involved in the advocacy of human rights not only on behalf of Israel, but on behalf of all people. In his Nobel Peace Prize acceptance speech Elie Wiesel affirmed the need to act when "human dignity is in jeopardy" and acknowledged that "Human rights are being violated on every continent."[69] Nonetheless, he says: "I have faith. Faith in God and even in His creation."[70] Therefore he calls on all men and women of good conscience to act on behalf of the victims of the world, so they may know they are not alone.

Notes

1.   Lowell W. Livezey notes that the Union of U.S. Hebrew Congregations, which represents Reform Judaism, "is the only major Jewish denomination that is active in the international human rights movement, and even its work in the human rights field is considerably less than that undertaken by cultural or 'secular' Jewish agencies such as the American Jewish Committee, the American Jewish Congress, B'nai B'rith International, and the Anti-Defamation League of B'nai B'rith." Livezey, "US Religious Organizations and the International Human Rights Movement," *Human Rights Quarterly* 11, no. 1 (February 1989):42.

2.   Daniel F. Polish, "Judaism and Human Rights," in *Human Rights in Religious Traditions* (New York: The Pilgrim Press, 1982), 40.

3.   Ibid., 46. Abraham Kaplan argues that while Judaism places moral responsibility upon the individual, it does not support an individualistic understanding of human rights. Kaplan, "Human Relations and Human Rights in Judaism," in *The Philosophy of Human Rights: International Perspectives*, ed. Alan S. Rosenbaum (Westport, Conn.: Greenwood Press, 1980), 57-59.

4.   David Daube, "The Rabbis and Philo on Human Rights," in *Essays on Human Rights: Contemporary Rights and Jewish Perspectives*, ed. David Sidorsky (Philadelphia: The Jewish Publication Society of America, 1979), 234-46.

5.   S. D. Goitein, "Human Rights and Jewish Thought and Life in the Middle Ages," in *Essays on Human Rights*, 249.

6.   Jacob Katz, "Post-Emancipation Development of Rights: Liberalism and Universalism," in *Essays on Human Rights*, 292.

7.   Daniel F. Polish, "Judaism and Human Rights," in *Human Rights in Religious Traditions*, 40. See R. J. Zwi Werblosky, "Judaism and Human Rights," in *Human Rights Teaching* 2, no. 1 (Paris: UNESCO, 1981), 7-9.

8.   Michael Fishbane, "The Image of the Human and the Rights of the Individual in Jewish Tradition," in *Human Rights and the World's Religions*, ed. Leroy S. Rouner (Notre Dame, Ind.: University of Notre Dame Press, 1988), 17.

9.   Daniel F. Polish, "Judaism and Human Rights," in *Human Rights in Religious Traditions*, 40.

10.   Ibid., 47-48.

11.   Ibid., 48.

12.   Ibid.

13.   Ibid., 49.

14.   Ibid., 50.

15.   Ibid.

16.   William A. Irwin, "The Rule of a Higher Law," in *Judaism and Human Rights*, ed. Milton R. Konvitz (New York: W. W. Norton & Company, 1972), 101. This book is copyrighted by the B'nai B'rith Commission on Adult Jewish Education.

17.   Ibid., 101-02.

18.   Lord Acton, "Kingship under the Judgment of God," in *Judaism and Human Rights*, 90.

19.   Milton R. Konvitz, "Editor's Note," in *Judaism and Human Rights*, 88.

20.   Quoted in Milton R. Konvitz, "Judaism and the Democratic Ideal," in *Judaism and Human Rights*, 138.

21.   Emanuel Rackman, "Judaism and Equality," in *Judaism and Human Rights*, 33.

22.   Milton R. Konvitz, "Judaism and the Democratic Ideal," in *Judaism and Human Rights*, 124-25.

23.   Ibid., 139.

24.   Emanuel Rackman, "Judaism and Equality," in *Judaism and Human Rights*, 34.

25.   Robert Gordis, *The Root and the Branch* (Chicago: University of Chicago Press, 1962), 81.

26.   Lenn Evan Goodman, "Equality and Human Rights: The Lockean and Judaic Views," *Judaism* 25 (Summer 1976):361-62.

27.   Ibid., 360.

28.   Ibid.

29.   Emanuel Rackman, "Talmudic Insights on Human Rights," *Judaism* 1 (152):158-63.

30.   Herbert Chanan Brichto, "The Hebrew Bible on Human Rights," in *Essays on Human Rights*, 225.

31.   Milton R. Konvitz, "Judaism and the Democratic Ideal," in *Judaism and Human Rights*, 121.

32.   Quoted in Milton Konvitz, "Judaism and the Democratic Ideal," in *Judaism and Human Rights*, 121.

33.   Milton Konvitz, "Judaism and the Democratic Ideal," in *Judaism and Human Rights*, 121.

34.   Michael Fishbane, "The Image of the Human and the Rights of the Individual in Jewish Tradition," in *Human Rights and the World's Religions*, 31.

35.   Haim H. Cohn, *Human Rights in Jewish Law* (New York: KTAV Publishing House, 1984), vii. This book was published for the Institute of Jewish Affairs in London.

36.   Ibid., 1.

37.   Ibid.

38.   Ibid., 18.

39.   Ibid., 18-19.

40.   Ibid., 20.

41.   Ibid., 21.

42.   Ibid.

43.   Ibid., v.

44.   Ibid., 157.

45.   Ibid., 160.

46.   Ibid., 165-66.

47.   Ibid., 166.

48.   Ibid., 167.

49.   Ibid., 170-71.

50.   Ibid., 189.

51.   Ibid., 198, 208 and 217.

52.   Article 29.2, Universal Declaration of Human Rights, in *Human Rights in International Law*, 13. Quoted in Haim H. Cohn, *Human Rights in Jewish Law*, 231.

53.   Haim H. Cohn, *Human Rights in Jewish Law*, 231.

54.   Ibid.

55.   Ibid.

56.   Ibid.

57.   Louis Henkin, "Human Rights: Reappraisal and Readjustment," in *Essays on Human Rights*, 87.

58.   Isaac Lewin, "On the Right of Everyone to Leave Any Country, Including His Own" (21 January 1963), in *Ten Years of Hope: Addresses before the United Nations* (New York: Shengold Publishers, 1971), 30.

59.   Michael Meerson-Aksenov, "The Influence of the Jewish Exodus on the Democratization of Soviet Society," trans. Gloria Donen Sosin, in *Essays on Human Rights*, 153.

60.   Ibid., 152.

61.   See also Yoran Dinstein, "Soviet Jewry and International Human Rights," in *Essays on Human Rights*, 126-43, and Paul Litvinov, "The Human-Rights Movement in the Soviet Union," in *Essays on Human Rights*, 113-25. Similarly, it is argued that the right to emigrate is the only protection Jews have in societies like Iraq. See Mitchell Knisbacher, "The Jews of Iraq and the International Protection of the Rights of Minorities (1856-1976)," in *Essays on Human Rights*, 157-78.

62.   David Sidorsky, "Introduction," in *Essays on Human Rights*, xxxiv. He attributes this to a letter by S. French to Herzl.

63.   Leslie C. Green, "Jewish Issues on the Human-Rights Agenda in the First Half of the Twentieth Century," in *Essays on Human Rights*, 298.

64.   Jacob L. Talmon, "Mission and Testimony: The Universal Significance of Modern Anti-Semitism," in *Essays on Human Rights*, 359. Jews argue that Israel's human rights record is better than their neighbors and that Israel has acted with restraint in the face of extreme provocation in the occupied territories. See Jerome J. Shestack, "Human Rights Issues in Israel's Rule of the West Bank and Gaza," in *Essays on Human Rights*, 193-209. To its credit, the Jacob Blaustein Institute has funded the Association for Civil Rights in Israel which defends the rights of Palestinian residents of the West Bank. Lowell W. Livezey, "U.S. Religious Organizations and the International Human Rights Movement," *Human Rights Quarterly* 11, no. 1 (February 1989):48-49.

65.   Walter Laqueur, "The Issue of Human Rights," in *Essays on Human Rights*, 9-10.

66.   Daniel P. Moynihan, "The Significance of the Zionism-as-Racism Resolution for International Human Rights," in *Essays in Human Rights*, 43.

67.   Ibid., 43-45.

68.   Sidney Liskofsky, "The United Nations and Human Rights: 'Alternative Approaches'," in *Essays on Human Rights*, 48. See Richard H. Schwartz, "Human Rights and Obligations," *Judaism and Global Survival* (New York: Atara Publishing Co., 1987).

69.   Elie Wiesel, "Wiesel's Speech: 'This Honor Belongs to All the Survivors'," *New York Times*, 1 December 1986, A-8. At the opening of a photo exhibit entitled "Auschwitz: A Crime against Mankind," on 10 December 1985, Human Rights Day, Wiesel said: "We remember Auschwitz for the sake of all victims everywhere who suffer. We remember our hunger so as to eliminate starvation today. We remember our anguish so as to proclaim the right of men and women everywhere to live without fear." Quoted in "Auschwitz Exhibit Underscores United Nations Commitment to Human Rights," *UN Chronicle* 23 (February 1986):93. The dedication of *Human Rights and the World's Religions* begins: "For Elie Wiesel, eloquent advocate for the human rights of all human beings."

70.   Ibid.

Chapter 7

MUSLIMS

When the Universal Declaration of Human Rights was approved in 1948 by the UN General Assembly, the government of Saudi Arabia abstained, on the grounds that the Declaration did not acknowledge rights to be the gift of God and violated the Qur'an by asserting a right to change one's religion. However, the Muslim foreign minister of Pakistan, Muhammed Zufrullah Khan, defended his country's support for the Declaration on the grounds that the Qur'an permits one to believe or disbelieve.[1]

This issue is one of several that continue to be debated among Muslims. Ann Elizabeth Mayer notes that Muslims "are currently deeply divided among themselves on the question of what kinds of human rights protections Islam provides."[2] Moreover, she argues that where contemporary governments have used Islamic criteria the result has been to limit the exercise of human rights. Yet today Muslim countries throughout the world have ratified international human rights covenants, and Muslim lawyers and scholars are quick to assert that Islam has always supported human rights.

In this chapter I will summarize arguments given by Muslims in support of human rights. I will describe in detail the general support of one leading Muslim for the Universal Declaration of Human Rights. Finally, I will review the recent declarations of human rights by Muslim advocates and intellectuals.

Muslim Lawyers

In 1980 a Seminar on Human Rights in Islam was organized by the International Commission of Jurists, together with the University of Kuwait

and the Union of Arab Lawyers. One purpose of the seminar was succinctly set forth in a sentence in its report: "The time has come to refute the idea that the initiation and continued development of the concept of human rights must be attributed exclusively to Western culture."[3]

The sixty-five participants in the seminar agreed upon several conclusions. They affirmed that

> Islam was the first to recognize basic human rights and almost 14 centuries ago it set up guarantees and safeguards that have only recently been incorporated in universal declarations of human rights.[4]

They acknowledged that contemporary Islamic practice in many respects does not conform to the true principles of Islam. However, they noted that "Islam was the first to safeguard personal rights and freedoms for religious minorities."[5] They asserted that because "human rights and freedoms are not attributed to Nature but are considered to be gifts of God in accordance with the Islamic faith,"

> This confers on them an added measure of veneration, prestige and sanctity to protect them from inroads by the ruling authorities, lends them the qualities of completeness and universality, and renders them inalienable and irrevocable.[6]

Moreover, they affirmed that Islam's codification of human rights constitutes "a solid foundation for an effective exercise of human rights and freedoms and protection against any infringement of them."[7]

The seminar made recommendations about economic, social and cultural rights as well as civil and political rights. Islamic states were called upon to implement standards in international law consistent with Islamic law and to reform their economic systems "to achieve social justice and guarantee human dignity."[8] In conclusion:

> The Seminar finally addressed itself to Almighty God in a fervent prayer that all Muslims be brought together in justice and goodness, and that this humanitarian effort be pursued until the dignity of man is assured, the foundations of his rights and his life firmly established, and consolidated, and the roots of arbitrariness and injustice eradicated from the world.[9]

Thus, in Islam, God-given human rights are seen as the means of assuring human dignity in the life of this world.

This theme was set forth clearly in the inaugural address of His Highness the Sovereign Emir of Kuwait. He noted that it was fifteen centuries since the Prophet and his followers "took refuge in Medina and set up a community where the exercise of human rights, previously a

mere aspiration and hope, became a reality."[10] This became possible "because of Islam's primary belief in human dignity, as emphasized by God, the Almighty, in the Qur'an where He says: 'and we have edified the progeny of Adam'."[11] The Emir thus affirmed that

> To preserve the dignity of man, it is necessary that society guarantees him food, drink, lodging, clothing, education and employment as well as his right to express his opinion, participate in the political life of his country and to be assured of his own security and that of his kin.[12]

The community has a duty to acquire the competence to ensure such rights. "Duties, in this way, are seen as another aspect of rights, as though rights and duties form the twin wings which enable society to soar to the horizons of its aspired future."[13]

In a major address Zouheir Al-Midani, Secretary-General of the Arab Lawyers' Union, noted that appeals to human rights are being made in the Third World as a part of the ideological struggle between capitalism and socialism. He asked the participants in the seminar:

> Would it be possible for us, as Muslims, to find our refuge in the spiritual values of Islam and escape being pulled right or left by embracing its concepts on human rights, basic freedoms, justice and equity, while upholding them as themes for our age, and by adhering to these fundamental doctrines of Islam which Muslims have constantly upheld?[14]

Thus he called for a return to the basic principles of Islamic faith as derived from the Qur'an and the Sunnah.

Basic Doctrines

Pakistani scholar Rashid Ahmad Jullundhri writes that "Islam wants to create a society based on a deep sense of moral responsibility and justice in order to preserve human dignity accorded to man by God," and he argues that "without the practical recognition of the basic rights of man all talk of human dignity will remain empty verbiage."[15] The task of the state then is to protect the rights of its citizens.

This is a religious duty as well. Jullundhri notes that the Arabic word *huquq* is used for human rights. *Huquq* is the plural of *haqq*. *Haqq* is also a divine name meaning the real. In Sufi usage *Haqq* means the Absolute.[16] This word is also used in the traditions of the Prophet, for the Prophet is quoted as saying: "O, God, you are the Truth."[17] Therefore, Jullundhri asserts:

> The Ulama [Judges] regarded human rights as an integral part of faith. A Man cannot be considered religious in the true sense of the word if he does not grant the rights of his fellowmen. The measure of judging a man's religiosity is how he deals with people, not how much he prays.[18]

As practice is the measure of all piety, belief "in human rights alone cannot make man free of fear and spiritual anxiety."[19] The truth must be lived as well as believed.

Mohammed Allal Sinaceur argues that contemporary human rights are recognized as compatible with Islam: "Human rights in Islam are human rights in the light of Islam, Islam as the outward medium through which its believers attain their true value, through which is realized the right to right [sic] and the right to truth."[20] He identifies five basic principles in Islam which legitimate human rights: the primacy of the life and dignity of the human person, the protection against restraint on religion, respect for the dwelling, the right of asylum, and the duty of care for others.

The text from the Qur'an fundamental to all human rights reads: "that whoso slays a soul not to retaliate for a soul slain, nor for corruption done in the land, shall be as if he had slain mankind altogether."[21] In Islam the human person has absolute value:

> Not merely because of man's resemblance to God as affirmed, for example, by Cicero, nor because of the Christian tradition, recalled to us in a hadith, that God created Adam in his own image, nor because the human individual is of more value than a whole material universe, nor because, as St. Thomas Aquinas put it, 'the relation between each individual person and the entire community is that of the part to the whole,' nor because the individual is above the community, nor because a single man typifies or exemplifies man, like Hamlet, who is neither you nor I but all of us.[22]

The value of the human person is absolute because the individual is humankind as a whole: "The value of the individual is neither numerical nor rational nor social; it is the gift of God himself, a gift to man as such—without regard either for attributes of civilization or for historic renown or for the excellence of his self-consciousness."[23]

Abdul Aziz Said begins his well-known essay, "Human Rights in Islamic Perspectives," with a challenging paragraph:

> Human rights are concerned with the dignity of the individual—the level of self-esteem that secures personal identity and promotes human community. While the pursuit of human dignity is universal, its forms are designed by the cultures of people. Politics is a cultural activity reflecting tradition and environment. The debate on human rights assumes that in spite of the differences that characterize the spectrum of world cultures, political conduct can

be conceptualized by certain common norms and attitudes. In the modern global system, Westerners have concentrated on discovering common denominators rooted in Judeo-Christian traditions and from which a calculus of human rights would emerge. This emphasis on Western common denominators projects a parochial view of human rights that excludes the cultural realities and present existential conditions of Third World societies.[24]

Politics is cultural, and human rights are political: "The character and nature of human rights are determined in the crucible of a specific sociopolitical culture."[25]

In an Islamic culture the state has the responsibility of enforcing the principles of the Shari'a: "the laws derived from the Qur'an, the Sunnah—the Hadith and decisions of Muhammad, Ijma'—the consensus of opinion of the Ulama (Judges) and Ijtihad—the counsel of judges on a particular case."[26] As sovereignty belongs to God, the state exists not merely to protect its citizens but to achieve social justice. Thus "it is the state's duty to enhance human dignity and alleviate conditions that hinder individuals in their efforts to achieve happiness."[27]

Said argues that the Western liberal emphasis on freedom from restraint is alien to Islam. Freedom in Islam is not the ability to act, but the ability to become:

> The jurists see human freedom in terms of personal surrender to the Divine Will. Freedom is not an inherent right. . . . The goal of freedom is human creativity. Freedom is defined as belonging to the community, and participating with the people in cultural creation.[28]

Basharat Ahmad proclaims: "It was the Holy Qur'an which for the first time preached the gospel of human freedom with such zeal and emphasis that the whole world woke up, as it were, from deep sleep."[29] However, this human freedom must be understood, as Seyyed Hossein Nasr clearly states in "The Concept and Reality of Freedom in Islam and Islamic Civilization," as the freedom to do what is right. For as pure freedom belongs to God alone, "the more we are, the more we are free."[30]

According to the Shari'a, human rights are "a consequence of human obligations and not their antecedent":

> We possess certain obligations toward God, nature, and other humans. . . . As a result of fulfilling these obligations, we gain certain rights and freedoms that are again outlined by the Divine Law.[31]

Thus democracy is understood differently in Islamic culture than in the West. As all members of a society are responsible to God, all share equally in delegating authority to the state. In the words of Pakistani Abul

A'la Mawdudi: "In Western democracy, the people are sovereign; in Islam sovereignty is vested in God and the people are His caliphs or representatives."[32]

Human rights then are justified because they are the gift of God and the responsibility of those who rule this world on behalf of God. This gives them ultimate authority:

> When we speak of human rights in Islam we mean those rights granted by God. Rights granted by kings or legislative assemblies can be withdrawn as easily as they are conferred; but no individual and no institution has the authority to withdraw the rights conferred by God.[33]

Mawdudi argues that the resolutions of the United Nations cannot be compared with the rights sanctioned by God for "the former are not obligatory on anybody, while the latter are an integral part of the Islamic faith."[34]

Fouad Zakaria also asserts that "the basic foundation of the concept of human rights, in the contemporary Muslim Arab mind, is religious."[35] He admits that this "sacredness" of human rights was fully recognized for only a brief time in Islam and that the rulers who came after the age of the Prophet and the four Rightful or Orthodox Caliphs have distorted "the true Islamic rule."[36] Thus in Islam human rights are not associated with history at all, but with the ancient precepts of the Qur'an and its early enforcement.

Zakaria summarizes the features which characterize the concept of human rights in Islam, as interpreted by contemporary Muslims in the Arab world:

> This concept is theocentric; in it man counts only as far as he is a reflection of divine nature. It is non-historical, or rather it freezes a certain moment of history and holds fast to it till the very end, thus doing away with dynamism, mobility and historical development. Finally, it is non-empirical; it does not depend on long and graduated practice in widening the scope of human rights, but seeks to imitate a theoretical and spiritual ideal, while completely disregarding the effect of practice on this theoretical ideal.[37]

Thus there is not only a great divide between theory and practice but few tools of interpretation are available in the tradition to bridge this gap.

The practical problems are aptly illustrated by conflict over freedom of religion. The conclusions of the 1980 Seminar in Kuwait call upon the Islamic state to guarantee the rights of non-Muslims, including their right

> to practice their religious beliefs, conduct their ceremonies, pursue their professions, vocations and other activities and benefit like everyone else from public revenues such as state assistance and aid.[38]

However, Muslim scholar Abdullahi Ahmed An-Na'im argues that "discrimination on grounds of religion or belief is fundamental to traditional Shari'a law."[39] And James Piscatori agrees.[40]

John Kelsay argues that, at least in the modern era, there is greater diversity of belief within Islam than Piscatori and others acknowledge. He notes that Muhammed Ali Jinnah, the "Great Leader" of Pakistan, affirmed freedom of religion in his presidential address to the Constituent Assembly of Pakistan on 11 August 1947. And Kelsay asserts: "Whatever the case for Jinnah's status as a religious thinker, it is certainly true that his statement in the 11 August speech, as well as Zafrullah Khan's comments at the United Nations, would have been in accord with certain tendencies in Indo-Pakistan Islam at the time."[41]

As evidence for this position he notes that the popular work by Amir 'Ali, *The Spirit of Islam*, which was first published in 1891 and went through several editions, presents a view of Islam which is not in conflict with modern notions of freedom of conscience. Amir 'Ali writes:

> By the laws of Islam, liberty of conscience and freedom of worship were allowed and guaranteed to the followers of every other creed under Moslem dominion. The passage in the Koran, "Let there be no compulsion in religion," testifies to the principles of toleration and charity inculcated by Islam. "If thy Lord had pleased, verily all who are in the world would have believed together." "Wilt thou then force men to believe when belief can come only from God?"[42]

Muhammed Zafrullah Khan, Muhammed Ali Jinnah, and Amir 'Ali all argue for freedom of conscience on the basis of the statement in the Qur'an that there is to be no compulsion in religion.[43]

Abdulaziz A. Sachedina argues that the division in Islam over freedom of religious belief and conscience can be traced back to a controversy between the Mu'tazilite and Ash'arite schools of dialectical theology. The first school supports the notion that religious belief and practice cannot be compelled, because it is God "who grants or withholds the gift of faith, who either makes the heart receptive to warnings or hardens it upon unsatisfactory actions or attitudes on the part of an individual."[44] In this tradition God's guidance may be known through the natural order, by reason, as well as through revelation.

The exegetes of the second school believe that the will of God is only known through Islamic law. Moreover, they interpret the Qur'an to mean that only the "People of the Book"—Jews, Christians, and Zoroastrians—are to be allowed freedom of religious practice, as these peoples have God's guidance through Scripture. They also point out that the Prophet supported compelling idol worshippers, as well as those who renounced Islamic faith, to accept it.

Clearly then, the Qur'an, as understood by some Muslim commentators, contains elements which may be used to support religious liberty. However, it must also be granted that many Muslim commentators do not take this position. Moreover, the practice within Islamic cultures has often denied freedom of religion and conscience.

In Islamic culture legal capacity has traditionally been determined by one's religion, with only Muslims being recognized as full citizens of the state. To be sure, the treatment of non-Muslims in Muslim countries has varied greatly from country to country and era to era. However, Muslims have often held that "A Muslim who abandons Islam, whether or not he or she subsequently embraces another faith, is guilty of the crime of apostasy, which is punishable by death under Shari'a law."[45] Christians and Jews, as believers in Scripture which Muslims believe to be divine, have frequently enjoyed a limited degree of independence, as "People of the Book" or *Dhimmas*. However, Abdullah Ahmad An-Na'im asserts that "even the best *Dhimma* system in conception and implementation would still discriminate against Christians and Jews and violate their religious freedom."[46]

An-Na'im argues that the Islamic tradition can be reformed, along the lines advocated by the late Sudanese scholar Ustadh Mahmoud Mohmed Taha, who "did not propose to discard any part of the Qur'an or undermine its divine nature" but suggested "that Muslims should undertake modern legislation to enact those verses of the Qur'an which were previously deemed to be abrogated in the sense that they were not made the source of legally binding rules (*ayat al-ahkam*)."[47] With respect to religious liberty, M. Taha argued:

> that the verses emphasizing freedom of choice and individual responsibility for such choice before God should be the bases of modern Islamic law. To do that, Muslims need to abrogate the verses of compulsion and discrimination against non-Muslims, in the sense of denying them legal efficacy in modern Islamic law. Such verses shall remain part of the holy Qur'an for all purposes except the purpose of legally binding rules. In other words, in the same way that early Muslim jurists employed the technique of abrogation (*naskh*) to rationalize and develop a body of law for their time, modern Muslim society should undertake a similar process in order to develop a body of law for modern society.[48]

Without changes in the Shari'a such as these, An-Na'im argues, it will hardly be an instrument of religious freedom. Furthermore, the "immediate and total implementation of Shari'a demanded by Muslim fundamentalists would make a difficult situation completely intolerable."[49]

Equality

Khalid Duran notes that M. Taha had great support among educated Sudanese, even for his position that the Qur'an supports equal rights for women.[50] Muslims have long held that historically the position of women in society was improved wherever Islam was practiced. For example, an Iranian report written in 1968 affirms: "Islam, a religion based on equality, regarded women as equal to men in the political, economic, and social spheres."[51] However, the report goes on to acknowledge that in Islamic society other ideologies have often resulted in unequal treatment of women.

Muslim Scholar Riffat Hassan also takes the position that, while Islamic society continues to treat women as unequal to men, the proper reading of the Qur'an leads to a very different conclusion:

Having spent seven years in study of the Qur'anic passages relating to women, I am convinced that the Qur'an is not biased against women and does not discriminate against them. On the contrary, because of its protective attitude toward all downtrodden and oppressed classes, it appears to be weighted in many ways in favor of women.[52]

However, she acknowledges that human rights are disappearing today "under the pressure of mounting fanaticism and traditionalism in many areas of the Muslim world":

I am particularly concerned about serious violations of human rights pertaining to the rights of women, the rights of minorities, the right of the accused to due process of law, and the right of the Muslim masses to be free of dictatorships. In the end we have what seems to be an irreconcilable gulf between Qur'anic ideals and the realities of Muslim living.[53]

Nonetheless, she affirms that while "others may or may not recognize our human rights . . . as human beings who have a covenantal relationship with God, we must strive under all circumstances to secure and to guard those rights which we believe have been given to us by God and which, therefore, no one else has the right to take away."[54]

If equality of men and women in Islam has often seemed to be a mere ideal, the Islamic affirmation of equality regardless of color or race has more often been put into practice. Mawdudi quotes the Prophet as saying:

No Arab has any superiority over a non-Arab, nor does a non-Arab have any superiority over a black man, or the black man any superiority over the white man. You are all the children of Adam, and Adam was created from clay.[55]

During his pilgrimage to Mecca, American Malcolm X was so impressed by the spirit of brotherhood among Muslims of different races and colors that he changed from a black nationalist to a black human rights advocate. He wrote:

> America needs to understand Islam, because this is the one religion that erases from its society the race problem. Throughout my travels in the Muslim world, I have met, talked to, and even eaten with people who in America would have been considered "white"—but the "white" attitude was removed from their minds by the religion of Islam. I have never before seen *sincere* and *true* brotherhood practiced by all colors together, irrespective of their color.[56]

Thus in a time when other black leaders in America spoke only of civil rights, Malcolm X asserted that "the salvation of America's very soul . . . can only be salvaged if human rights and dignity, in full, are extended to black men."[57]

A Sufi Commentary

To mark the twentieth anniversary of the Universal Declaration of Human Rights, Sultanhussein Tabandeh of Gunabad, Iran, leader of the Ne'ematullahi Sultanalishahi Sufi Order which was founded about 1400, wrote *A Muslim Commentary on the Universal Declaration of Human Rights* and had it delivered to every Islamic representative who attended the 1968 Tehran International Conference on Human Rights.

Sultanhussein Tabandeh describes the Universal Declaration as "a masterpiece" of the United Nations, but suggests "most of its provisions were already inherent in Islam."[58] Denying any involvement in politics and confessing ignorance as to the political implications of the Declaration, he asserts his concern is "only the religious angle, and in particular the relation to the sacred theology of Islam and of Shi'a belief."[59] He suggests this is particularly appropriate, as the "Declaration was greeted by private individuals of all races as a gospel proclaimed for their protection by the jurists and the liberals of the world."[60]

After reviewing the "genesis" of the Universal Declaration, Sultanhussein Tabandeh suggests:

> The UN became the Ka'aba of peaceloving hopes. It has performed great services, one of which was its publication of the Universal Declaration of Human Rights. Like any human institution, this Declaration has its defects, as indeed at its very inception was pointed out by the representative of Syria in the first debate in the General Assembly. It does not guarantee all the longings of mankind: nonetheless it is a great step forward in the right direction towards

the foundation of the human society of peace, freedom and equality which men of vision have aimed at through the millennia.[61]

He then proceeds to discuss each article in detail "in order to show that what all good people hold in common, Islam possesses in itself; and offers to humanity for the benefit of all."[62]

Sultanhussein Tabandeh argues that occasionally the Declaration is at variance with Islamic law.[63] He asserts that Islam forbids the marriage of a Muslim to a polytheist, an idolater or an infidel, and that a Muslim woman has no right to marry any non-Muslim man. Moreover, he argues that Islamic law limits the right of divorce to the husband, and in other ways does not recognize the equal rights of men and women who are naturally "adapted to different natural functions, and capable of different duties in life."[64] He defends the different rights and duties assigned to husband and wife by Islamic law as necessary for the protection of the family, which the Universal Declaration affirms is "the natural and fundamental group unit of society and is entitled to protection by society and the State."[65] Moreover, he is extremely critical of Muslim representatives to the UN who agreed to the provisions of Article 16 of the Universal Declaration which affirm equal rights in marriage.

Freedom of thought, conscience and belief are acceptable within Islamic law, he notes, but only to the extent consistent with Islamic teachings: "No one's freedom gives him the right to blaspheme or to curse God, His Prophets or His Saints."[66] Thus religious minorities "who follow the one true God and the revelation given to a prophet of His," such as Jews, Christians and Zoroastrians, can pursue their religious practice freely:

> But followers of a religion of which the basis is contrary to Islam, like those who demand Islam's extirpation, have no official rights to freedom of religion in Islamic countries or under an Islamic government, nor can they claim respect for their religion, any more than in certain countries definite political parties which are contrary to the ideology of the regime can claim freedom since they are declared to be inimical to the welfare of that land and people.[67]

In addition to stressing that the common good limits religious liberty, Sultanhussein Tabandeh argues—much as Augustine did in the fourth century—that freedom of religion should not be interpreted as allowing people to reject the truth, for no one would knowingly endanger his or her salvation. Thus conversion is restricted to giving up "some other religion than Islam in order to accept Islam's sound faith."[68]

The rest of the Declaration is found to conform to Islamic teaching. Sultanhussein Tabandeh concludes:

the Universal Declaration of Human Rights has not promulgated anything that was new nor inaugurated innovations. Every clause of it, indeed every valuable regulation needed for the welfare of human society ever enacted by the law-givers, already existed in a better and more perfect form in Islam.[69]

In faith he affirms that "Islam is the summit and nothing excels it!"[70]

Recent Declarations on Human Rights

In the Islamic perspective, human rights are seen as "rights which all human beings *ought* to have" because "These rights are so deeply rooted in our humanness that their denial or violation is tantamount to a negation or degradation of that which makes us human."[71] These rights are right, because they are from God. They are to be respected as a matter of religious obligation, that is, as a matter of one's faith in God.

It is to be expected that the practice of these rights falls short of the ideal, for that is true of all life in this world. Nonetheless, human rights are to be proclaimed, because they are true. Richard Antoun notes that this approach may be reflected in the declaratory judgments in Islamic courts, where certain deviations are allowed out of respect for local customs:

> Indeed, deviations from the ideal standard are always expected. What is important is to proclaim that standard and repeat that proclamation in its most elevated form in order to provide a constant guide for the community of believers.[72]

As in most religious traditions, words as well as deeds are believed to shape the nature of reality.

Perhaps this declaratory approach explains two recent proclamations of human rights by Muslim intellectuals. The first, the "Universal Islamic Declaration of Human Rights," is published by the Islamic Foundation in London.[73] It provides a sufficiently authoritative list of human rights in the Islamic tradition to be cited in a Shari'a court decision in Pakistan.[74]

The second recent declaration is the "Draft Charter on Human and People's Rights in the Arab World," developed by a group of Arab experts in December of 1986. This draft received the unanimous support of the fifteen hundred members of the Arab Union of Lawyers (which claims a membership of one hundred thousand) who were present at its annual meeting in 1987.[75] Its supporters reaffirm "their faith in the principles proclaimed in the Charter of the United Nations and the International Bill of Human Rights," but also affirm an Islamic interpretation of human rights that they feel is best suited to the particular needs of the modern Arab world.[76]

Conclusion

Clearly then, there is support for human rights in the Muslim world, although there is also great concern about the modernization of Islamic culture. Thus there is support in the Muslim world to develop what Abdul Aziz Said calls "a global conception of human rights."[77] This new conception of human rights needs to allow for major cultural differences. Said asserts that this "concept of human rights must incorporate Islamic and other Third World traditions or it will continue to provoke irreconcilable quarrels."[78]

Rights must be linked with duties, and individual claims must be reconciled with the common good. In the Islamic view human rights are universally true, and yet implementation of these rights may require various forms: "As law reflects the achievement of society so too the 'rightness' of human rights is determined by time, place, and experience."[79]

The "confluence between Islam and human rights" today is clearly based on

> internal Westernizing forces and modernist movements, on the influence exerted by non-Muslim authorities in Islamic countries that have, in self-defense, taken over into Islamic usage the themes, terminology and various meanings pertaining to the concepts given expression in the various Declarations of Human Rights.[80]

Challenged by the West, Islamic societies are rediscovering their own tradition in new ways. While grounding human rights in their own faith, Muslims nonetheless affirm the universality of human rights.[81] In addition, a number of Muslims have been stirred to action by the lack of protection for fundamental human rights, in their own societies as well as in the rest of the world.

Notes

1.   See A. David Gurewitsch, *Eleanor Roosevelt: Her Day* (New York: Interchange Foundation, 1973), 25.

2.   Ann Elizabeth Mayer, "The Dilemmas of Islamic Identity," in *Human Rights and the World's Religions*, ed. Leroy S. Rouner (Notre Dame, Ind.: University of Notre Dame Press, 1988), 94.

3.   *Human Rights in Islam* (Geneva: International Commission of Jurists, 1982), 3.

4.   Ibid., 9.

5.   Ibid., 11.

6.   Ibid., 9.

7.   Ibid., 11.

8.   Ibid., 13.

9. Ibid., 21.

10. Ibid., 25.

11. Ibid.

12. Ibid.

13. Ibid.

14. Ibid., 33.

15. Rashid Ahmad Jullundhri, "Human Rights and Islam," in *Understanding Human Rights: An Interdisciplinary and Interfaith Study*, ed. Alan D. Falconer (Dublin: Irish School of Ecumenics, 1980), 34.

16. Muhammad al-Thanawi, *Kashshaf instilahat al-Funun* (Calcutta: 1864); Sarskhsi, *Usul* (Cairo: 1954) 2, 332-40. Quoted in Jullundhri, "Human Rights and Islam," 35.

17. In fact, these words were spoken by Salman to his companion. Later he informed the Prophet, who endorsed Salman's saying. See Bukhari, *Al-Jam'i al-Sahih*, ed. Rudolph Krehl (Leiden: 1862), I, 490. Quoted in Jullundhri, "Human Rights and Islam," 35.

18. Jullundhri, "Human Rights and Islam," 35.

19. Ibid., 42.

20. Mohammed Allal Sinaceur, "Islamic Tradition and Human Rights," in *Philosophical Foundations of Human Rights* (Paris: UNESCO, 1986), 211. However, James P. Piscatori argues that traditional Islamic beliefs are unlike modern concepts of human rights in that rights are understood as God-given rather than as natural to persons and as subject to governmental control rather than as a check on governmental power. Piscatori, "Human Rights in Islamic Political Culture," in *The Moral Imperatives of Human Rights: A World Survey*, ed. Kenneth W. Thompson (Washington, D.C.: University Press of America, 1980), 142.

21. Ibid., 212. (Qur'an 5:32)

22. Ibid., 213.

23. Ibid.

24. Abdul Aziz Said, "Human Rights in Islamic Perspectives," in *Human Rights: Cultural and Ideological Perspectives*, ed. Adamantia Pollis and Peter Schwab (New York: Praeger Publishers, 1979), 86. For instance, unlike the Christian tradition, Islamic law has never had a doctrine of natural law and makes no claim to govern the conscience. Sinaceur, "Islamic Tradition and Human Rights," in *Philosophical Foundations of Human Rights*, 204-05.

25. Ibid. See also Abdul Aziz Said, "The Islamic Context for Human Rights," *Breakthrough* 10, nos. 2-3 (Winter/Spring 1989):39-41.

26. Ibid, 87.

27. Ibid.

28. Abdul Aziz Said and Jamil Nasser, "The Use and Abuse of Democracy in Islam," in *International Human Rights: Contemporary Issues*, ed. Jack L. Nelson and Vera M. Green (Stanfordville, N.Y.: Human Rights Publishing Group, Earl M. Coleman, 1980), 76-77. See Mansour Farhang, "Fundamentalism and Civil Rights in Contemporary Middle Eastern Politics," in *Human Rights and the World's Religions*, 64.

29. Basharat Ahmad, "Qur'anic View of Human Freedom," *The Islamic Review* 5, nos. 1, 2, and 3 (October, November, December 1984):9.

30. Seyyed Hossein Nasr, "The Concept and Reality of Freedom in Islam and Islamic Civilization," in *The Philosophy of Human Rights*, ed. Alan S. Rosenbaum (Westport, Conn.: Greenwood Press, 1980), 96. On 26 November 1982, before the Third Committee of the UN General Assembly, Mr. Zarif of the Islamic Republic of Iran asserted that "the Islamic Revolution in his own country was aimed, *inter alia*, at the promotion of human rights on a world-wide scale." He maintained that "Defending human rights, whose status was so exalted in the eyes of Islam, was a difficult task, particularly since corruption and absurdity

had become common practice in contemporary societies through the gross neglect and compromising of liberties in the name of individual freedom; unfortunately, freedom had become synonymous with decadence. Consequently, all rules regarding human rights must be founded exclusively on principles of divine ethics, and justice must be defined in terms of external moral principles." "Summary Record of the 56th Meeting of the Third Committee," A/C.3/37/SR.56, English, 15.

31.   Ibid., 97.

32.   Abul A'la Mawdudi, *Human Rights in Islam* (Leicester, U.K.: Islamic Foundation, 2d ed. 1980), 10.

33.   Ibid., 15. Chaudri Nazir Ahmad Khan asserts that "a fundamental drawback in the whole concept of human rights was the idea that these rights were being granted by man to man, as if they were a gift. We must realize that every child wherever born and of whatever color, caste or creed, brings into the world all these rights at the time of his birth, as a direct blessing from Allah—the Creator. They are sacred and inviolable." Khan, "Address," in *The International Observance: World Law Day—Human Rights: 1968* (Geneva: World Peace through Law Center, 1968), 8.

34.   Ibid., 16. See Ihsen Hamid Al-Mafregy, "Islam and Human Rights," in *Human Rights Teaching* 2, no. 1 (Paris: UNESCO, 1981), 11-14. Mawdudi's Islamic Party (*Jama'at-e Islami*) rejected liberal notions of natural law and liberty of conscience and regarded Muhammed Zufrullah Khan as a heretic. John Kelsay, "Saudi Arabia, Pakistan, and the Universal Declaration of Human Rights," in *Human Rights and the Conflict of Cultures: Western and Islamic Perspectives on Religious Liberty* (Columbia, S.C.: University of South Carolina Press, 1988), 49.

35.   Fouad Zakaria, "Human Rights in the Arab World: the Islamic Context," in *Philosophical Foundations of Human Rights*, 228.

36.   Ibid., 230.

37.   Ibid., 237. Zakaria observes that the Iranian Revolution represents a notable exception.

38.   *Human Rights in Islam*, 7-8. Mohammed Allal Sinaceur argues that this conclusion is supported by the Qur'anic affirmation (2:256): "No constraint in religion." Sinaceur, "Islamic Tradition and Human Rights," in *Philosophical Foundations of Human Rights*, 215-16.

39.   Abdulahi Ahmed An-Na'im, "Religious Freedom in Egypt: Under the Shadow of the Islamic *Dhimma* System," in *Religious Liberty and Human Rights in Nations and in Religions*, ed. Leonard Swidler (Philadelphia: Ecumenical Press, Temple University, 1986), 55. See also his article, "Religious Minorities under Islamic Law and the Limits of Cultural Relativism," *Human Rights Quarterly* 9, no. 1 (February 1987):1-18.

40.   James P. Piscatori, "Human Rights in Islamic Political Culture," in *The Moral Imperatives of Human Rights*, 144-46.

41.   John Kelsay, "Saudi Arabia, Pakistan, and the Universal Declaration of Human Rights," in *Human Rights and the Conflict of Cultures: Western and Islamic Perspectives on Religious Liberty*, 43-44.

42.   Amir 'Ali, *The Spirit of Islam* (London: Methuen, 1967), 212; quoted in John Kelsay, "Saudi Arabia, Pakistan, and the Universal Declaration of Human Rights," in *Human Rights and the Conflict of Cultures*, 45. Wilfred Cantwell Smith acknowledges that *The Spirit of Islam* was widely circulated among liberal Muslims, but argues that it is superficial. He asserts that Muhammad Iqbal not only "saw through the liberal sham of democracy, to its exploitation," but communicated a revolutionary message to Indian Muslims through his poetry. In *Sultanat* Iqbal writes: "The West's republicanism is the same old instrument, In its strings there are no tunes but those of Kaiserism. The demon of exploitation dances in republican garb, And you suppose that it is the fairy of liberty. Constitutional bodies,

reforms, privileges, rights, Are sweet-tasting western soporifics." Quoted in Smith, *Modern Islam in India: A Social Analysis* (London: Victor Gollancz Ltd., 1946), 110-11.

43. David Little asserts: "Presumably genuine submission or surrender to Allah's will, along with the appropriate dispositions of gratitude, devotion, steadfastness, etc., must come from the heart, must involve the deepest and most intimate kind of personal consent and commitment. If that is true, then compulsion and external interference would appear to be the antithesis of Islamic faith." Little, "The Western Tradition," in *Human Rights and the Conflict of Cultures*, 29.

44. Abdulaziz A. Sachedina, "Freedom of Conscience and Religion in the Qur'an," in *Human Rights and the Conflict of Cultures*, 67.

45. Ibid.

46. Ibid., 56. See James Dudley, "Human Rights Practices in the Arab States: The Modern Impact of Shari'a Values," *Georgia Journal of International and Comparative Law* 12 (1982):55-93.

47. Ibid, 59. Ustadh Mahmoud was executed by former President Numeiri of Sudan on 18 January 1985, because he opposed the immediate total implementation of Islamic Shari'a law without undertaking the reform process he advocated. Numeiri was overthrown three months later.

48. Ibid., 59. Pakistani scholar Muhammad Asad similarly argues for a reformed statement of Islam in his study, *The Principles of State and Government in Islam* (Berkeley and Los Angeles: University of California Press, 1961). See also M. Talbi, "Religious Liberty: A Muslim Perspective," *Islam o Christiana* 2 (1985):99-113.

49. Ibid.

50. Khalid Duran, "Religious Liberty and Human Rights in the Sudan," in *Religious Liberty and Human Rights in Nations and Religions*, 74.

51. *Iran and Human Rights: A Brief Account of the Achievements of the Last Few Years* (Iran: Compiled under the Auspices of the Iranian Coordinating Committee for the International Year for Human Rights, 1968), 95.

52. Riffat Hassan, "On Human Rights and the Qur'anic Perspective," in *Human Rights in Religious Traditions*, ed. Arlene Swidler (New York: The Pilgrim Press, 1982), 63. Nikki R. Keddie notes that those presenting such "modernist" arguments often assert that the Qur'an has many meanings, a traditional position in Islam, and so call for "reform" in the circumstances of modern society. "An allied argument is to stress the spirit of the Qur'an—to use the book title of the South Asian reformer Ameer Ali—and to say that the Qur'an is egalitarian (largely true) and favors human rights, and that these general principles were meant to be extended to women's rights. There is also extensive reinterpretation of particular verses and passages. The Qur'an in the same chapter says that men can marry up to four wives if they can treat the wives equally, and later that no matter how hard they try men will not be able to treat wives equally. Putting the two together, it is logically held by the modernists that the Qur'an was against polygamy, as the conditions it lays down as requirements for polygamy it then says are impossible to meet. More generally, various passages are interpreted to refer to male-female equality." Nikki R. Keddie, "The Rights of Women in Contemporary Islam," in *Human Rights and the World's Religions*, 86.

53. Ibid., 65. James P. Piscatori argues to the contrary that the Qur'an clearly supports inequitable treatment of men and women. Piscatori, "Human Rights in Islamic Political Culture," in *The Moral Imperatives of Human Rights*, 144.

54. Ibid., 55.

55. Quoted in Abdul A'la Mawdudi, *Human Rights in Islam*, 22.

56. Quoted in Alex Haley, *The Autobiography of Malcolm X* (New York: Ballantine Books, 1965), 340.

57. Ibid., 377.

58.   Sultanhussein Tabandeh, *A Muslim Commentary on the Universal Declaration of Human Rights*, trans. F. J. Goulding (London: F. T. Goulding & Company, English edition, 1970), 1. However, Mansour Farhang argues that the concept of human rights in the Universal Declaration is essentially Western: "It is a preconception of the Universal Declaration of Human Rights that in spite of the diversity of culture and differences in existential conditions in the world, a common standard of rights can be established for all peoples and nations." Farhang, "Fundamentalism and Civil Rights in Contemporary Middle Eastern Politics," in *Human Rights and the World's Religions*, 64.

59.   Ibid. Mr. Zarif's statement on behalf of the Islamic Republic of Iran is clearly more political, although it also is concerned to defend religious rights. Mr. Zarif stated that the Universal Declaration and the major human rights covenants were "not necessarily incompatible with the principles of justice and ethics"; however, the Declaration "appeared to relegate religion to the realm of an individual's private affairs, thereby precluding the possibility of establishing a religious Government." Moreover, "Specific provisions in the Declaration and the Covenants with regard to matters such as marriage were a blatant violation of the inherent right of everyone to practice his religious beliefs. In view of the fact that most religions had their own guidelines concerning issues such as marriage, the Declaration clearly promoted the abandonment of religion even in the sphere of personal and private matters, unfortunately under the guise of religious freedom." As the Declaration reflects the Western liberalism of its time, he argued that "the Western world must set aside its traditional cultural chauvinism and consider alternative approaches to the question of human rights." "Summary Record of the 56th Meeting of the Third Committee," 26 November 1982, A/C.3/37/SR.56, English, 16.

60.   Sultanhussein Tabandeh, *A Muslim Commentary on the Universal Declaration of Human Rights*, 3.

61.   Ibid., 9.

62.   Ibid., 14.

63.   During the drafting of the Universal Declaration the Egyptian delegate also raised objections on the basis of Islamic law. See United Nations, *Yearbook of the United Nations 1948-49* (New York: Columbia University Press in cooperation with the United Nations, 1950), 532; and James Frederick Green, *The United Nations and Human Rights* (Washington, D.C.: The Brookings Institute, 1956), 32.

64.   Ibid., 37-40. He notes that "Jesus Christ, too . . . decried the lovelessness which is the sin that leads to the inauguration of legal separation of a married couple."

65.   Article 16, 3d clause, Universal Declaration of Human Rights, 10.

66.   Ibid., 70.

67.   Ibid.

68.   Ibid., 72. Abdullahi Ahmed El Naiem notes the same distinction, but argues for a radical reform of the Shari'a. El Naiem, "A Modern Approach to Human Rights in Islam: Foundations and Implications for Africa," in *Human Rights and Development in Africa*, ed. Claude E. Welch, Jr. and Ronald I. Meltzer (Albany: State University of New York, 1984), 75-89.

69.   Ibid., 85.

70.   Ibid.

71.   Riffat Hassan, "On Human Rights and the Qur'anic Perspective," in *Human Rights in Religious Traditions*, 54.

72.   Richard T. Antoun, "The Islamic Court, The Islamic Judge, and the Declaration of Traditions: A Jordanian Case Study," *International Journal of Middle East Studies* 12 (1980):455-67. Mohammed Allal Sinaceur suggests that contemporary human rights derive their "mystic sustenance" from their "declaratory character." Sinaceur, "Islamic Tradition and Human Rights," in *Philosophical Foundations of Human Rights*, 194.

73. *Universal Islamic Declaration of Human Rights* (London: Islamic Foundation, 1981). It is published in *Human Rights Sourcebook*, ed. Albert P. Blaustein, Roger S. Clark, and Jay A. Sigler (New York: Paragon House Publishers, 1987), 917-26. Riad Daoudi, Professor of Law at the University of Damascus, notes that this Declaration is an important point of reference in teaching human rights in countries like Saudi Arabia where Muslim law is the only source of national legislation. See Daoudi, "Teaching of Human Rights in Arab Countries," in *Frontiers of Human Rights Education*, ed. Asbjørn Eide and Marek Thee (New York: Columbia University Press, 1983), 69-71.

74. Ansar Burney v. Federation of Pakistan (Aftab Hussain, CJ), Feb. 1983, vol. 35, no. 2, *The All Pakistan Legal Decisions*, Federal Shariat Court, 73-93, Shariat Petition No. K-4 of 1982, decided on 10 August 1982, 93.

75. Comments by Munzer Anabtawi, professor at the University of Jordan, at the International Institute of Human Rights, Strasbourg, France, 21 July 1987, notes by author.

76. Unpublished copy received at the International Institute of Human Rights, Strasbourg, France, July 1987.

77. Abdul Aziz Said, "Human Rights in Islamic Perspectives," in *Human Rights: Cultural and Ideological Perspectives*, 96.

78. Ibid.

79. Ibid., 97.

80. Mohammed Allal Sinaceur, "Islamic Tradition and Human Rights," in *Philosophical Foundations of Human Rights*, 208.

81. "From the point of view of Islam, what is today recognized as human rights has, below the surface, so much in common with truth that it may be identified essentially with the ethical foundations of human society." Ibid., 220.

Chapter 8

HINDUS AND BUDDHISTS

Hindus

Hindu scholar Mark Juergensmeyer begins an essay on "Dharma and the Rights of Untouchables" with the statement: "If by 'human rights' one means minority rights, then Hindu society can be said to have a human rights tradition, for it has always had a way of incorporating the poor and socially ostracized into the social whole."[1] The caste system can be understood as a reflection of dharma or "the moral order" in Hindu society, which at its best maintains "reciprocal relationships of mutual economic and social benefit. Each group respects the rights and dignity of the others."[2] Of course, as Juergensmeyer acknowledges, the reality has very often been otherwise.

On the other hand, Kana Mitra argues that traditional codes of conduct in the Hindu tradition are on their face contrary to human rights. Manu's *Dharma Sutra*, which is considered authoritative in this regard, relates all rights to duties specified by caste, age, and sex. Traditional rights then are privileges of status and position. However, for twenty-five hundred years there have been rebellions within the Hindu tradition against its hierarchical order, and today most Hindus believe Manu's code needs revision.

The key to reform is *dharma*. Manu uses the Sanskrit word *adhikara* to describe the notion of a just claim or right; however, only Brahmans have such rights. Thus deriving a notion of human rights within the Hindu tradition requires turning to the general concept of duty, or *dharma*, which is central to the *Dharma Sutras*. Mitra writes: "*Dharma* implies justice and propriety as does the word 'right' of the U.N. Declaration, although the connotation of a 'just claim' is not explicitly present."[3]

The revolts against traditional Hinduism reinterpret *dharma*. For instance, some *bhakti* groups assert that

All humans are equal as God's creation but are not the same; therefore, all should give and receive according to their own nature. These groups uphold the idea of following one's own nature (*svadharma*) as advocated in the *Bhagavad-Gita*.[4]

The various vedanta groups within Hindu orthodoxy also hold that one should follow one's own nature to realize perennial truth. Mitra argues, "They uphold human rights on the basis of all human beings having the same essence."[5] Humans may be potentially divine, but may not have realized this potentiality. Thus while asserting essential nonduality, most vedanta schools also embrace Manu's rules of conduct for life in this world.[6]

In addition to these ancient reinterpretations of Hindu tradition, Western notions of individual rights have entered Indian society, initially through British law and education. There have been many efforts to combine modern notions of rights with Hindu notions of rights and duties. Rammohan Roy, founder of the Brahmo Samaj movement, advocates equality for all persons regardless of caste or sex, on the basis that all humans are God's creatures. Vivekananda, leader of the Ramakrishna movement, advocates equality on the basis of vedanta thought and thus does not, like Roy, reject Manu. "Rabindranath Tagore is another influential name in the human-rights movement."[7]

Most of those who led the independence movement in India sought some accommodation between Western notions of individual rights and the Hindu tradition of duty and caste. The Indian Constitution, largely drafted by B. R. Ambedkar, who was an untouchable, abolished untouchability and affirmed individual civil and political rights. Legislation was even passed to reserve places in government and schools for untouchables. The caste system itself, however, was left intact.

John Carmen notes that the Indian Constitution guarantees more rights than the American Bill of Rights. The preamble speaks of securing "the dignity of the individual" and sections which follow it include: "Right to Equality," "Right to Freedom," "Right against Exploitation," "Right to Freedom of Religion," "Cultural and Educational Rights," "Right to Property," and "Right to Constitutional Remedies."[8] Clearly, many of these rights directly challenge the system of unequal privileges which is fundamental to the Hindu tradition of caste.

Carmen argues that although the Indian Constitution contains an impressive list of fundamental rights, "it does not ground them in anything, whether in individual human nature, the requirements of human community, or the creative intention of God."[9] In short, "the constitution does not recognize the fundamental *dharma* affirmed by the Hindu tradition and sets no spiritual obligation for the state itself or for the people."[10]

In the face of persisting untouchability in India despite these efforts to eradicate it, reformers who turn again to the notion of *dharma*

> have found in the ancient Indian concept the basis for ideas that are quite similar to those of socially sensitive Westerners, and yet are rooted in the Indian religious tradition. In short, they have discovered dharmic reforms appropriate to the modern world.[11]

For example, members of the Arya Samaj movement have argued that the original Vedic teachings are casteless and thus have fashioned "a notion of *dharma* based on universal, rather than caste-specific, obligations to social values."[12]

Mitra writes that "Mahatma Gandhi is the epitome of the human-rights movement within traditional Hinduism," for his "fight for the rights of the untouchables was based on his ideas of human rights."[13] Gandhi considered himself an orthodox Hindu. He believed that whether God is understood in theistic or nontheistic terms, Hindu theology could not be used to justify inequality of human beings. As Mitra affirms: "Theistic Hinduism upholds human equality on the basis that all are God's creatures. Nontheistic Hinduism emphasizes the identity of the essence of all humans."[14]

Gandhi included untouchables in his ashrams and movement. Yet he accepted Manu's idea that rights and duties, one's *dharma*, are to be understood in his terms of *svadharma*, one's natural situation in life. Mitra writes:

> The idea of *svadharma*, if not understood as a rigid code or law, can be a contribution in the field of human rights in its suggestion that differences be taken seriously. Manu offers suggestions in taking it in a nonrigid way. *Dharma*, he says, is what "is followed by those learned of the Vedas and what is approved by the conscience of the virtuous who are exempt from hatred and inordinate affection." Tradition, conscience, and reason must all be consulted to determine the rights and duties of humans. Rights and duties of different people in different situations are different, but each human being deserves and should have equal consideration and concern.[15]

Thus Gandhi was not advocating "individual rights" in the Western sense, but rather *dharma*: "an ethic of community, responsibility and loyalty."[16]

Gandhi's emphasis on tradition and duty are clear. When asked what he thought of the proposed Universal Declaration of Human Rights, he replied:

> I learnt from my illiterate but wise mother that all rights to be deserved and preserved came from duty well done. Thus, the very right to live accrues to us only when we do the duty of citizenship of the world. From this one

fundamental statement, perhaps it is easy enough to define the duties of Man and of Woman and correlate every right to some corresponding duty to be first performed.[17]

His position, as always, was rooted in religious commitment rather than political expediency.

However, he did speak of learning "to stand up for human dignity and rights," and even affirmed that everyone "has an equal right to the necessaries of life. . . ."[18] Thus Gandhi affirmed human rights in the context of his Hindu tradition:

> If we all discharge our duties, rights will not be far to seek. If leaving duties unperformed, we run after rights, they will escape us like a will o' the wisp. . . . The same teaching has been embodied by Krishna in the immortal words: "Action alone is thine. Leave thou the fruit severely alone." Action is duty, fruit is the right.[19]

While others have turned to the Bible or to the Qur'an to find justification for human rights, Gandhi turned within his own Hindu tradition to the sacred text of the *Bhagavad Gita.*

Gandhi's legacy includes a multitude of movements for social change within India which emphasize *swaraj* or self-rule. "The Indian human rights movement grew out of this tradition of autonomous social organization and is linked to other social movements, many also of Gandhian inspiration, both through shared personnel and because the victims of human rights violations are often activists in those movements."[20] Barnett Rubin concludes that, given the caste tradition and all the problems of Indian society, any success of human rights protection in India "is a strong argument for the potential universality of the movement."[21]

R. C. Pandeya, too, stresses that for the Indian all rights are derived from duties, and thus he suggests that the first principle of human rights is buried in Article 29 of the Universal Declaration of Human Rights: "Everyone has duties to the community in which alone the free and full development of his personality is possible."[22]

In Hindu philosophy this notion of duty follows from the nature of man and may be articulated in two ways:

> Negatively formulated, it will state that a man ought not to act in such a way as to obscure his true nature. In other words his duty would consist in withdrawing or refraining from all such acts as were likely to obscure any aspect of the totality of his being. The same idea formulated in positive terms would amount to saying that man ought to act in order to fulfill his total nature. In this alternative formulation his duty would consist in a complete knowledge of self.[23]

These two different emphases in the formulation of duty lead to a fork in the road in Indian philosophy: the path of renunciation, represented by Buddhism, and the path of realization of being as being, represented by vedanta.

Pandeya argues that both of these paths are reflected in the Universal Declaration of Human Rights:

> The Declaration, with its emphasis on freedom and equality of men and the consequent denunciation of distinctions contrary to the basic spirit of equality and freedom, represents a highly balanced blending of the two paths mentioned above. This is a philosophical tribute to the thoughtfulness and wisdom of the framers of the Declaration.[24]

The Declaration "reaches almost to the combined goal of Buddhism and Vedanta," he claims, but because of constraints in the modern world the Universal Declaration fails to specify the duties which generate human rights.[25]

Clearly, modern concepts of human rights are a reflection of Western influence and interfere with traditional notions of *dharma*.[26] Yet Hindu reformers seek to interpret *dharma* in ways which support the notion of human rights. This is not easily done. Perhaps this is why the Indian Constitution sets forth the major human rights affirmed in the Universal Declaration without providing any philosophical foundation for them. "The fact remains, however, that most educated Hindus not only accepted these fundamental rights but insisted that they expressed age-old Hindu principles."[27] Hindus affirm both *dharma* and human rights.

Buddhists

An analysis of Buddhist affirmations of human rights might also begin in India, the birthplace of Buddhism. There in 1956 another Hindu, B. R. Ambedkar, converted to Buddhism and took some four million other untouchables with him.[28]

Sangharakshita, a Buddhist who played an important role in the mass conversion movement that Ambedkar set in motion, writes of Ambedkar that:

> In the end, after years of unsuccessful struggle for the basic human rights of his people, he was forced to recognize that there was going to be no change of heart on the part of the Caste Hindus, and that the casteless, "Protestant" Hinduism of which he had sometimes spoken so enthusiastically was only a dream.[29]

As early as 1935 Ambedkar had threatened to leave Hinduism, when in a speech to a conference of the depressed classes he "spoke bitterly of the failure of their attempts to secure their basic human rights as members of the Hindu community."[30]

Ambedkar had considered conversion to Sikhism, but finally admitted that only the personalities of the Buddha and Christ captivated him. However, because the caste system was observed in the Christian churches of Southern India and the Christian community had not fought against social injustice, he turned to Buddhism.[31]

Ambedkar wrote that his philosophy was "enshrined" in three words: liberty, equality, and fraternity.

> Let no one however say that I have borrowed my philosophy from the French Revolution. I have not. My philosophy has roots in religion and not in political science. I have derived them from the teachings of my master, the Buddha.[32]

He suggested that fraternity was only another name for democracy, which is "essentially an attitude of respect and reverence towards [one's] fellow men."[33] Buddha transformed attitudes of respect and obedience contained in the ethnic Hindu notion of *dharma* into a universal morality. By admitting members of lower castes and women into the Bhikshu Sangha, the Buddha took "concrete steps to destroy the gospel of inequality."[34]

Ambedkar argued that for Buddhists the *dharma* is that

> universal morality which protects the weak from the strong, which provides common models, standards, and rules, and which safeguards the growth of the individual. It is what makes liberty and equality effective. . . ."[35]

For Ambedkar, fraternity "is nothing but another name for brotherhood of men which is another name for morality. This is why the Buddha preached that Dhamma [*dharma*] is morality and as Dhamma is sacred so is morality."[36]

Many Buddhists are reluctant to identify the *dharma* with human rights. Buddhist scholar Masao Abe writes that "the exact equivalent of the phrase 'human rights' in the Western sense cannot be found anywhere in Buddhist literature."[37] The Western concept of human rights concerns only humans. By marked contrast, in Buddhism

> a human being is not grasped only from the human point of view, that is, not simply on an anthropocentric basis, but on a much broader trans-homocentric, cosmological basis. More concretely, in Buddhism human beings are grasped as a part of all sentient beings or even as a part of all beings, sentient and nonsentient, because both human and nonhuman beings are equally subject to transiency or impermanency.[38]

Therefore, the human self is also impermanent, or relative.

The notion of absolute self-identity or substantial, enduring selfhood is an unreal, conceptual construction created by human self-consciousness. Buddhism calls it *maya*, or illusion, and emphasizes the importance of awakening to no-self by doing away with this illusory understanding of the self.[39]

Though self and nature are different from one another on the relative level, "on the absolute level they are equal and interfuse with one another because of the lack of any fixed, substantial selfhood."[40]

Thus Buddhism, Abe tells us, differs radically from the monotheistic religious traditions.

In the Judeo-Christian tradition the problem of human rights and human duty to other people must be considered in relation to the exclusive commandment of the supreme God, whereas in Buddhism the same problem should be grasped in relation to all living beings in the universe. This difference entails that in Buddhism conflict between human rights and religious freedom becomes much less serious. . . .[41]

It also means that for Buddhists nature is no more subordinate to human beings than human beings to nature. Buddhism offers an ecological view of life: "Under the commandment 'Not to destroy any life,' the rights of animals and plants are as equally recognized as are human rights."[42]

On the basis of this Buddhist analysis, Abe makes the following recommendations to foster human rights and overcome religious intolerance. First, attachment to doctrine and dogma should be eliminated, for this is the cause of intolerance. Second, wisdom rather than justice should be emphasized, as this is the basis of compassion and love. Third, monotheistic traditions must come to understand the Oneness of ultimate reality in a nondualistic way in order to avoid exclusivistic and intolerant attitudes toward other traditions.[43]

Similarly, Kenneth Inada acknowledges the importance of human rights, but suggests that for Buddhists human rights are "ancillary to the larger or more basic issue of human nature."[44] Human nature is understood as part of the process of "relational origination (*paticcasamupada*)," which is the greatest doctrine of Buddhism:

It means that, in any life-process, the arising of an experiential event is a total, relational affair. A particular event does not arise in a vacuum, nor does it result by the imposition of external forces of elements. It is a unique arisal which is vitally dependent on or related to all the elements present within the surroundings. Thus, in the process there is nothing which is fragmentary or has

any gaps, since it relates with the complete fullness of all the elements present. Each relationship is full insofar as the process is concerned. This means that relational origination is a most concrete way in which life-process goes on.[45]

This is the *Dhamma* (*dharma*), for the Buddha said: "He who sees relational origination sees the *Dhamma* and he who sees the *Dhamma* sees relational origination."[46] Therefore, "there is an intimate and vital relationship of the Buddhist norm or *Dhamma* with that of human rights."[47]

The Bodhisattva personifies the ideal existence, for it goes to the heart of human nature:

> In its concern for fellow beings, it demonstrates the best concrete illustration of the doctrine of relational origination—in which every being is involved in every other being . . . It is not only the beginnings of harmony with other beings, but more important, the sustenance of harmony within the changing ambient world.[48]

The Bodhisattva ideal reminds us that there is no actual, individual experience, for it "speaks to us of "equality, liberty, and security from the total perspective."[49]

Human rights are an extension of human nature. Thus in the Buddhist perspective they flow from right human relations.

> Human rights are legal matters which can be legislated, but only to a certain extent, especially so in a divided world. Human nature, however, is an existential matter which can neither be legislated nor measured; therefore, one must resort to persuasion and self-realization in order to seek one's unique existence.[50]

Inada concludes that "when governments, singly or in consortium, are able to provide an ambience conducive to individual life-fulfillment by way of an open and free contact to all, the question of human rights based on human nature should be eased considerably, if not solved."[51]

Taitetsu Unno asserts: "The fact that the Buddhist tradition in its past history has had little to say about personal rights in the current sense of the term does not mean that Buddhists were not concerned with human well-being, with the dignity and autonomy of the spirit."[52] Moreover, he argues that contemporary Buddhism "must clarify what it has to offer to the concept of personal rights and its realization for all people."[53]

The key to the Buddhist contribution, Unno believes, is its notion of the human person. The human person is a part of the interdependence of all life. Thus the Buddhist teaching of no-self (*anatman*) makes possible an appreciation of persons as more than entities or individuals.

This awareness liberates a person from the enslaving concepts and practices of culture and religion, such as those imposed by the Hindu tradition of caste.

By negating the metaphysical basis of traditional values and practices the Buddha affirmed instead the crucial nature of human conduct and *virtus* [sic] as determining what is truly human. He also stressed reliance on the powers of analysis and autonomous reason and rejected revelation, authority, and tradition as sources of knowledge.[54]

The Sangha was to model this image of the human person, as "a society of equals—regardless of birth or lineage or whether one was rich or poor, man or woman."[55] People are human in relation to others and nature, by virtue of their conduct and character.

Rights are a reflection of this interdependent reality. When one realizes the interconnectedness of all life, one realizes that rights are fundamental not only for people but equally for all sentient beings, as well as for nature itself. Thus Unno asserts:

respect for the individual and the recognition of rights is not a static but a dynamic fact which makes it imperative that as we affirm our own individual rights we must also be willing to give up ourselves in order to affirm the rights of others. When, however, we affirm only our own rights at the expense of the rights of others—including the rights of humanity over nature, one nation or one race over another, one belief or view over others—we become tyrannical and oppressive.[56]

Only with such an understanding of interdependent reality will assertions of human rights contribute to a society of equals. For only in this way will we see that the person is not "one among the many, but one as the absolute subject, the negation of the many; and the many is not simply a collection of ones, but many as the common good, the negation of separate ones going their different ways."[57]

While the Bodhisattva is exceptional, all persons may live with a sense of gratitude for the interdependence of reality in the recognition that "one lives by virtue of the working and sacrifices of countless others, including the blessings of nature."[58] The common Japanese expression "*Okagesama*" reflects just this kind of humble gratitude.

Thus, from a Buddhist perspective, human rights need to be grounded in what today might be described as an ecological view of nature and humanity, and rights need to be conceived for other forms of life and not just for humans, if the ego-centeredness often associated with personal rights is to be avoided. In this respect, religion has often been a stumbling block:

The most subtle forms of disguised self-centeredness appear in all world religions; we see it in sectarianism and triumphalism, classism and sexism. How can we root out this radical egocentricity, all the more difficult because it is affirmed in noble language? How can we affirm plurality, cherishing our own beliefs without negating those of others? Good will and tolerance have been inadequate as evidenced in the world today. What is necessary is a new understanding of reality, a new vision of the ideal community, based on the interdependence and interconnectedness of life. . . .[59]

Unno concludes "that it is necessary for contemporary Buddhism to come forth with a clear and unequivocal statement on personal rights," to aid in the development of an adequate foundation for human rights.[60]

Similarly, Robert Thurman argues that the Buddhist experience has much to offer human rights considerations: "the principles of human rights were all there in the Buddha's earliest teachings" and were embodied in the Sangha; however, they never led to an institutional democracy until modern times, and then only when there was outside help.[61]

Thurman asserts: "The Buddhist 'individual,' as a living, relative, social, conventional being emerges as the center of the Buddha's Teaching since there is no such thing as an unchanging, ultimate, isolated, intrinsically identifiable 'individual'."[62] Thus in Buddhism

the individual human who possess rights is presented as a spiritual as well as physical being of unique accomplishments and valuable opportunities. We have earned our rights through suffering and transcending egotism in the sea of evolution, and no one can deprive us of them, since no one conferred them upon us. Societies cease to be truly human when they cease to acknowledge that each individual's fulfillment is the purpose of the whole. And humans are free also to give away their rights in furtherance of the fulfillment of others. Indeed it is by the supreme generosity of giving even one's life that one evolved into a human out of lower forms. Thus talk of rights quickly passes over into talk of responsibilities, as the self-fulfilled (that is, enlightened as to selflessness) individual automatically wills to share that happiness of release with others by aiding them in their own quest of enlightenment.[63]

As persons assume responsibility, there is less need to talk about or enforce human rights.

Thurman argues that several texts provide the foundation for a Buddhist social philosophy and notes that the stone-carved edicts of Emperor Ashoka (third century B.C.E.) set forth five basic principles of Buddhist politics: "(1) individualistic transcendentalism, (2) nonviolent pacifism, (3) religious pluralism with an educational emphasis, (4) compassionate welfare paternalism, and (5) reliance on a powerful central authority to affirm the rights of individuals over claims of intermediate

groups."[64] He also discusses Tibet as a "long-term Buddhist experiment" in "furthering human social and cultural rights."[65]

Apart from these theoretical considerations, Buddhists have begun to speak of human rights in various ways.[66] Buddhists protest "human rights violations" in China, Tibet, Laos, and Korea.[67] Buddhists join with other members of religious traditions in conferences concerned with human rights.[68] Buddhists participate in resolutions on human rights, such as the Seoul Declaration of the Asian Conference on Religion and Peace, which declared: "Human dignity must be safeguarded by human rights, through which human dignity can be fully manifested."[69]

The late U Thant, a Burmese Buddhist who served as Secretary-General of the UN, on at least one occasion reiterated Eleanor Roosevelt's comment that the Universal Declaration of Human Rights was the "Magna Carta of Mankind."[70] Furthermore, he wrote of the family:

> The Universal Declaration of Human Rights describes the family as the natural and fundamental unit of society. It follows that any choice and decision with regard to the size of the family must irrevocably rest with the family itself, and cannot be made by anyone else. But this right of parents to free choice will remain illusory unless they are aware of the alternatives open to them. Hence, the right of every family to information and the availability of services in this field is increasingly considered as a basic human right and as an indispensable ingredient of human dignity.[71]

In a statement that clearly reflects Buddhist philosophy, at least as articulated by Abe and Inada, U Thant urged: "We must all foster and encourage a climate of opinion in which human rights can flourish. We must be alive to any encroachment upon the rights and freedoms of any individual. And, above all, we must practice tolerance, and respect the rights and freedoms of others."[72]

Dr. Tilokasundari Kariyawasam, President of the World Fellowship of Buddhist Women and Deputy Director General of Education in Sri Lanka, also strongly supports human rights: "Buddhism is an all pervading philosophy and a religion, strongly motivated by human rights or rights of everything that exists, man, woman, animal and the environment they live in."[73] She writes of the influence of Buddhist thought on the woman "*as an individual born free and equal in dignity and rights,*" claims that the "*rights, the Buddhist woman has enjoyed for centuries are revolutionary and daring,*" and suggests that concern "for human rights is seen in the efforts of women to ensure great equality of access to and participation in Buddhism."[74]

Thai Buddhist Sulak Sivaraksa, in writing of the Sangha as an ideal for human society, translates the basic ethical precepts of Buddhism into modern terms. He suggests that the precept to speak the truth is taking

new collective forms today: "Out of the networking of the global peace, justice and human rights movements arises a radical discourse, a pluralistic, insurgent understanding, a dynamic truth which threatens the power of the forces of violence, greed and ignorance."[75] As a Buddhist he asserts: "The defense of human rights and justice takes ethical precedence over national sovereignty."[76] Thus he urges Buddhist involvement in international issues, the United Nations, and development in the Third World.[77]

Moreover, in a Sri Lankan village Buddhists and Roman Catholics have found a common cause in human rights. In 1981, before a thousand people gathered to celebrate the triple light festival of Vesak, recalling the birth, enlightenment and the *mahaparinibbana* of the Buddha, a Christian speaker suggested: "if we violate human rights for food, clothing, shelter, justice, then we violate the first precept: *pranatipata vera mani sikkha. . . .*"[78] The Venerable Kotaneluwe Upatissa of the ancient Happoruwa temple, who was present for the festival at Suba Seth Gedara on this occasion, replied: "Let me say that this Catholic priest expounded *dhamma* well."[79]

Similarly, when Buddhists and Christians joined together to seek help for farmers who had lost their harvest due to severe drought, the Venerable Alutwela Piyananda—although pressured by local officials not to participate in the petition—affirmed instead his unity with the Christians in their common cause: "For whom did Jesus live and die? for man. For whom did the Buddha work? for man, for men and women. Now let us get together and work for human rights."[80]

Thus Buddhists do affirm human rights, as central to their understanding of the *dharma* and the living out of the Buddhist precepts. Despite the conceptual difficulties of justifying human rights, as central to Buddhist faith, at least some Buddhists find human rights language expressive of their religious commitment to the Three Refuges: the Buddha, the Dharma, and the Sangha.

It may not be surprising then to find exiled Tibetan leader, the Dalai Lama, suggesting that "we all have an equal right to be happy"[81] because of our common humanity: "This shared humanness and thus the shared aspiration of gaining happiness and avoiding suffering, as well as the basic right to bring these about, are of prime importance."[82] Thus he concludes that

> Universal responsibility is based on an understanding of the desire, the right, and the possibility of achieving happiness for all beings. When we recognize the importance of this outlook, a true sense of compassion becomes possible, and, eventually, a natural reality.[83]

For Buddhists then, recognition and protection of human rights may be seen not only as the fruits of wisdom and compassion but as means of attaining both.

Notes

1. Mark Juergensmeyer, "Dharma and the Rights of the Untouchables," unpublished essay, 8 March 1986, 1.
2. Ibid.
3. Kana Mitra, "Human Rights in Hinduism," in *Human Rights in Religious Traditions*, ed. Arlene Swidler (New York: The Pilgrim Press, 1982), 79. Raimundo Panikkar argues that the Hindu notion of dharma requires: 1) that human rights are not only the rights of individuals or even humans, 2) that human rights involve duties and relate us to the whole cosmos, and 3) that human rights are not absolute but are relative to each culture. Panikkar, "Is Human Rights a Western Concept? A Hindu/Jain/Buddhist Reflection," *Breakthrough* 10, nos. 2-3 (Winter/Spring 1989):33-34. An expanded version of this article appeared in the UNESCO publication *Diogenes* (Winter 1982).
4. Ibid., 80-81.
5. Ibid., 81.
6. Barnett R. Rubin also argues that respect for human rights in India does not necessarily mean abolition of the caste system, and that "The plurality of *dharmas* can also legitimate rights and social and political pluralism." He claims that "the biggest obstacle to human rights is not caste itself but untouchability, which, while outlawed, is still widely practiced and relegates a whole section of the community to 'unclean' status." Rubin, "India," in *International Handbook of Human Rights*, ed. Jack Donnelly and Rhoda E. Howard (Westport, Conn.: Greenwood Press, 1987), 137.
7. Ibid. However, Ralph Buultjens asserts: "The Western concept of human rights has been advocated by relatively few leaders of myth-figure stature in Indian history. Two such recent advocates have been Rabindranath Tagore and Jawaharlal Nehru. However, neither Tagore nor Nehru evokes the passionate fervor that attaches to Krishna-Chaitanya-Bose-Gandhi and projects them as exemplars." Buultjens, "Human Rights in Indian Political Culture," in *The Moral Imperatives of Human Rights: A World Survey*, ed. Kenneth W. Thompson (Washington, D.C.: University Press of America, 1980), 116.
8. John B. Carmen, "Duties and Rights in Hindu Society," in *Human Rights and the World's Religions*, ed. Leroy S. Rouner (Notre Dame, Ind.: University of Notre Dame Press, 1988), 117. The late P. V. Kane writes: "The Constitution makes a complete break with our traditional ideas. . . . The Constitution engenders a feeling among common people that they have rights and no obligations and that the masses have the right to impose their will and to give the force of law and justice to their own ideas and norms formed in their own cottages and tea shops. . . . The Constitution of India has no chapter on the duties of the people to the country or to the people as a whole." Kane, *History of Dharmasastras*, 2d ed., rev. and enl. (Poona: Bhandarkar Oriental Research Institute, 1968), 1664-65. Quoted in Carmen, "Duties in Hindu Society," 119.
9. Ibid., 120.
10. Ibid.
11. Barnett R. Rubin, "India," in *International Handbook of Human Rights*, 137.
12. Ibid.
13. Kana Mitra, "Human Rights in Hinduism," in *Human Rights and Religious Traditions*, 82.

14. Ibid.

15. Ibid., 83. Bühler, *Laws of Manu,* 2:1.

16. Mark Juergensmeyer, "Dharma and the Rights of the Untouchables," 28. A. Push-parajan, who argues that both Hindus and Christians have failed miserably to overcome untouchability in India, supports the program outlined by Gandhi. See his article, "Harijans and the Prospects of Their Human Rights," *Journal of Dharma* 8 (October-December 1983):391-405.

17. Quoted in German Arciniegas, "Culture—A Human Right," in *Freedom and Culture,* ed. Julian Huxley (London: Wingate, 1951), 32.

18. Gandhi, *Young India,* 21 August 1924, and *Young India,* 26 March 1931, in *The Essential Gandhi: His Life, Work, and Ideas,* ed. Louis Fischer (New York: Vintage Books, 1983), 200 and 284.

19. Gandhi, *Young India,* 8 January 1925. Max L. Stackhouse asserts that Gandhi "worked with others to get socialist as well as Western democratic statements of human rights included in the constitution." Stackhouse, *Creeds, Society, and Human Rights: A Study in Three Cultures* (Grand Rapids, Mich.: William B. Eerdmans Publishing Company, 1984), 254.

20. Barnett R. Rubin, "India," in *International Handbook of Human Rights,* 154.

21. Ibid., 156.

22. R. C. Pandeya, "Human Rights: An Indian Perspective," in *Philosophical Foundations of Human Rights* (Paris: UNESCO, 1986), 274.

23. Ibid., 275.

24. Ibid., 277. Another Indian, Prem Kirpal, disagrees. He argues that the Universal Declaration is largely the result of Western political thought and neglects "the wisdom and faith" found in "the older experience of Asian civilizations and several world religions." Kirpal, "The Contemporary Situation—Looking Ahead," in *Philosophical Foundations of Human Rights,* 280-82.

25. Ibid.

26. For instance, John Carmen describes a mid-nineteenth century conflict between Brahmins and a group of outcastes who had become Christian. The Brahmins asked the British magistrate to require the outcastes to pull a temple car as part of a traditional festival, claiming that it was the outcastes' *dharma.* The magistrate held that, as Christians, the outcastes had a duty not to participate in the practice of Hindu religion and so upheld their right to refuse. Carmen, "Duties and Rights in Hindu Society," in *Human Rights and the World's Religions,* 115.

27. Ibid., 127. Ralph Buultjens suggests: "it may be that the special accommodative genius of Hindu culture will create a new synthesis and produce the type of adjustment it has achieved in other areas. Perhaps both Indian political culture and Western political ideals can transcend their historical constrictions, taking lessons from the ways in which India has already adopted and adapted forms of democracy in the past three decades." Buultjens, "Human Rights in Indian Political Culture," in *The Moral Imperatives of Human Rights: A World Survey,* 121.

28. Four hundred thousand converted with him, one hundred thousand more converted after his cremation. As his ashes were distributed around India, hundreds of thousands of others converted. Sangharakshita, *Ambedkar and Buddhism* (Glasgow, Scotland: Windhorse Publications, 1986), 162-63.

29. Ibid., 59.

30. Ibid., 60.

31. Ibid., 68.

32. Quoted in Dhananjay Keer, *Dr. Ambedkar: Life and Mission,* 2d ed. (Bombay: 1962), 106. In Sangharakshita, *Ambedkar and Buddhism,* 76. Robert Aiken agrees that "the

Buddha's own teaching was egalitarian and democratic to the core." Aiken, "The Lay Zen Buddhist Sangha in the West," *The Pacific World*, New Series no. 4 (Fall 1988):77.

33.   B. R. Ambedkar, *Writings and Speeches*, 1 (Bombay: 1979), 57. Quoted in Sangharakshita, *Ambedkar and Buddhism*, 113.

34.   B. R. Ambedkar, *Buddha and the Future of His Religion*, 3d ed. (Jullundur: 1980), 7. Quoted in Sangharakshita, *Ambedkar and Buddhism*, 109.

35.   Sangharakshita, *Ambedkar and Buddhism*, 157.

36.   B. R. Ambedkar, *The Buddha and His Dhamma*, 2d ed. (Bombay, 1974), 234. Quoted in Sangharakshita, *Ambedkar and His Religion*, 156.

37.   Masao Abe, "Religious Tolerance and Human Rights: A Buddhist Perspective," in *Religious Liberty and Human Rights in Nations and in Religions*, ed. Leonard Swidler (Philadelphia: Ecumenical Press, Temple University, 1986), 202.

38.   Ibid.

39.   Ibid., 204.

40.   Ibid., 205.

41.   Ibid. Ali A. Mazrui argues that the three monotheistic religious traditions contribute to the process of psychic subhumanization which precedes human rights violations, for these monotheisms create the "greater danger to human rights," that is, "the dichotomy between 'us' and 'them'." He concludes: "Western civilization has become increasingly secularized, yet its two greatest challenges are, on one side, militantly monotheistic (Islam) and, on the other, self-consciously atheistic (Marxism). But Marxism, Western civilization and Islam are in any case interrelated. The dialectic in Marxism is dualistic; so is the constant tension between good and evil in both Christianity and Islam. The map of world power today is a map covered by Islam, Western civilization and Marxist systems. All three cultural universes betray the historic and normative impact of monotheism and its derivative patterns of cognition. 'In the beginning was the Word, and the Word was of God, and the Word was God.' But perhaps the word was of man, and the word was man. And in the beginning were the rights of man." Mazrui, "Human Rights and the Moving Frontier of World Culture," in *Philosophical Foundations of Human Rights*, 243 and 264.

42.   Ibid., 205.

43.   Ibid., 206-11.

44.   Kenneth K. Inada, "The Buddhist Perspective on Human Rights," in *Human Rights in Religious Traditions*, 70. Saneh Chamarik makes the same argument in "Buddhism and Human Rights," in *Human Rights Teaching* 2, no. 1 (1981), 14-20.

45.   Ibid., 70.

46.   Majjhima-nikaya, I, 190-91. *The Collection of the Middle Length Sayings*, trans. I. B. Horner (London: Luzac & Co., 1954), 1, 236-37. Quoted in Inada, "The Buddhist Perspective on Human Rights," 71.

47.   Ibid.

48.   Ibid., 75.

49.   Ibid.

50.   Ibid., 76.

51.   Ibid.

52.   Taitetsu Unno, "Personal Rights and Contemporary Buddhism," in *Human Rights and the World's Religions*, 129.

53.   Ibid., 130.

54.   Ibid., 131.

55.   Ibid.

56.   Ibid., 140.

57.   Ibid.

58.   Ibid. Kenko Futaba argues that this sense of gratitude is central to the teachings

of Shinran, who founded the Jodo Shinshu community on the principle of equality: "Any power structure that trampled on human dignity was absolutely contrary to the Nembutsu way which proclaimed equality of all human beings." Shinran's objective "was to realize Buddhahood and live dynamically in the flow of history in harmony with Amida's Primal Vow. Thus, he opened a world where all peoples could live equally in truth. He took issue with any social condition that obstructed the realization of human dignity—the complete fulfillment of the human person in the way of the Buddha." Kenko Futaba, "Shinran and Human Dignity: Opening an Historic Horizon," *The Pacific World*, New Series no. 4 (Fall 1988):57-58. This translation by Rev. Kenryu T. Tsuji is the first chapter of a book entitled *All of Shinran (Shinran no Subete)*, edited by Kenko Futaba.

59.   Ibid., 145.
60.   Ibid.
61.   Robert A. F. Thurman, "Social and Cultural Rights in Buddhism," in *Human Rights and the World's Religions*, 148.
62.   Ibid., 150. Similarly, Henry Rosemont, Jr. maintains that the Confucian concept of the person, as "the totality of roles" one lives "in relation to specific others," is contrary to the Western notion of a freely choosing individual who has rights. Rosemont, "Why Take Rights Seriously? A Confucian Critique," in *Human Rights and the World's Religions*, 177.
63.   Ibid., 152-53.
64.   Ibid., 156. Aryasanga's *The Stages of the Bodhisattva*, trans. Jampel Thardod et al. (American Institute of Buddhist Studies, manuscript translation), sanctions revolutions against an oppressive king; Nagarjuna's *Friendly Epistle* and *Jewel Rosary of Royal Advice*, written to the Satavahana King Udayi in the second century C.E. contains detailed prescriptions for government according to Buddhist principles; *The Teaching of the Manifestations of Liberative Strategies in the Repertoire of the Bodhisattvas*, which survives only in Tibetan and Chinese versions, conveys the teachings of Satyavadi on good government; and the *Universal Vehicle Scripture of Kshitigarbha Bodhisattva, the Ten Wheels of Government* describes all of social life from a Buddhist perspective. See Thurman, "The Politics of Enlightenment," *Lindisfarne Letter* (1975) and "Buddhist Social Activism," *Eastern Buddhist* (1983), and also Ven. Samdong Rinpoche, "Social and Political Strata in Buddhist Thought," in Samdong Rinpoche, *Social Philosophy of Buddhism* (Sarnath, 1972).
65.   Ibid., 161.
66.   See Bhikshu Shih Tao-an, "La Doctrine du Bouddha et les Droits de l'Homme," *Revue des Droits de l'Homme/Human Rights Journal* 10, nos. 1-2 (1977):5-13.
67.   *A North American Buddhist Resolution on the Situation in Asia*, prepared for the Conference on World Buddhism in North America by Buddhists Concerned for Social Justice and World Peace (Ann Arbor, Mich.: Zen Lotus Society, 10 July 1987).
68.   "Seeking Solidarity Beyond Religious Differences: World Conference on Religion and Peace Discusses Disarmament, Development, and Human Rights," *Dharma World* (Special Issue October 1986):50-51.
69.   "Asian Conference on Religion and Peace III Held in Seoul," *Dharma World* 13 (September/October 1986):7. Two pages earlier in the same issue, in an article entitled "Promotion of Human Dignity and Humanization," it was reported that "Discussion focussed on the religious significance of human dignity, from which concepts of human rights originate."
70.   Quoted in Egan Schwelb, *Human Rights and the International Community: The Roots and Growth of the Universal Declaration of Human Rights, 1948-1963* (Chicago: Quadrangle Books, 1964), 7. See U Thant, *View from the UN* (Garden City, N.Y.: Doubleday, 1978).
71.   U Thant, *Population Newsletter*, April 1968, 43. Quoted in *Human Rights Aspects of Population Programs: With Special Reference to Human Rights Law* (Paris: UNESCO, 1977), 111.

72.   Quoted in *The International Observance: World Law Day—Human Rights: 1968* (Geneva: World Peace through Law Center, 1968), 37.

73.   Tilokasundari Kariyawasam, "Feminism in Theravada Buddhism," paper presented at the conference, "Buddhism and Christianity: Toward the Human Future," Berkeley, Calif., 8-15 August 1987, 1.

74.   Ibid., 3-4. See also pages 8 and 9, where she writes of equal rights "*as to marriage, during marriage, womanhood etc.*" and of rights "*of freedom of peaceful assembly and association.*" Emphasis in the original.

75.   Sulak Sivaraksa, "Being in the World: A Buddhist Ethical and Social Concern," paper presented at the conference, "Buddhism and Christianity: Toward the Human Future," Berkeley, Calif., 8-15 August 1987, 6.

76.   Ibid., 7.

77.   See also Sulak Sivaraksa, "Buddhism and Development—A Thai Perspective," *Ching Feng* 26, nos. 2-3 (August 1983):123-33.

78.   Rev. Dr. Michael Rodrigo, O.M.I., "An Example of Village Dialogue of Life," paper presented at the conference, "Buddhism and Christianity: Toward the Human Future," Berkeley, Calif., 8-15 August 1987, 3. Tragically, Dr. Rodrigo became a martyr for human rights soon after returning to Sri Lanka from the Berkeley conference, for he was killed in an ambush by those opposed to his work for village reform.

79.   Ibid., 4.

80.   Ibid. The Sarvodaya movement in Sri Lanka employs Buddhist concepts to undergird the basic human rights of villagers. See Joanna Macy, *Dharma and Development: Religion as Resource in the Sarvodaya Self Help Movement* (West Hartford, Conn.: Kumarian Press, 1983).

81.   His Holiness the Dalai Lama, "Hope for the Future," in *The Path of Compassion: Contemporary Writings on Engaged Buddhism,* ed. Fred Eppsteiner and Dennis Maloney (Berkeley, Calif.: Buddhist Peace Fellowship, 1985), 2.

82.   His Holiness the Dalai Lama, "Spiritual Contributions to Social Progress," in *The Path of Compassion,* 10. In a speech on 15 June 1988 at the European Parliament in Strasbourg, which is available from the U.S. Tibet Committee, the Dalai Lama called for "respect for human rights and democratic ideals" in Tibet and pledged that a Tibetan government would adhere "to the Universal Declaration of Human Rights." The Dalai Lama received the 1989 Nobel Peace Prize.

83.   His Holiness the Dalai Lama, "The Principle of Universal Responsibility," in *The Path of Compassion,* 17.

Chapter 9

AFRICANS

In 1972 Kéba Mbaya, President of the Senegal Supreme Court, asserted the "right to development," which he defined as "The recognized prerogative of every individual and every people to enjoy in just measure the goods and services produced thanks to the effort of solidarity of the members of the community."[1] This right of development reflects communitarian values indigenous to the African cultures, as well as modern notions of human rights.

In this chapter I will review some of the arguments made for the protection of human rights within traditional African cultures. In addition, I will discuss recent attempts to develop new concepts of human rights which draw both on traditional values and values which Africans have adopted from Western culture.

Traditional Human Rights

Musa Ballah Conteh suggests that the history of human rights in Africa is best described in three phases. He argues that human rights were present in the first phase of traditional society, although in a context quite unlike that of the West. In the words of Mbaya, he affirms that "Traditional Africa does possess a coherent system of human rights, but the philosophy underlying that system differs from that which inspired [in France] the Declaration of the Rights of Man and of the Citizen."[2] The traditional African system of human rights not only affirmed the rights to life and to freedom of expression and association and religious liberty, but also the obligation to provide for those without the means of sustenance. Rights were derived from duties.

The denial of these rights, first by foreign slave traders and then by colonial powers, led to the second phase of the development of human rights concepts in Africa. Beginning with the latter part of the nineteenth century, human rights claims were advanced by African intellectuals on behalf of the black peoples of Africa. As Conteh notes, "the cardinal concern of all six Pan-African Congresses, held between 1900 (when the concept of Pan-Africanism itself was born) and 1974, was the pursuit of freedom and dignity by the 'black man'."[3] In this phase there was little concern for universal rights.

The third phase in the evolution of the idea of human rights involves a "synthesis of human and peoples rights," which Conteh asserts began with the adoption of the Universal Declaration of Human Rights and was reinforced by effective decolonization: "The liberal and individual aspects of human rights became progressively integrated or merged with the collective human rights efforts and demands of African peoples, now organized as single independent states in the world society."[4] The process continues today.

African scholar Claude E. Welch, Jr. agrees that recognition as well as "protection of human rights certainly existed in the precolonial period."[5] He identifies six major sets of rights in traditional society: "the right to life, the right to education, the right to freedom of movement, the right to receive justice, the right to work, and the right to participate in the benefits and decision making of the community."[6] He notes that in contrast to European conceptions stressing individual protection, African conceptions have emphasized collective expression. The web of kinship, of family and clan, provided the framework in which individuals asserted their rights and accepted their responsibilities. Understandably then, during colonial rule, "conflicts emerged between indigenous and European conceptions" and therefore, since independence, Africa has been involved in what Welch calls the "redomestication" of human rights.[7]

Similarly, Yougindra Khushalani, former human rights officer of the United Nations Center for Human Rights in Geneva, asserts that traditional Africa "does possess a coherent system of human rights," including the right to life, the right to receive justice, the right to participation, freedom of religion, freedom of association, and freedom of expression.[8] She asserts that in traditional African culture the right to life

> stems from the scrupulous respect which Africans have for their traditional religious beliefs. It includes not only the life of man, but even that of animals. A man kills only from necessity, in self-defense, to provide food, to perform a sacrifice, or to protect another's life or a possession. But respect for life is governed not only by negative rules, such as not to kill, but also by responsibilities. The right to life implies an obligation to provide those who do not

possess the means of subsistence with what is necessary to ensure their survival.[9]

She notes that human rights, whether individual or collective, were protected through custom rather than by written texts, but often involved well-defined procedures.

In contrast to Western traditions, African procedures have the character of conciliation, arbitration and mediation rather than formal judgment:

> This conciliatory approach reflects the importance of community cohesiveness in traditional societies as well as the likely existence of kinship ties between the litigants which would render a nonconsensual decision even more disruptive to family and communal life. The traditional system often sought to discover truth directly rather than through the clash of an adversary process in which each side supports its own position before an impartial and disinterested judge.[10]

In addition, she argues that in traditional society, "besides having the right to select their leaders, Africans had the right to depose them and had methods and mechanisms for resolving issues affecting their societies as a whole."[11]

Furthermore, Khushalani asserts that traditional African society recognized freedom of movement, the right to work, and the right to education. These rights were not stated in adversarial terms, but were derived from the responsibilities of various members of the community. Thus she concludes that traditional African society recognized the rights of both individuals and groups and through consensual procedures provided "an almost sacred protection" of fundamental human rights.[12]

Iba Der Thiam argues that the precolonial Wolof societies in Africa recognized the freedoms of assembly, of association, and of expression as well as the rights to own property and to work, to education and to one's culture, to privacy, to collective solidarity, and to go to law. He also argues that Islam reinforced most of the norms already in existence in Africa, but that the slave trade and colonization of the Senagambian kingdoms undermined the rights of the people.[13]

Chris Mojekwu reports that in traditional African culture all able-bodied members shared both the responsibility of maintaining and protecting their community and the right to use its resources. He argues that

> Human rights as a basic concept was very much present in precolonial African society well before the eighteenth and nineteenth centuries. The difference was that the concept of human rights in Africa was fundamentally based on ascribed status. It was a person's place of birth, his membership or belonging to a particular locality and within a particular social unit that gave content and meaning to his human rights—social, economic, and political.[14]

Thus in traditional Africa a person without membership in a social unit, an outcast or a stranger, "lived outside the range of human rights protection by the social unit."[15]

Mojekwu says that the modern African states are the result of European intervention "which destroyed the precolonial African authority structure and choked its concept of human rights."[16] He asserts that the right of self-determination so clearly established through United Nations resolutions and covenants should be understood as the right of a *people* to constitute itself rather than as the right of a *state* to choose its own political and economic system, a position clearly in conflict with both orthodox liberal and socialist doctrines. Finally, rather than shaping African realities to Western models, he affirms that the "African view of communal rights" can employ "African flexibility to accommodate Western conceptions in rights."[17]

Paulin J. Hountondji suggests that generally both the originality and coherence of Western civilization is overestimated:

> Europe certainly did not invent human rights, any more than it invented the idea of human dignity. It was simply able to conduct on this theme—and this was its merit—systematic research which took the form of an open progressive discussion. It thus produced, not the thing, but discourse about the thing, not the idea of natural law or of human dignity but the work of expression concerning this idea, the project of its formulation, explanation, analysis of its presuppositions and its consequences, in short, the draft of a philosophy of human rights.[18]

He argues that the task in African studies is not to look for elements comparable to Western society but to understand African societies more clearly, "in order better to appreciate and transform them."[19] Thus he calls on both Africans and Westerners, in Paul Ricoeur's words, "first to realize the relativity of their pretensions, then to qualify their relativism itself by reaching down to the root of the struggle for human rights—simply humanity itself."[20]

Lakshman Marasinghe argues for traditional notions of human rights in much the same way:

> It is a popular myth to assume that traditional societies of Africa are devoid of any conception of human rights and that when one refers to human rights the modern societies of the West are the exclusive custodians of this universal concept.[21]

He cites the attack by American political scientist Jack Donnelly, who argues that what are described as human rights in traditional African and Asian society are merely privileges granted by a ruling elite: "most

non-Western cultural and political traditions lack not only the practice of human rights but the very concept. As a matter of historical fact, the concept of human rights is an artifact of modern Western Civilization."[22] Marasinghe argues that Donnelly's position is shown to be false by empirical research demonstrating that there is a greater chance of enforcing human rights in traditional societies than in nontraditional societies.[23] He notes:

> Constitutions protecting human rights can be ended, suspended, or amended. The extended family, on the other hand, is a permanent institution which must exist as long as the individuals who form a part of it exist. To that extent the vulnerability of the traditional conceptions of human rights is minimized.[24]

Thus he asserts that in traditional African culture there is, in fact, "enormous satisfaction as to the basically democratic way in which the society protects its own human values."[25]

Josiah A. M. Cobbah suggests that these African values may be helpful in developing international human rights norms for the Third World as a whole:

> Ultimately what is important to an international community of cultures is for all peoples to feel that all voices are genuinely being heard in the human rights discussion. I have attempted to point out that Africans do not espouse a philosophy of human dignity that is derived from a natural rights and individualist framework. African societies function within a communal structure whereby a person's dignity and honor flow from his or her transcendental role as a cultural being. Within a changing world, we can expect that some specific aspects of African lifestyles will change. It can be shown, however, that basic Africentric core values still remain and that these values should be admitted into the international debate on human rights.[26]

The issue is not whether Western lifestyles should be adopted by others, but whether "cultural values" in Africa and other parts of the Third World "provide human beings with human dignity."[27]

African Human Rights Charter

In 1981 the African States in the Organization of African Unity (OAU) took the first step in establishing a distinctively African perspective on human rights by approving the African Charter on Human and Peoples' Rights.[28] The charter states that the members of the OAU reaffirm "their adherence to the principles of human and peoples' rights and freedoms contained in the declarations, conventions and other instruments adopted

by the Organization of African Unity, the Movement of Non-Aligned Countries and the United Nations"; and establish an African Commission on Human and Peoples' Rights which

> shall draw inspiration from international law on human and peoples' rights, particularly from the provisions of various African instruments on human and peoples' rights, the Charter of the United Nations, the Charter of the Organization of African Unity, the Universal Declaration of Human Rights, other instruments adopted by the United Nations and by African countries in the field of human and peoples' rights as well as from the provisions of various instruments adopted within the Specialized Agencies of the United Nations of which the parties to the present Charter are members.[29]

In the charter the African states take "into consideration the virtues of their historical tradition and the values of African civilization which should inspire and characterize their reflection on the concept of human and peoples rights."[30]

Richard Gittleman notes that in the protection of human rights, "the Charter reflects a strong preference for mediation, conciliation, and consensus as opposed to confrontation or adversarial procedures."[31] It is apparent that in this Charter African governments are seeking to embrace both Western and traditional notions of human rights—to claim rights for Africans which are universal and yet rooted in the traditions of the African peoples.

Thus Africans commonly affirm that "the core elements of the concept of human rights are not alien to non-Western cultures."[32] As Kenneth Kaunda proclaimed, while president of the Republic of Zambia:

> Human dignity is a concept which is as old as man himself. It is basic in every human life. It refers to the intrinsic worth of man; it underlines his importance as the center of creation, probably the highest expression of God's image in the whole of creation and the pivotal agent in the ceaseless stream of events in our changing environment. In a large measure I think it is true to say that this quality, which is inherent in man and not imparted to him by any human action, makes him different from other animals. It is the most important element among the qualities which confer upon man the inalienable rights which have since been defined in more precise and unequivocal terms, in the Universal Declaration of Human Rights, the principles of which have been incorporated in the Charter of the United Nations.[33]

Kaunda challenges us to prove by our actions "our faith in the principles governing our conduct in fostering harmonious relations among peoples and nations" and "our faith in the United Nations and its *Charter.* . . ."[34]

Conclusion

The histories of Africa and the North American and Western European continents are very different. Until quite recently, human rights law was articulated in terms derived almost entirely from the West. However, now human rights instruments are being promulgated which draw heavily on the traditional values of African and other cultures of the Southern Hemisphere.

Based on the African experience, Mbaya argues that the right to development, although only recently asserted, is a "fundamental human right, without which life in a society is not worth living."[35] His voice, and all those voices crying out for justice from Africa and the other Southern continents of the Third World, deserve to be heard.

Notes

1.   Quoted in *Development, Human Rights and the Rule of Law*, Report of a conference held in The Hague, 27 April-1 May 1981, International Commission of Jurists (Oxford: Pergamon Press, 1981), 5. Mbaya first asserted this right in an address to the International Institute of Human Rights in Strasbourg, France.

2.   Musa Ballah Conteh, "Human Rights Teaching in Africa: The Socio-Economic and Cultural Context," in *Frontiers of Human Rights Education*, ed. Asbjørn Eide and Marek Thee (New York: Columbia University Press, 1983), 58. Rhoda Howard analyzes various human rights comparisons to which Africa is often subjected in "Evaluating Human Rights in Africa: Some Problems of Implicit Comparisons," *Human Rights Quarterly* 6, no. 2 (May 1984):160-79.

3.   Ibid., 59.

4.   Ibid.

5.   Claude E. Welch, Jr., "Human Rights as a Problem in Contemporary Africa," in *Human Rights and Development in Africa*, ed. Welch and Ronald I. Meltzer (Albany: State University of New York Press, 1984), 11.

6.   Ibid., 16. Thomas M. Franck writes: "It is certainly not to a jurisprudential desert that the sturdy oak of the common law has been transplanted. Particularly in the area of procedural human rights, much that the common law posits is also indigenous to tribal or 'native' customary law." Franck, "Introduction: Western Law in Non-Western Nations," in *Human Rights in Third World Perspectives*, vol. 1 (London: Oceana Publications, Inc., 1982), xvi.

7.   Ibid., 11.

8.   Yougindra Khushalani, "Human Rights in Asia and Africa," *Human Rights Law Journal* 4, no. 4 (1983):415.

9.   Ibid., 415-16.

10.   Ibid., 416-17.

11.   Ibid., 417.

12.   Ibid., 418.

13.   Iba Der Thiam, "Human Rights in African Cultural Traditions," in *Human Rights Teaching* 3 (Paris: UNESCO, 1982), 4-10.

14.   Chris C. Mojekwu, "International Human Rights: The African Perspective," in *International Human Rights: Contemporary Issues*, ed. Jack L. Nelson and Vera M. Green

(Stanfordville, N.Y.: Human Rights Publishing Group, Earl M. Coleman Enterprises, 1980), 86.

15.   Ibid., 86-87.

16.   Ibid., 88. Dunstan M. Wai also argues that the authoritarian character of modern African governments is the result of colonial exploitation which disrupted the protection of human rights by traditional forms of authority and decision making. Wai, "Human Rights in Sub-Saharan Africa," in *Human Rights: Cultural and Ideological Perspectives*, ed. Adamantia Pollis and Peter Schwab (New York: Praeger Publishers, 1979), 115. See Warren Weinstein, "Africa's Approach to Human Rights at the United Nations," *Issue: A Quarterly Journal of Opinion* 6, no. 4 (Winter 1976):17 and Richard F. Weisfelder, "The Decline of Human Rights in Lesotho: An Evaluation of Domestic and External Determinants," *Issue: A Quarterly Journal of Opinion* 6, no. 4 (Winter 1976):23.

17.   Ibid., 93.

18.   Paulin J. Hountondji, "The Master's Voice—Remarks on the Problem of Human Rights in Africa," in *Philosophical Foundations of Human Rights* (Paris: UNESCO, 1986), 323.

19.   Ibid.

20.   Paul Ricoeur, "Introduction," in *Philosophical Foundations of Human Rights*, 28.

21.   Lakshman Marasinghe, "Traditional Conceptions of Human Rights in Africa," in *Human Rights and Development in Africa*, 42.

22.   Jack Donnelly, "Human Rights and Human Dignity: An Analytic Critique of Non-Western Conceptions of Human Rights," *American Political Science Review* 76 (1982):303. Quoted in *Human Rights and Development in Africa*, 42. Donnelly's general Western approach is reiterated in "Cultural Relativism and Universal Human Rights," *Human Rights Quarterly* 6, no. 4 (November 1984): 401. His position is strongly criticized by Josiah A. M. Cobbah in "African Values and the Human Rights Debate: An African Perspective," *Human Rights Quarterly* 9, no. 3 (August 1987):309-31.

23.   Lakshman Marasinghe, "The Relationship between the Social Infrastructure and the Working of the Legal System: A Case Study on Access to Justice in Northern Nigeria," *Verfassung und Recht in Ubersee* 14 (Hamburg: Forschungstelle fur Volkerrecht und auslandishes öffentliches Recht, 1981).

24.   Lakshman Marasinghe, "Traditional Conceptions of Human Rights in Africa," in *Human Rights and Development in Africa*, 43.

25.   Ibid. Asmarom Legesse argues that the collective ownership of land by African peoples such as the Amhara of northern Ethiopia, who distribute the use of land by inheritance equally to sons and daughters from both their mothers and fathers, "enshrines the most basic idea of 'human rights'." Legesse, "Human Rights in African Political Culture," in *The Moral Imperatives of Human Rights: A World Survey*, ed. Kenneth W. Thompson (Washington, D.C.: University Press of America, 1980), 126.

26.   Josiah A. M. Cobbah, "African Values and the Human Rights Debate: An African Perspective," *Human Rights Quarterly* 9, no. 3 (August 1987):331.

27.   Ibid.

28.   See "African Charter on Human and Peoples' Rights," in *Human Rights Teaching* 3 (Paris: UNESCO, 1982), 11-17.

29.   African Charter on Human and Peoples' Rights, Preamble and Chapter IV, Article 60, in *Human Rights in International Law: Basic Texts* (Strasbourg: Directorate of Human Rights, 1985), 207 and 223. However, Asmarom Legesse argues that the Universal Declaration of Human Rights is universal only in intent: "If Africans were the sole authors of the Universal Declaration of Human Rights, they might have ranked the rights of communities above those of individuals. . . ." Legesse, "Human Rights in African Political Culture," in *The Moral Imperatives of Human Rights*, 128.

30.   Ibid., 207.

31.   Richard Gittleman, "The African Convention of Human and Peoples' Rights: Prospects and Procedures," in *Guide to International Human Rights Practice*, ed. Hurst Hannum (Philadelphia: University of Pennsylvania Press, 1984), 161. See Gittleman, "The Banjul Charter on Human and Peoples' Rights: A Legal Analysis," and Edward Kannyo, "The Banjul Charter on Human and Peoples' Rights: Genesis and Political Background," in *Human Rights and Development in Africa*, 152-76 and 128-51. See also B. Obinna Okere, "The Protection of Human Rights in Africa and the African Charter on Human and Peoples' Rights: A Comparative Analysis with the European and American Systems," *Human Rights Quarterly* 6, no. 2 (May 1984):141-59, and James C. N. Paul, "Human Rights and Legal Development: Observations on Some African Experiences," in *International Human Rights Law and Practice: The Roles of the United Nations, the Private Sector, the Government and Their Lawyers* (Philadelphia: International Printing, 1978), 23-37.

32.   Edward Kannyo, "Human Rights in Africa: Problems and Prospects," a report prepared for the International League of Human Rights (May 1980), 4. R. Ogbonna Ohuche, professor of education at the University of Nigeria, writes in his foreword to Nwachukwuike S. S. Iwe's history of human rights: "Here in Nigeria, we have for sometime been conscious of the expectation of the Black man wherever he may be that the nations should face the challenge of restoring the dignity of man fouled up by years of slavery and centuries of colonialism, imperialism and oppression. Our successive Governments have re-stated time and again our national belief in the fundamental rights of man." In Iwe, *The History and Contents of Human Rights: A Study of the History and Interpretation of Human Rights* (New York: Peter Lang, 1986), 6.

33.   Kenneth O. Kaunda, *The Imperative of Human Dignity*, address at the inaugural session of the Non-Governmental Organizations International Conference on Human Rights (Paris: 15 September 1968), 4. See Josiah Cobbah and Munyanzwe Hamalengwa, "The Human Rights Literature on Africa: A Bibliography," *Human Rights Quarterly* 8, no. 1 (February 1986):115-25.

34.   Ibid., 12.

35.   Quoted in *Development, Human Rights and the Rule of Law*, 5.

Chapter 10

ASIANS

It is commonplace to distinguish Eastern and Western cultures. It is also frequently argued that human rights are the product of Western culture. However, Saneh Chamarik, professor of political science in Bangkok, argues "that the growth and development of human rights have their roots in human nature itself."[1] Moreover, he suggests that "in the Third World one also finds a situation of human aspiration for freedom and dignity which is inexorable, although—unlike in the West—without the historical background of radical social transformation."[2]

> Economic and social rights were practically unknown to the natural rights thinkers of the 18th century because the notion of rights was born, historically and philosophically, as the ideology of the haves and the affluent, that is, the rising middle class. Thus the Western brand of liberalism needs to be over-hauled, not just because of its original sin of self-aggrandizement in the past and present, but because of the global and interdependent nature of contemporary problems and solutions.[3]

For Chamarik, democracy is a developmental process closely related to particular cultures and political realities, which will therefore take different forms in Asia than in the West. However, fundamental human aspirations for human dignity are universal, because they are rooted in human nature.

For Francis Loh Kok Wah, social scientist at the University of Malaysia, this means the challenge is:

> to return to our various religious and philosophical traditions to emphasize those *universal spiritual values* that all these traditions share, for example, truth, justice, compassion and peace. By emphasizing these common values, we will, in the same effort, be building bridges among the different communities. This latter task is especially important in view of movements of religious revivalism which until now have largely focused on narrow ritualistic aspects

which emphasize our differences and thereby threaten our unity even more. Yet another advantage would be the development of a powerful counter-argument to those leaders who go around denouncing human rights as "western derived" and attacking defenders of human rights as serving "western interests." Freedom, justice, solidarity, we must argue, are neither western or eastern values; they are universal. In fact, they stem from belief in a superior moral force—God. Loyalty to these values transcends loyalty to particular ethnic groups, governments or nations.[4]

Thus, while universal human rights affirmations may be expressed in indigenous cultural forms, they may nonetheless be grounded in values common to the great religious traditions of the world.

Nagendra Singh sees the end of European colonial rule in Asia as the triumph of human rights. Singh asserts that in "one sense human rights are as ancient as the civilization of man," and thus he affirms that Pandit Motilal Nehru and the other Indian patriots, who before 1947 in India "constantly endeavored to uphold the right of people to freedom, progress and prosperity," were emphasizing the principles of ancient Hindu scripture.[5]

Filipino Raúl Manglapus asserts that the substance, if not the form, of human rights is present in traditional society all throughout Asia. He objects to the comment by William Buckley, Jr., that "democracy" and "civic virtue" are "beyond comprehension by the Oriental mind," and counters by asserting:

> This should be startling news to Indonesians, Malaysians, Urdu, Punjabi, and Persians who have used the Arabic word *hagg*, the Hindi and Bengali who have their *adhikar* and the Sanskrit *svetve*, the Thais their *sitthi*, the Koreans their *kooahri*, and the Filipinos their *karapatan*—all mean "rights."[6]

Manglapus notes that the Universal Declaration of Human Rights does not affirm the institutions Westerners often equate with human rights, such as parliaments or supreme courts, but rather allows for various cultural forms by simply setting forth "those political, social, and economic rights that contribute to the dignity of the individual person."[7]

The Chinese Context

Peter K. Y. Woo argues that the "issue of human rights becomes a problem only when it is present in our awareness as a privation."[8] Then the struggle begins. However, the struggle for human rights clearly takes different forms within different cultures, even within the different cultures of Asia.

Chinese culture has traditionally been shaped by Confucian, Taoist and Buddhist views of life.

Within the formulation of the ideal of harmony and unity, the issue of human rights cannot obtain the status of an independent and genuine problem, because the relations among men are only a step toward a much higher goal of the harmony of all beings. Whatever grievance an individual person may have must be reconsidered in relation to the value of universal unity. Hence, conceptually, not only were the actual experiences of human relations ignored, but the issue of human rights never arose. For example, the ideal of righteousness was not regarded as the central idea to deal with human relations. The harmony and the consequent equality of men were to be arrived at through compassion and the mutual, conscious striving for harmony.[9]

In traditional Chinese society any attempt to conceive of persons as autonomous individuals was repudiated.[10]

Woo identifies the demonstrations for political and economic self-determination on 4 May 1919 as "virtually the beginning of a consideration of the problem of human rights in China."[11] These demonstrations reflected a new consciousness which was to produce a people's revolution led by Dr. Sun Yat-sen and the establishment of a new form of government modeled after Western constitutional practices. Woo writes that the "Three Principles of the People" proclaimed by Sun Yat-sen became "the conceptual bridge between the ideals of universal harmony and the independence and freedom of the individual," and thus that

Early twentieth-century China was imbued with an enthusiasm for human rights, ranging from a concern with the nature of the family and its components of individual persons, and the status of women in society, to the balancing of the rights of individuals with the community as a whole. The efforts in dealing with these problems led necessarily to more reforms, most significantly, in education and in the consciousness of what it means to be a person.[12]

Before this century the Chinese had accepted government by privileged individuals. However, with this new consciousness they felt entitled to rights such as freedom of speech, of religion, of assembly, and choice of residence—all proclaimed in "The Three Principles of the People"—and to the forms of government necessary to guarantee them.

War and revolutionary struggle have resulted in a Chinese-controlled government on Taiwan, which espouses a liberal tradition of human rights, and in the People's Republic of China on the mainland, which asserts a socialist view. Mab Huang writes:

In the field of human rights traditional Chinese political culture and contemporary communist ideology reinforce each other in the denial of political and civil rights while they converge to promote the satisfaction of the basic needs of the people. They both emphasize the collective instead of the individual and duties instead of rights. Moreover they both stress the nurturing role of the state and the reciprocal relations between the state and individuals, giving an impetus toward egalitarianism and a concern for the social welfare of citizens.[13]

Mao Tse-tung asserted that the Chinese "cannot use 'the natural rights of man'. . . [but] can only use Western technology."[14] He espoused the socialist view that:

Both democracy and freedom are relative, not absolute, and they come into being and develop in specific circumstances. . . . Our democratic centralism means the unity of democracy and centralism and the unity of freedom and discipline. Under this system, the people enjoy a wide measure of democracy and freedom, but at the same time they have to keep themselves within the bound [*sic*] of socialist discipline.[15]

The Communist victory in the late 1940s over the forces of Chiang Kai-shek, who claimed to be fighting for liberal democracy, was also in part a defeat for Sun Yat-sen's "Three Principles of the People."

However, during the 1970s there was a revival in China of interest in civil and political rights, as well as social and economic rights, which culminated in what has been described as the "fifth modernization." From November 1978 to March 1979 a democratic movement, centered in Beijing but engulfing cities throughout the nation, rallied peasants and workers as well as students until it was crushed by the government.

In the publications and wall posters that appeared during this period, the values of the West were prominent. Rousseau and Montesquieu were quoted, the American and French revolutions were lauded, the United States and Britain were used as models of nations that govern by elections, even a public letter to President Carter was authored. Traditional Chinese culture was often strongly criticized. "A Call to Arms" published by the Enlightenment Society is typical in its confessional claim that "The words 'human rights' cannot be found in China's history" and in its call for the victory of Western forms of mass "democracy and human rights."[16]

Occasionally, the demand for the rule of law and democracy was described as the rescue of the traditional teachings of Confucius—supporting "benevolent government" and asserting that "an oppressive government is worse than a tiger"—from autocratic government:

We must reject the dregs of Confucianism, that is, the fantasy that tyrants can ever be persuaded to practice benevolent government. But the *essence* of Confucianism, which we do want to keep, is the concept that people are born with equal rights.[17]

However, more commonly those advocating human rights spoke as "citizens of the world" representing "the free spirit of mankind."[18]

Marxist practices were attacked, but socialism was understood as essentially democratic:

socialism in its original sense should first insure equal rights for individuals in their livelihood. These rights can be realized only through free organization and coordination with democratic politics. Therefore, socialism is essentially inclined toward democracy.[19]

On 8 January 1979, several thousand farmers marched through the capital demanding freedom and food with banners that read: "We want human rights and democracy."[20] Li Jiahua describes the "movement of socialist mass democracy," which began with the demonstrations of 4 April 1976 against the rule of the Gang of Four, as the culminating development of the protest movements of 4 May 1919: "If the May Fourth Movement is regarded as a banner to oppose imperialism and feudalism, then the April Fifth Movement can be called a movement against autocracy and dictatorship and for basic human rights and democracy in socialist China."[21] The human rights movement in China was being renewed and reformed.

The student and worker demonstrations in the spring of 1989 thus represent a resurgence of support for human rights which has often been repressed. Fang Lizhi, an astrophysicist and one of China's most outspoken dissidents, argues that recent reforms in China have both allowed people to appreciate human rights and revealed that human rights are necessary for reform to succeed. He writes: "improvement in the situation of human rights is an indispensable key to releasing China from its current predicament of stalled reform. The changes should begin with respect for freedom of thought and belief, freedom of speech, freedom of the press, and freedom of assembly."[22]

The crackdown on students, workers, and other dissidents in China will not easily destroy the Chinese human rights movement. Chinese around the world have been galvanized into action. The government did destroy the goddess of democracy statue raised by the students in Tiannanmen Square in Beijing, but this statue has been resurrected by Chinese in other cities around the world. As one Chinese student leader in Beijing put it: "Our call for democracy has reached the living rooms of largely apolitical people. It has planted seeds of the ideas of freedom and democracy and human rights."[23]

While the recent protests in China stress civil and political rights, the Chinese ought not to be seen as simply asserting Western values. James Hsiung suggests that in East Asia human rights are understood in consensual rather than adversarial terms. The rights of individuals are not seen in opposition to the welfare of the community. He suggests that an analysis of East Asian societies is helpful in seeing that "while the idea of human rights is universally accepted, the exact meaning of these rights is culture-specific."[24]

One incident from the 1989 demonstrations in Beijing vividly illustrates this point. A photograph of a lone Chinese student stopping a column of tanks was widely publicized in the West. This act of courage might simply be seen to represent individual freedom over against collective society. However, Chinese-born CBS consultant Bette Bao Lord suggests that the Chinese see it differently: "The Chinese are not an individualistic people. When that young man went out there, he was taking his ancestors with him."[25] For the Chinese, individual action is always an assertion of community values.

In words which remind us of other Asian affirmations, Hung-chao Tai writes: "To most people in the Third World, to justify human rights solely in terms of Western individualism is inconsistent with their cultural tradition."[26] In Chinese culture human rights must be a matter of consensus, because of the Confucian culture which has shaped for centuries the life and understanding of the people. Yet Chinese also affirm individual rights and the rule of law. Hung-chao Tai charges Chinese intellectuals with "the responsibility for achieving the convergence of the two political cultures" and suggests they "would honor both a Chinese tradition and exercise Western-inspired human rights if they could use their freedom of thought to advance an appropriate political theory sustaining human rights in Taiwan."[27]

The Japanese context is similar in many respects to that of the Chinese, for a consensual model of human rights has developed in a society traditionally shaped by Confucian and Buddhist values.[28] Noboru Toishi writes that "originally, Japanese people were not familiar with the thought of human rights," but during the past several years "the thought of human rights is gradually penetrating into and fixing on the consciousness of Japanese people."[29] Furthermore, Yasuhiko Saito notes that it took years of lobbying in Japan by human rights advocates and nongovernmental organizations to help form among the Japanese people "a consensus to enable the Diet's ratification" of the two international human rights covenants.[30]

The Filipino Context

A study of attitudes toward human rights in the Philippines reinforces the notion that Western forms of human rights are the result of recent history, but that human rights are universal claims which find expression to some extent in all cultural traditions. In 1977 the University of the Philippines Law Center and the Philippines Council for Policy Science sent a questionnaire to a variety of leaders in the Philippines, including lawyers, government officials, scholars, artists, business leaders, labor leaders, and political activists. Each person was asked to respond in a total of three thousand words to six questions.

The first question addressed the controversial issue of universality:

> What do you understand by "human rights"? Do you believe that human rights are inherent in man or that they are granted by the State? What is your view on the subject?[31]

The second question focussed on the notion of tradition:

> Is there a tradition of human rights in the Philippines? Some believe that the concept of human rights is essentially a Western importation; others believe that the notion of human rights runs through Philippine history. What is your own view on the matter?[32]

Almost all of the forty-eight respondents claim that human rights are inherent in humankind and are not merely granted by the state. In addition, almost all affirm that human rights are rooted in the traditions of the Filipino people.

Reynaldo S. Capule, a political leader in the Bulacan area, responded to the first question as follows:

> Human rights are inherent or natural and are not granted by the state. Even at the beginning of history, people existed in a society where every member has equal rights, for example, equal rights in making use of the land, equal rights to the products of labor, equal rights in the protection of the security of the individual or of the society as a whole and other rights needed in order to live.[33]

However, he notes that "as society developed and the concept of the state evolved, there has been unequal enjoyment of inherent human rights," as is clear in Western societies where only those in power enjoy these rights.[34]

Romulo de Guzman, an agricultural leader, responded to the same question in this way:

> First of all, human rights is [sic] the right to live free from hunger and fear, to enjoy the right to exercise one's free will, and the right to think according to one's own belief. It also means the right to involve one's self in an organization geared towards the development of the society of which he is part, and the right to participate in the formulation and implementation of measures to develop the politics, the economy and culture of the people.[35]

Furthermore, de Guzman suggests that when "the different sectors or classes emerged, the state which formally established the rights of man also appeared" and, as a result, "human rights became a responsibility of the state. . . ."[36]

Political activist Filomena Tolentino stresses that "Human rights are conceived, recognized, developed and achieved in society" and include "the freedom to work, freedom from exploitation, freedom to live, and freedom to organize together, with the freedom to say and publish one's views and opinions."[37] Human rights are thus "inherent in social life" and are "not awarded by anyone or any power, including the State. . . ."[38]

In answer to the second question Adrian E. Cristobal, vice chairman of the Philippine Center for Advanced Studies and Chairman of the Social Security Commission, wrote:

> There is definitely a tradition of human rights in the Philippines. The writings of patriots, scholars, jurists and literary men attest to this. But it should be noted that the consciousness of human rights emerged as a people's natural reaction to foreign domination.[39]

He acknowledges that there is a sense "in which the concept of human rights is a western notion, mainly of the question on the form of government which can best promote these rights under specific historical and social circumstances."[40]

Teresita Saldivar-Sali, professor of political science, suggests: "it is probably more accurate to say that there is a tradition of aspiration for rights in the Philippines, rather than a tradition of their actuality."[41] Similarly, Manuel F. Bonifacio, professor of sociology, notes: "The struggle for human rights in the Philippines is, for the most part, a struggle against a colonial power."[42] Yet he affirms that "the recognition of human rights is a reality in the Philippine society," in that "our idea of human rights ties in very neatly with the idea of what is correct or appropriate or obligatory."[43]

It is recognized by many that certain forms of human rights are imports from the West, but that some of these are now a part of the Filipino value system. For instance, Alfredo Nem Singh of International Harvester wrote: "I earnestly believe that there is a tradition of human rights in the Philippines," but he also acknowledges "that Western influence especially American influence with its emphasis on the democratic way of life, had

a big hand in making us realize the existence of these freedoms."[44] Thus he suggests "the blending of these two—the inherent Filipino ideals of human rights and the Western contributions—is very significant in our study of human rights."[45]

Finally, there is near consensus in answering the fourth question of the survey:

> What is the relationship between human rights and development? One view is that economic and social development in the Third World requires that priority be given to economic, social and cultural rights over civil and political rights; another is that these two sets of rights are closely linked together and must support each other in order to ensure balanced national development. What are your views on the subject?[46]

Felicidad Espina, president of the Centro Excolar University Faculty Club, answered:

> I believe these two sets of rights are closely linked together and must support each other in order to ensure balanced national development. The nation is as strong only as the citizens that comprise it. And the strength of each individual citizen is dependent not only on his social and economic well-being but on his civil and political well-being as well.[47]

Similarly, Judge Milagros A. German wrote: "Closely linked together, both rights must support each other to ensure the economic development of the country."[48]

Conclusion

Thus, in Asia, human rights are proclaimed as inherent truths which are commonly violated, but which are central both to the history and development of each society and to the general welfare of its members. Many, if not most Asians, would agree with Hiroko Yamane:

> In almost all the countries of Asia, ageless beliefs, institutions and social practices structure the everyday life of the people beneath the thin layer of the legacy of colonialism which brought about, among other things, the modern and legalistic idea of human rights.[49]

These old traditions reflect universal values that affirm human dignity. Therefore, she and others support an approach to human rights education in Asia which emphasizes both commitment to the realization of fundamental human rights and the contribution of Asians in developing new forms of human rights.

Notes

1. Saneh Chamarik, "Some Thoughts on Human Rights Promotion and Protection," in *Access to Justice: Human Rights Struggles in South East Asia*, ed. Harry M. Scoble and Laurie S. Wiseberg (London: Zed Books, 1985), 9. Similarly, Shao-chuan Leng writes: "Human rights are not just a Western concern but have a universal validity, with contributions from all the major civilizations." Leng, "Human Rights in Chinese Political Culture," in *The Moral Imperatives of Human Rights: A World Survey*, ed. Kenneth W. Thompson (Washington, D.C.: University Press of America, 1980), 81.

2. Ibid., 19.

3. Ibid., 16.

4. Francis Loh Kok Wah, "Human Rights in Malaysia: Reflections and Approaches," in *Human Rights Activism in Asia: Some Perspectives, Problems and Approaches*, ed. Asian Coalition of Human Rights Organizations (ACHRO) (New York: Council on International and Public Affairs in cooperation with the International Center for Law in Development, 1984), 46.

5. Nagendra Singh, *Human Rights and the Future of Mankind* (Atlantic Highlands, N.J.: Humanities Press, 1982), 1-2.

6. Raúl S. Manglapus, "Human Rights Are Not a Western Discovery," *Worldview* 21 (October 1978):4. He does not explain more precisely the meaning of these terms, nor respond to the obvious question of whether or not they are conceptually equivalent. For instance, Alasdair MacIntyre argues that the concept of "a right," used to refer to the notion of rights "which are obliged to belong to human beings as such," lacks "any means of expression in Hebrew, Greek, Latin or Arabic, classical or medieval, before about 1400, let alone in Old English or in Japanese even as late as the mid-nineteenth century." MacIntyre, *After Virtue: A Study in Moral Theory* (Notre Dame, Ind.: University of Notre Dame Press, 2d edition, 1984), 68-69. He asserts: "From this it does not of course follow that there are no natural or human rights; it only follows that no one could have known there were." Ryosuke Inagaki notes that there was no word in Japanese for "right" until translators of Dutch books in the nineteenth century had to create a term. Ryosuke Inagaki, "Some Aspects of Human Rights in Japan," *Philosophical Foundations of Human Rights* (Paris: UNESCO, 1986), 191.

7. Ibid. He rejects the notion that the poor of Asia are uninterested in fundamental freedoms and human rights, and tells the story of an Indian farmer who, when asked if he was voting in the upcoming elections, replied: "Just because I am poor and maybe cannot read does not mean I do not care for human rights."

8. Peter K. Y. Woo, "A Metaphysical Approach to Human Rights from a Chinese Point of View," in *The Philosophy of Human Rights: International Perspectives*, ed. Alan S. Rosenbaum (Westport, Conn.: Greenwood Press, 1980), 113.

9. Ibid., 116. Roger T. Ames argues for the superiority of a society in which rights and duties are enforced by social pressures rather than legal punishments. Ames, "Rites as Rights: The Confucian Alternative," in *Human Rights and the World's Religions*, ed. Leroy S. Rouner (Notre Dame, Ind.: University of Notre Dame Press, 1988), 199-216.

10. Shao-chuan Leng argues that traditional Chinese culture contains *some* democratic traits: "Taoism as a philosophy advocated naturalism and condemned government meddling. As popular religions, both Taoism and Buddhism were concerned with the fate or salvation of the individual and stood for spiritual autonomy and freedom. Even Confucianism, while stressing man's particular place in society, exalted the moral worth of the individual and the attainment of his full development through self-cultivation." Moreover, education was open to all who were able, regardless of class. Leng, "Human Rights in Chinese Political Culture," in *The Moral Imperataives of Human Rights*, 82.

11.   Ibid., 117.

12.   Ibid., 117-18.

13.   Mab Huang, "Human Rights in a Revolutionary Society: The Case of the People's Republic of China," in *Human Rights: Cultural and Ideological Perspectives*, ed. Adamantia Pollis and Peter Schwab (New York: Praeger Publishers, 1979), 63.

14.   Mao Tse-tung, speech at Hangchow, 21 December 1965. Quoted in *Chairman Talks to the People*, ed. Stuart Schram (New York: Pantheon, 1975), 234-35.

15.   Mao Tse-tung, *On Correct Handling of Contradictions among the People* (Peking: Foreign Language Press, 1957). Quoted in John Lewis, *Major Doctrines of Communist China* (New York: W. W. Norton, 1964), 101-02.

16.   *The Fifth Modernization: China's Human Rights Movement, 1978-1979*, ed. James D. Seymour (Stanfordville, N.Y.: Human Rights Publishing Group, 1980), 29. See *Beijing Street Voices: The Poetry and Politics of China's Democracy Movement*, ed. David S. G. Goodman (London: Marion Boyars, 1981). For a report on human rights in China today, see Seymour, "China," in *International Handbook of Human Rights*, ed. Jack Donnelly and Rhoda E. Howard (Westport, Conn.: Greenwood Press, 1987), 75-98.

17.   Wei Jingsheng, "The Fifth Modernization," in *The Fifth Modernization*, 68. Hung-chao Tai similarly claims: "In contrast to the diverse origins of the Western concept of human rights, the origin of the Chinese concept of human rights is simple, deriving from the Confucian ethical code." Hung-chao Tai, "Human Rights in Taiwan: Convergence of Two Political Cultures," in *Human Rights in East Asia*, ed. James C. Hsiung (New York: Paragon House Publishers, 1985), 89.

18.   James D. Seymour, *The Fifth Modernization*, 3 and 26.

19.   Wei Jingsheng, "The Fifth Modernization," 62.

20.   James D. Seymour, *The Fifth Modernization*, 19.

21.   Ibid., 267. Shao-chuan Leng writes: "The political ferment in China today illustrates the existence of a universal yearning for human rights and the fallacy of the proposition that a society can trade off individual rights for economic development with impunity." Leng, "Human Rights in Chinese Political Culture," in *The Moral Imperatives of Human Rights*, 100. See also R. Randle Edwards, Louis Henkin, and Andrew J. Nathan, *Human Rights in Contemporary China* (New York: Columbia University Press, 1986).

22.   Fang Lizhi, "Human Rights and the New China," *The Oakland Tribune*, 17 April 1989, B-7. This article first appeared in the *Los Angeles Times* and was translated by Perry Link.

23.   Quoted in "China's Dark Hours," *Time*, 19 June 1989, 14. Another Chinese student leader, Wu'er Kaixi, speaking in exile in San Francisco, told guests at a dinner to raise funds for the Front for a Democratic China: "I hope that all peace-loving people in the world will link our [*sic*] hands together because peace, freedom and human rights belong to the human race. . . ." Quoted in William Wong, "China's Dissidents Resume the Mission," *The Oakland Tribune*, 11 August 1989, A-13.

24.   James Hsiung, *Human Rights in East Asia*, vii. Henry Rosemont, Jr. argues that the notion of universal human rights is inconsistent with any concept of culture-specific rights. Thus he holds that the Universal Declaration of Human Rights reflects a Western orientation which is antithetical to the Confucian way of thinking and to other traditional cultures. Rosemont, "Why Take Rights Seriously? A Confucian Critique," in *Human Rights and the World's Religions*, 167. However, Wm. Theodore de Bary asserts that human rights language is changing Chinese culture as well as being changed by Chinese culture. See de Bary, "Human Rights—An Essay on Confucianism and Human Rights," *China Notes* 23, no. 4 (Fall 1984):307-13.

25.   Quoted in Bill Mann, "TV Makes Us Eyewitnesses to History," *The Oakland Tribune*, 6 June 1989, C-1. Joan Baez, human rights activist and folk singer, clearly

understands this for in her song "China" she sings: "And Wang Wei Lin, you remember him/All alone he stood before the tanks/A shadow of forgotten ancestors in Tiananmen Square." Quoted in Jacqueline Cutler, "Remembering Tiananmen: Thousands in S.F. Rally for Democracy," *The Oakland Tribune*, 11 September 1989, A-8.

    26.   Hung-chao Tai, "Human Rights in Taiwan: Convergence of Two Political Cultures," in *Human Rights in East Asia*, 85. In his recent book, *China Watch*, John King Fairbank is critical of the use of Western human rights language to describe the struggles in China. While sympathetic to this concern, Franklin Woo suggests that Fairbank's analysis overly emphasizes the unique, cultural characteristics of China. See "On Books," *China Notes* 25, nos. 2 and 3 (Spring and Summer 1987):441-42.

    27.   Ibid., 102. Fang Lizhi recently observed: "Two or three years ago, the phrase human rights was seldom heard in Chinese political discourse. Today everyone—not only supporters of human rights but also those who regard them as a headache—has to admit that the question of human rights has become an intrinsic part of Chinese political life." Fang Lizhi, "Human Rights and the New China," trans. Perry Link, *The Oakland Tribune*, 17 April 1989, B-7.

    28.   Ryosuke Inagaki asserts that although the original human rights documents were developed primarily by Western nations, "The ideas of basic human rights, with the underlying emphasis upon the dignity of the human person, expressed in this constitution [1946], represent the substantial consensus of the Japanese people. The idea that the first and principal aim of government is to protect and promote the rights of people seems to have taken root in the thinking of people." Ryosuke Inagaki, "Some Aspects of Human Rights in Japan," in *Philosophical Foundations of Human Rights*, 182.

    29.   Noboru Toishi, "Recent Trends in Human Rights in Japan," in *Recent Trends in Human Rights*, ed. Lawasia Human Rights Standing Committee (Sydney: The Law Association for Asia and the Western Pacific, 1982?), 25. Christians in Japan have led the way in this regard. For example, since it was founded in 1953, the International Christian University in Tokyo has required all entering students to sign a Human Rights Pledge based on the Universal Declaration of Human Rights. "Japanese Students Sign Human Rights Pledge," *Breakthrough* 10, nos. 2-3 (Winter/Spring 1989):81.

    30.   Yasuhiko Saito, "Japan and Human Rights Covenants," *Human Rights Law Journal* 2, nos. 1-2 (1981):106. Yuji Iwasawa argues that ratification of the international human rights covenants has begun to change Japanese law. See "Legal Treatment of Koreans in Japan: The Impact of International Human Rights Law on Japanese Law," *Human Rights Quarterly* 8, no. 2 (May 1986):131-79.

    31.   Purificacion Valera-Quisumbing and Armando F. Bonifacio, ed. *Human Rights in the Philippines: An Unassembled Symposium* (Diliman, Quezon City: University of the Philippines Law Center, 1977), ix.

    32.   Ibid.

    33.   Ibid., 210.

    34.   Ibid.

    35.   Ibid., 214.

    36.   Ibid.

    37.   Ibid., 229.

    38.   Ibid.

    39.   Ibid., 53.

    40.   Ibid.

    41.   Ibid., 76.

    42.   Ibid., 52.

    43.   Ibid.

    44.   Ibid., 72.

45.   Ibid.
46.   Ibid., ix.
47.   Ibid., 131.
48.   Ibid., 133.
49.   Hiroko Yamane, "Development of Human Rights Teaching and Research in Asia," in *Frontiers of Human Rights Education*, ed. Asbjørn Eide and Marek Thee (New York: Columbia University Press, 1983), 45. See also Yamane, "Human Rights for the Peoples of Asia," in *Human Rights Teaching* 3 (Paris: UNESCO, 1982), 18-22.

PART III

FATIH IN HUMAN RIGHTS

Chapter 11

THE CORNERSTONE

François Refoulé writes that Pope Paul VI wanted to make the Universal Declaration of Human Rights "the corner-stone of all his work."[1] For Paul VI, the Universal Declaration was "the path that must not be abandoned if mankind today sincerely wants to consolidate peace"; and he never lost an opportunity to express his "complete moral support for the common ideal contained in the Universal Declaration."[2]

In this chapter I will show that religious leaders have not only accepted the Universal Declaration of Human Rights as the cornerstone of the human rights movement, but were active in cutting and laying the stone in place. First, I will review the history of involvement by religious leaders in the development of the Universal Declaration. Then I will survey support in religious literature for the Universal Declaration of Human Rights.

Laying the Cornerstone

Philip Potter writes that the Protestant effort on behalf of the Universal Declaration of Human Rights began as early as 1943, when the Federal Council of Churches and the Foreign Missions Conference (which later merged to become the National Council of Churches of Christ in the U.S.A.) established a Joint Committee on Religious Liberty, with O. Frederick Nolde as its executive secretary.[3] The following year a statement on religious liberty was sent to the president of the United States and his secretary of state, all members of Congress, fifty-three heads of diplomatic missions, and the leaders of thirty-five churches abroad.

In 1945 three memoranda prepared by the Joint Committee on Religious Liberty were among those considered by the Conference on

International Organization at San Francisco. The first related religious liberty to Roosevelt's Four Freedoms, which Nolde describes as a "cornerstone" for human rights.[4] The second emphasized the relationship between religious liberty and civil rights. The third urged that

> if the Dumbarton Oaks proposal to create an economic and social council under the general assembly admits of prompt realization . . . our government take immediate steps to the end that this council give consideration to human rights and fundamental freedoms; and further, in order to permit such forthright action as world conditions demand and as agreement among the nations will permit, that a specialized agency under this council . . . be established with responsibility in the area of human rights and fundamental freedoms.[5]

Additional support for this proposal came from the International Round Table at Princeton in July 1943, involving sixty-one Christian leaders from twelve countries in North America, Europe, and Asia and from Australia and New Zealand; support also came from the second National Study Conference on the Churches and a Just and Durable Peace, which met in January 1945 and recommended, as an amendment to the Dumbarton Proposals, that "A special commission on Human Rights and Fundamental Freedoms should be established."[6]

The Federal Council of Churches assigned Nolde the responsibility of pressing human rights concerns at the San Francisco Conference in 1945. On May 2nd, after it had become obvious "that prompt and virtually drastic action was needed if substantial provisions for human rights were to be inserted in the Charter," Nolde led a delegation of nongovernmental representatives to a meeting with U.S. Secretary of State Stettinius.[7] The secretary of state indicated there was little chance of securing additional human rights provisions in the Charter, but Nolde made a strong statement urging reconsideration. The representative of the American Jewish Committee, Judge Proskauer, also firmly supported the human rights additions.[8]

The effect of this intervention was summarized in an article in the *Philadelphia Inquirer* on 4 May 1945:

> The rights of individuals, as well as the rights of nations, will be incorporated in the San Francisco Charter it was learned today, largely as the result of the efforts of a Philadelphia clergyman [Nolde, who was a professor in the Lutheran Theological Seminary there]. . . . The "revolt" from the "little people," who had previously been complaining that they were completely out of touch with the American delegation and were not being consulted although they are consultants, reportedly made a great impression on Mr. Stettinius.[9]

This report is confirmed by Edward Duff, who claims the private papers of Senator Vandenberg support Nolde's assertion that "an international

Christian influence played a determining part in achieving the more extensive provisions for human rights and fundamental freedoms which ultimately found their way into the Charter."[10]

In 1946 the Academy of Political and Social Science devoted its January issue of *The Annals* to the question of "Essential Human Rights." Of the twenty-five contributors, Nolde was asked to write the final article on "Possible Functions of the Commission of Human Rights." Nolde argued that the first task of the commission was to develop "an international declaration or bill of rights."[11] Copies of this issue of *The Annals* were flown to London and made available to the members of the Economic and Social Council as they deliberated on the Commission on Human Rights, and early in the first session of the General Assembly, copies were given to all delegations. Nolde suggests: "A very substantial similarity exists between the terms of reference as finally adopted and the proposals contained in the January 1946 issue of *The Annals.*"[12]

The Commission of the Churches on International Affairs (CCIA) was established in 1946 as a joint agency of the World Council of Churches, which was in the process of forming, and the International Missionary Council. Nolde became its first director, while continuing to serve as the executive secretary of the Joint Committee on Religious Liberty. Throughout 1946 and 1947, Nolde led the work of both groups in lobbying for clearer language with respect to "freedom of religion" in the peace treaties with Germany and Italy.[13]

The CCIA was early granted consultative status with the Economic and Social Council, and thus churches in the ecumenical movement increasingly channeled their communications on UN matters through the CCIA. Archive materials reveal how extensively the CCIA was involved with the UN Commission on Human Rights, with governmental representatives, and with church leaders concerned that an international declaration of human rights include freedom of religion.[14]

During the drafting of the Universal Declaration the CCIA worked hard to be certain

> that the preamble should reflect a basic approach to the observance of human rights which was acceptable from the Christian standpoint, even though it did not contend that a Christian position had to be enunciated therein. . . . As the drafting of the Universal Declaration progressed, the CCIA unflaggingly emphasized the principle that governments could not grant human rights, but could only recognize the human rights which man, by virtue of his being and destiny, already possessed.[15]

In a paper prepared for the Amsterdam Assembly of 1948, Nolde argued that there was an "immediate and urgent need for the development of the Christian view on human rights in terms which will apply to all men and

which can be used in representations to national and international political authorities."[16] This position of the CCIA was "formalized later in relation to the covenants."[17]

In a statement prepared by Nolde for the CCIA, the omission of any reference to God in the Universal Declaration was acknowledged as a concern for many Christians. However, the statement continues, as "it is the distinct task of the churches to bring men to faith and to a profession of that faith," Christians "cannot expect the United Nations to accomplish by legal fiat that which must be the expression of a prevailing conviction."[18] Furthermore, "In interpreting the Declaration, the Christian has an obligation to contend that such rights as man claims in society derive from the Christian view of man's nature and destiny, by virtue of his creation, redemption, and calling."[19]

Seán MacBride, human rights leader and Nobel and Lenin Peace Laureate, notes that during this same period Monsignor Roncalli, who subsequently became Pope John XXIII, "played an important part in the formulation of the draft Universal Declaration of Human Rights," for as the Papal Nuncio in Paris he participated with René Cassin in the deliberations of the French delegation.[20] In addition, numerous Jewish groups promoted the idea of an international declaration of human rights.[21]

For Eleanor Roosevelt, who chaired the UN Commission on Human Rights which drafted the Universal Declaration, the document was a "moral and spiritual" milestone for the world reflecting, if indirectly, "the true spirit of Christianity."[22] Some Christians, however, were far less enthusiastic. A front-page editorial in the Vatican newspaper, *L'Osservatore Romano*, initialed by Count Giuseppe dalle Torre, the editorial director, declared:

> The new ethical-juridical edifice in which the man of the United Nations era is to find the security of a fortress, bears on its threshold the ancient warning: If God be not the builder of the house, its building will be in vain.[23]

Given this resistance, and the historic distrust by the Roman Catholic Church of secular declarations of rights, it is remarkable that the Universal Declaration is affirmed in *Pacem in Terris* and also that it was John XXIII's clear wish that "the precise and juridical character" of the Declaration be supported "on the level of justice and legislation and not only on that of humanitarian assistance."[24]

Global Support

As is evident from the preceding chapters, the Universal Declaration is affirmed by numerous religious leaders. In 1968 the YMCA published a

book "to secure through group action solid implementation of the principles of the Universal Declaration."[25] In 1971 the Roman Catholic Synod of Bishops added the weight of the episcopal college to that of the pope: "Let the United Nations Declaration of Human Rights be ratified by all Governments who have not yet adhered to it, and let it be fully observed by all."[26] Methodist José Míguez Bonino writes:

> the drive toward universality implicit in our Christian faith, which found partial expression in the quest of the American and French revolutions, the aspirations expressed in the *UN Declaration*, finds its historical focus today for us in the struggle of the poor, the economically and socially oppressed, for their liberation. At this point the biblical teaching and the historical junction coalesce to give the Christian churches a mission.[27]

Presbyterian Robert Smylie asserts that "the Universal Declaration is not only a profoundly religious document worthy of support, but a discerning spiritual challenge to Christians and the Church."[28]

Similarly, Muslim Riffat Hassan describes as "truly remarkable" the passage of the Universal Declaration by the United Nations and suggests that though it is "secular" in terminology it is more "religious" in essence than many "*fatwas*" given by Islamic authorities.[29]

Frequently, conferences will reaffirm the Universal Declaration of Human Rights. The members of the International Consultation on Human Rights, sponsored by the Irish School of Ecumenics, urged in their final statement that Christian organizations at all levels "reaffirm their support for the *Universal Declaration of Human Rights*."[30] In 1978 representatives of churches participating in the International Symposium on "The Dignity of Man: His Rights and Obligations in Today's World" joined in "Carta de Santiago" (Charter of Santiago) which declared that the Universal Declaration of Human Rights still stands as "a common ideal toward which all peoples and nations should strive," for it "proclaims the fundamental concepts of the human being and of society, capable of being shared by those of all races, creeds and convictions."[31]

The International Association for Religious Freedom has urged governments to support the Universal Declaration of Human Rights by ratifying international human rights covenants.[32] And in 1979, in "The Princeton Declaration" of the World Conference on Religion and Peace, the participants stated:

> Adhering to different religions, we may differ in our objects of faith and worship. Nevertheless, in the way we practice our faith, we all confess that the God or the truth in which we believe transcends the powers and divisions of this world. . . . We are all commanded by our faiths to seek justice in the world in a community of free and equal persons. . . . We reaffirm our commitment . . . to the U.N.

Declaration of Human Rights, and we deplore the denial of human rights to any individual or community.[33]

In 1985 the Conference on Religious Liberty and Human Rights, which included Buddhist, Hindu, Islamic, Christian and Jewish scholars, urged in its final statement that all governments disseminate in their national languages the Universal Declaration of Human Rights as well as other pertinent UN declarations and covenants on promoting religious liberty.[34]

On behalf of the Agudas Israel World Organization, Isaac Lewin made numerous references to the Universal Declaration of Human Rights in the struggle to resist anti-Semitism and other forms of religious tolerance.[35] Moreover, Shimon Shetreet reports that "in dealing with questions of religious freedom, as well as other human rights, the Israeli courts have also resorted to the Universal Declaration of Human Rights and the International Covenant on Political and Civil Rights."[36]

In 1975 Methodist pastors in Bolivia "formed an internal human rights committee for Bible study" and the next year the Permanent Assembly on Human Rights was organized, representing Roman Catholic and Lutheran as well as Methodist leaders, "for the purpose of enforcing the Universal Declaration of Human Rights."[37] Similarly, in a "Declaration on Human Rights and Social Justice," the Associated Members of the Episcopal Conferences of Eastern Africa in 1970 affirmed the Universal Declaration of Human Rights as a basis for the right of parents to choose the education for their children and the right of free expression and association.[38]

In Taiwan the General Assembly Executive Committee of the Presbyterian Church issued a declaration in 1977 affirming: "Our church confesses that Jesus Christ is Lord of all mankind and believes that human rights and a land in which each one of us has a stake are gifts bestowed by God."[39] The statement concludes: "As we face the possibility of an invasion by Communist China we hold firmly to our faith and to the principles underlying the United Nations Declaration of Human Rights."[40]

On the thirty-sixth anniversary of the Universal Declaration of Human Rights in 1984, the first Asian regional human rights mechanism was convened in Japan. The "Asian Human Rights Commission" appointed Clement John, secretary for international affairs of the Christian Conference of Asia, as Secretary General of the Commission.[41] In 1987, speaking at a public rally in Japan protesting the fingerprinting of Koreans, Clement John asserted: "For Christians, protection and safeguarding of human rights is a matter of faith. Our involvement in the struggle of the marginalized groups is an affirmation of our faith in the crucified Jesus. . . ."[42]

The Universal Declaration of Human Rights is also affirmed by Asian writers who are not Christians. For instance, Indian Fali Narman argues

that there "are no Eastern and Western Human Rights," but "only Universal Human Rights declared by the U.N. in 1948 and accepted and adopted by all its members—both in the East and West."[43] He asserts that the "true essence of the idea of human rights as embodied in the Universal Declaration is the concept which gives priority to the recognition and protection of the fundamental rights of the individual."[44] Moreover, he suggests that this notion of inalienable human rights, which protect the individual against the ruler or in a democracy even against the will of the majority, is established in the "great American and French texts (of 1776 and of 1789 and 1791) which heralded modern democracy. . . ."[45]

Provisions of the Universal Declaration have been incorporated into the constitutions of many Asian countries.[46] However, constitutional government in Asia is weak. In addition to the problem of limitations on human rights provisions in the constitutions, there is no history of true constitutional government in many Asian countries. For example, the dean of the Faculty of Law at the University of Malaya, Azmi Khalid, writes:

The nation and society of Malaysia have sworn to uphold belief in the supremacy of the Constitution as well as the rule of law as both are enshrined in the Principles of the Nation. If we desire that the principles of nationhood be realized, then the legal system must emphasize not just the letter of the Malaysian Constitution but also a spirit of constitutionalism showing love of freedom, justice, and truth.[47]

Perhaps because there is no indigenous tradition of respect for the law of a state, Asians frequently turn to international conventions and standards as statements of "higher law."

This is evident in a paper on human rights entitled "Declaration of the Basic Duties of member states of ASEAN Peoples and Governments," issued in 1983 by the Regional Council on Human Rights in Asia, a nongovernmental organization of jurists from member states of ASEAN (Association of Southeast Asian Nations).[48] After deploring the violations of human rights throughout Asia, the Council urged protection of the rights set forth in the Universal Declaration of Human Rights, the international human rights covenants, and all other international instruments. It based its position on three principles:

1. Human rights are not merely ideals or aspirations. They are claims that inhere in all persons and all peoples by virtue of their human dignity, claims that all other persons, peoples and government have the duty to honor. The concept of human rights is universal and dynamic. It is not the exclusive property of any one people, place, or region of the world. Its content enlarges as the needs of human beings and communities expand. But at its core is always the deep recognition of the inalienable human dignity inherent in every man, woman and child.

2. Every person and every people have the right to self-directed development. The primary goal of development must be both to wipe out poverty . . . and to provide an improving quality of life in all its aspects, material and spiritual, for all the people. Consequently, authentic development cannot be attained without respect for basic individual and collective human rights.

3. Human rights are violated not only by unjust acts but also by unjust national and international structures. To work for human rights then is not only to combat instances of injustice, it is also to seek to change structures that exploit not merely individuals and peoples but nature itself. One such structure is authoritarian government that denies the right of peoples to participate in making decisions that affect their life and the future of their children.[49]

As a summary of the Asian perspective on human rights, this statement of principles illustrates the kind of synthesis of traditions which is occurring throughout the Third World.

Commentaries

The Universal Declaration is even the subject of commentaries by scholars in different religious traditions, a surprising fact, as the commentary is more traditionally the form used for discussion of religious texts. Sultanhussein Tabandeh of Gunabad, Iran wrote *A Muslim Commentary on the Universal Declaration of Human Rights*. And Israeli legal scholar Haim H. Cohn has written a commentary on the Universal Declaration from the Jewish perspective. Both of these commentaries have been discussed in detail earlier in Part Two.

I am not aware of a comparable commentary on the Universal Declaration of Human Rights in the Christian tradition, although we have seen enumerations of human rights compared to the Universal Declaration by Protestant theologian John Warwick Montgomery in *Human Rights and Human Dignity* and by Roman Catholic theologian David Hollenbach in *Claims in Conflict*.[50] Furthermore, in *The Ten Commandments and Human Rights* Walter Harrelson argues, much as does Cohn, that human rights can be derived from biblical duties:

> In that sense, the Bible has much to say about human rights. It is possible to see in the basic understandings of human rights, reflected in, for example, the United Nations' Universal Declaration of Human Rights, a large measure of the biblical understanding of human obligation under God.[51]

Harrelson goes on to argue for the development of a contemporary Decalogue to "contribute to the refashioning of a *communal* life under God in the world."[52]

He suggests that in our modern secular world the basis for such a Decalogue can be drawn from Jewish and Christian understandings of the Bible. "The way is open to such an understanding. It would be analogous to the Bill of Rights in the United States Constitution. That list of amendments has very much the form and the force of Israel's Decalogue."[53] To meet the needs of our time he suggests the following set of commands:

1. Do not have more than a single ultimate allegiance.
2. Do not give ultimate loyalty to any earthly reality.
3. Do not use the power of religion to harm others.
4. Do not treat with contempt the times set aside for rest.
5. Do not treat with contempt members of the family.
6. Do not do violence against fellow human beings.
7. Do not violate the commitment of sexual love.
8. Do not claim the life or goods of others.
9. Do not damage others through misuse of human speech.
10. Do not lust after the life or goods of others.[54]

He concludes by affirming that such a list can be supplemented by modern human rights statements:

> The Universal Declaration of Human Rights . . . with its supplemental compacts and accords, offers a marvelous set of guidelines for the fulfilling of our commitment to fellow human beings in community. So also do the many summary statements concerning human rights and responsibilities that have been developed by the Christian churches, some of them in direct dependence upon the Decalogue.[55]

Therefore, he believes the time is right "for the Christian community to reaffirm its commitment to such summary lists and to their restatement, study, and regular re-presentation within the churches."[56] However, the language of the Universal Declaration of Human Rights is not the language of Scripture:

> Despite the religious bases for universal moral community in each of the traditions, the language of human rights in the Universal Declaration is not the language of the Hebrew Bible, the Christian scriptures or the Muslim Qur'an. It is not the language that any of the three holy books uses to speak of the universal moral community of all persons.[57]

The Universal Declaration of Human Rights is a summary statement which reflects the deepest aspirations of the peoples of the world. It is not the creed of a new world religion, but it is an affirmation of faith which has

gained the support of many within the various religious traditions of the world.

Conclusion

Additional evidence might be offered, but the point is already made. The Universal Declaration of Human Rights is the cornerstone for efforts all over the world by religious as well as secular leaders to build a system of law so that the moral imperatives of human rights might be promoted, respected and enforced. It was created as much by religious as by secular leadership, it is understood within various religious traditions as reflecting the values of sacred texts and authoritative teachings, and it is defended and proclaimed by men and women of faith as the foundation in our troubled time for justice and peace on earth.

Notes

1. François Refoulé, "Efforts made on behalf of the Supreme Authority of the Church," in *The Church and the Rights of Man*, ed. Alois Müller and Norbert Greinacher (New York: The Seabury Press, 1979), 78.
2. Ibid.
3. Philip Potter, "Religious Liberty—A Global View," *Journal of Ecumenical Studies* 14, no. 4 (Fall 1977):125 [693].
4. O. Frederick Nolde, *Free and Equal: Human Rights in Ecumenical Perspective* (Geneva: World Council of Churches, 1968), 18.
5. Ibid., 20.
6. Ibid.
7. Ibid., 22.
8. See Joseph M. Proskauer, *A Segment of My Times* (New York: Farrar and Straus, 1950).
9. Archives of the Commission of the Churches on International Affairs, "Human Rights Varia 1945-1968," 428.3.25, World Council of Churches, Geneva, Switzerland.
10. Edward Duff, S.J., *The Social Thought of the World Council of Churches* (New York: Association Press, 1980), 276-77. Quoted in O. Frederick Nolde, *Free and Equal*, 25.
11. Ibid., 28.
12. Ibid., 29.
13. Ibid., 33.
14. See CCIA Archives, "Human Rights" and "UN International Bill of Human Rights, 1947-1948," 428.3.24, World Council of Churches, Geneva, Switzerland. In addition to those in the United States and Europe, the CCIA corresponded with church leaders from the Methodist Mission in Portuguese East Africa and the Methodist Overseas Mission in Fiji, Pyramid House in Cairo, the Christian Council of Kenya, and groups in the Union of South Africa, Australia, China, India, Iraq, Lebanon, and New Zealand.
15. O. Frederick Nolde, *Free and Equal*, 38. Representatives of other religious traditions presented similar arguments. In 1947 the National Spiritual Assembly of the Baha'is of the United States submitted "A Baha'i Declaration of Human Obligations and Rights." Mary

Ellen Togtman-Wood, "Prerequisites to Human Rights: A Baha'i Perspective," *Breakthrough* 10, nos. 2-3 (Winter/Spring 1989):41-42.

16.   Quoted in *Man's Disorder and God's Design*, 4, 148 in *The Amsterdam Assembly* series, 5 vols., ed. W. A. Visser 't Hooft (New York: Harper and Brothers, 1949), and in Paul Bock, *In Search of a Responsible World Society: The Social Teachings of the World Council of Churches* (Philadelphia: The Westminster Press, 1974), 66.

17.   O. Frederick Nolde, *Free and Equal*, 38.

18.   O. Frederick Nolde, "The United Nations Acts for Human Rights," release by the American Committee for the World Council of Churches, in the *Michigan Christian Advocate*, 30 December 1948, CCIA Archives, "UN International Bill of Human Rights, 1947-1948," 428.3.24, World Council of Churches, Geneva, Switzerland.

19.   Ibid.

20.   Seán MacBride, "The Universal Declaration—Thirty Years After," in *Understanding Human Rights: An Interdisciplinary and Interfaith Study*, ed. Alan D. Falconer (Dublin: Irish School of Ecumenics, 1980), 9. See Philippe de le Chapelle, *La Déclaration Universelle des Droits de l'Homme et le Catholicisme* (Paris: Librairie Générale de Droit et de Jurisprudence, 1967).

21.   Rita Hauser, "The Dream and Its Deceptions," in *Essays on Human Rights: Contemporary Rights and Jewish Perspectives*, ed. David Sidorsky (Philadelphia: The Jewish Publication Society of America, 1979), 22.

22.   "Human Rights Bill is Voted by United Nations Committee," subtitled "Mrs. Roosevelt Acclaims It as 'Moral and Spiritual' Milestone for the World," *New York Herald Tribune*, 7 December 1948, CCIA Archives, "Human Rights Varia 1945-1968", 428.3.25, World Council of Churches, Geneva, Switzerland. Max L. Stackhouse describes the drafting of the Universal Declaration as the "political appropriation of human rights as a creed" and asserts: "Not since the pre-Reformation councils had such an assemblage of national representatives attempted to define what is universally valid as a creed for all." Stackhouse, *Creeds, Society, and Human Rights: A Study in Three Cultures* (Grand Rapids, Mich.: William B. Eerdmans Publishing Company, 1984), 104. For a brief summary of the development of the Universal Declaration see Peter Mayer, "How the International Bill of Rights Was Born," *Breakthrough* 10, nos. 2-3 (Winter/Spring 1989):16-17, excerpted from *The Internatonal Bill of Human Rights* (Glen Ellen, Calif.: Entwhistle Books, 1981).

23.   "Vatican Hits U. N. Group," subtitled "Assails Omission of God's Name in Human Rights Draft," 31 October 1948. CCIA Archives, "Human Rights Varia 1945-1965," 428.3.25, World Council of Churches, Geneva, Switzerland.

24.   "Reflections by Cardinal Maurice Roy on the Occasion of the Tenth Anniversary of the Encyclical 'Pacem in Terris' of Pope John XXIII (11 April 1973)," in *The Gospel of Peace and Justice: Catholic Social Teaching since Pope John*, ed. Joseph Gremillion (Maryknoll, N.Y.: Orbis, 1976), 540.

25.   Stanley I. Stuber, *Human Rights and Fundamental Freedoms in Your Community* (New York: National Board of Young Men's Christian Associations, 1968), 5.

26.   *Justice in the World*, no. 64, in *The Gospel of Peace and Justice*, 88. In *Sollicitudo Rei Socialis*, John Paul II acknowledges the positive influence of the Universal Declaration in promoting respect for human rights. "Encyclical Letter of the Supreme Pontiff John Paul II: *Sollicitudo Rei Socialis*," *L'Osservatore Romano*, English edition, 29 February 1988, 6.

27.   José Míguez Bonino, "Religious Commitment and Human Rights: A Christian Perspective," in *Understanding Human Rights*, 32.

28.   Robert F. Smylie, "Christianity and Human Rights: A View from the United States," *Breakthrough* 10, nos. 2-3 (Winter/Spring 1989):37. He goes on to claim that the Universal Declaration "should make us realize that every violation of human rights that persists, be it civil, political, economic or social, is a violation of the right of the Creator to the Creation,

and a violation of his Son, the Redeemer, who is identified with and in all, and whose love encompasses all."

29.   Riffat Hassan, "On Human Rights and the Qur'anic Perspective," in *Human Rights in Religious Traditions*, ed. Arlene Swidler (New York: The Pilgrim Press, 1982), 53. Munzer Anabtawi asserted on 21 July 1987 at the International Institute of Human Rights in Strasbourg, France that the "Draft Charter on Human and People's Rights in the Arab World" drew upon the "common standards" of the Universal Declaration as well as the international human rights covenants. Notes of author.

30.   In *Understanding Human Rights*, 237.

31.   "Carta de Santiago" (Charter of Santiago), 25 November 1978, in *Human Rights: A Challenge to Theology* (Rome: CCIA and IDOC International, 1983), 59. See John F. Dearden, "The Modern Quest for Human Rights," in *Human Rights and the Liberation of Man in the Americas*, ed. Louis M. Colonnese (Notre Dame, Ind.: University of Notre Dame Press, 1970), 3-12.

32.   IARF World, no. 2 (1989):12.

33.   "The Princeton Declaration," 3d assembly of the World Conference on Religion and Peace, *Church and Society* 71 (November/December 1980-January/February 1981):37-39.

34.   In *Religious Liberty and Human Rights in Nations and in Religions*, ed. Leonard Swidler (Philadelphia: Ecumenical Press, Temple University, 1986), 246.

35.   Isaac Lewin, *Ten Years of Hope: Addresses before the United Nations* (New York: Shengold Publishers, 1971).

36.   Shimon Shetreet, "Freedom of Conscience and Religion in Israel," in *Essays on Human Rights: Contemporary Rights and Jewish Perspectives*, ed. David Sidorsky (Philadelphia: The Jewish Publication Society of America, 1979), 180.

37.   "The Gospel and the Aymara People," in *Human Rights: A Challenge to Theology*, 84. As noted earlier, the Salvation Army affirms the Universal Declaration. See *Human Rights and the Salvation Army* (London: The Campfield Press, 1968), 23.

38.   "Declaration on Human Rights and Social Justice," in *Exchange*, Bulletin of Third World Christian Literature 12, no. 45 (December 1986):39-40.

39.   "A Declaration of Human Rights by the Presbyterian Church in Taiwan," in *Asian Christian Theology: Emerging Themes*, ed. Douglas J. Elwood (Philadelphia: Westminster Press, 1980), 330.

40.   Ibid., 331.

41.   Masahiko Kurata, executive secretary of the National Christian Council of Japan's Center for Christian Response to Asian Issues, "Asian Perspective—Human Rights—a Western Standard?" *Asia Lutheran News* 3 (May-June 1985):11.

42.   "Human Rights: Their Basis and Their Protection," *CCA News* 22, no. 2 (15 February 1987):4.

43.   Fali S. Narman, "Human Rights in India—Recent Trends," in *Recent Trends in Human Rights*, ed. Lawasia Human Rights Standing Committee (Sydney: Law Association for Asia and the Western Pacific, 1981?), 1. He argues that even poor Indians support universal values and relates a story told by Mother Teresa of a destitute woman in Calcutta who, though without food for her family for three days, shared the meager ration given to her with other families in need. If, as Mother Teresa asserts, the right to live is the most fundamental of all human rights, the poor are concerned with the protection of this right not only for themselves but also for others.

44.   Ibid.

45.   Fali S. Narman, "Protecting the Rights of Minorities in Society," in *Studie-en Informatiecentrum Mensenrechten Special* 5 (Netherlands Institute of Human Rights, February 1985), 43. See *Seminar on National, Local and Regional Arrangements for the Promotion and Protection of Human Rights in the Asian Region* (New York: UN, 1982).

46.   See H. J. C. Princen, "Access to Justice," in *Access to Justice: Human Struggles in South East Asia*, ed. Harry M. Scoble and Laurie S. Wiseberg (London: Zed Books, 1985), 80 and 81; Asmi Khalid, "Law and the Decline of Freedom in Malaysia," in *Access to Justice*, 97; Participatory Research and Organization of Communities through Educational and Self-Help Services, Inc. (PROCES), "Human Rights Activism in Relation to Landless Rural Workers in the Philippines," in *Human Rights Activism in Asia: Some Perspectives, Problems, and Approaches* (New York: Council on International and Public Affairs, June 1984), 37 and 41; and Rajesware Kanniah, "Perceptions of Human Rights Activism," in *Human Rights Activism in Asia*, 48.

47.   Azmi Khalid, "Law and the Decline of Freedom in Malaysia," in *Access to Justice*, 92.

48.   Indonesia, Malayasia, the Philippines, Thailand, and Brunei Darassalem are represented in ASEAN. See "Declaration of the Basic Duties of ASEAN Peoples and Governments," in *Human Rights Sourcebook*, ed. Albert P. Blaustein, Roger S. Clark, Jay S. Sigler (N.Y.: Paragon House Publishers, 1987), 646-57.

49.   Scoble and Wiseberg, *Access to Justice*, 206-07.

50.   Dom Helder Camara comments on several articles of the Universal Declaration in "Human Rights and the Liberation of Man in the Americas: Reflections and Responses," in *Human Rights and the Liberation of Man in the Americas*, 259-68.

51.   Walter Harrelson, *The Ten Commandments and Human Rights* (Philadelphia: Fortress Press, 1980), xv.

52.   Ibid., 190.

53.   Ibid.

54.   Ibid., 192.

55.   Ibid., 192-93. Erich Weingärtner suggests that the Universal Declaration of Human Rights provides a modern "Ten Commandments" in that it is "an easily understood standard of conduct whose respect alone already constituted in large part its fulfillment." Weingärtner, *Human Rights on the Ecumenical Agenda: Report and Assessment* (Geneva: CCIA, World Council of Churches, 1983), 10.

56.   Ibid., 193.

57.   David Hollenbach, *Justice, Peace, and Human Rights: American Catholic Social Ethics in a Pluralistic Context* (New York: The Crossroad Publishing Company, 1988), 113.

Chapter 12

THE COMMON GOOD

The Universal Declaration of Human Rights begins by asserting that "recognition of the inherent dignity and of the equal and inalienable rights of all members of the human family is the foundation of freedom, justice and peace in the world. . . ." The image of "the human family" is perhaps a rhetorical flourish, but it suggests that human rights are seen as the legal ordering of the common good. Human rights are not merely the claims which individuals have against the state or other citizens, but are ways of ordering life in the human family so as to ensure human dignity for all of its members.

This image of human rights is sometimes lost in the fray of ideological debate. However, it is embraced and articulated by religious leaders who affirm human rights as an expression of their faith. That is, religious leaders see human rights not only as means of protecting the individual from oppression by the state, but as the way of creating justice within states and peace within the world community.

In this chapter I will describe briefly the political debate over human rights, between members of the First, Second and Third Worlds and the shift in emphasis that has taken place in the human rights efforts of the United Nations. I will suggest that human rights advocates in the Third World are bringing together diverse notions of human rights into a new synthesis. Finally, I will review the support in the religious communities for this reformed notion of human rights.

The Liberal and Socialist Debate

Hersch Lauterpacht argues that the heart of the doctrine of human rights, as it has developed in the West, is that "The sovereign was

subjected to the higher law conceived as the guarantor of the inalienable rights of man."[1] This "first generation" of human rights, using the phrase introduced by French jurist Karel Vasak, is concerned with the civil and political rights of the individual.[2] It is concerned with the freedom of the individual from interference by the state, with what are often called "negative rights" for they involve assertions of what the government cannot do.

These rights dominate the text of the Universal Declaration of Human Rights and are set forth in Articles 2-21, which include:

> freedom from racial and equivalent forms of discrimination; the right to life, liberty, and the security of the person; freedom from slavery or involuntary servitude; freedom from torture and from cruel, inhuman, or degrading treatment or punishment; freedom from arbitrary arrest, detention, or exile; the right to a fair and public trial; freedom of movement and residence; the right to asylum from persecution; freedom of thought, conscience, and religion; freedom of opinion and expression; freedom of peaceful assembly and association; and the right to participate in government, directly or through free elections.[3]

The Universal Declaration also includes the right to own property and the right not to be deprived arbitrarily of property, rights central to the struggle in both the American and French revolutions and to the rise of capitalism.

This expression of the Western liberal view of human rights stresses the rights of the individual over against the state, as necessary conditions for human dignity. Maurice Cranston argues that this view precludes any notion of rights which requires positive action by the state, and so he concludes that social and economic rights are not human rights at all.[4] More recently, Jack Donnelly and Adda Bozeman have vigorously asserted that human rights are grounded in a concept of the individual that is lacking in the cultures of Africa and Asia.[5]

The history of the development of human rights in the United States suggests that this is not merely an academic debate. James Sellers argues that in America it is the ideas of Hobbes rather than those of Locke that came to predominate: that what shaped American political thought most was "not natural law, or the common good, or the humanitarian impulse toward community" but "the absolute right of the individual."[6] This impulse has until very recently not only limited American understanding of human rights to civil rights, but to the narrowest reading of civil rights which stresses the rights of the individual in a society in which the state is conceived as guaranteeing protection only by not intervening in the lives of its citizens.

This is the context which President Roosevelt challenged in his annual message to Congress on 6 January 1941, which affirmed the Four Freedoms that were to receive wide sanction a year later in the Joint Declaration of the United Nations. He said:

> We look forward to a world founded upon four essential human freedoms. The first is freedom of speech and expression—everywhere in the world. The second is freedom of every person to worship God in his own way—every-where in the world. The third is freedom from want—which, translated into world terms, means economic understandings which will secure to every nation a healthy peaceful life for its inhabitants—everywhere in the world. The fourth is freedom from fear—which, translated into world terms, means a world-wide reduction of armaments to such a point and in such a thorough fashion that no nation will be in a position to commit an act of physical aggression against any neighbor—anywhere in the world.[7]

Freedom of speech and expression and freedom of worship are clearly established in American constitutional law. However, freedom from fear is largely left to an informed public, and freedom from want is tradi-tionally understood as the goal of charity rather than as the responsibility of government.

Arthur Holcombe argues that in the newly formed United States of America in the late eighteenth century:

> There were no provisions in any of the state bills of rights for securing a right to work and nothing about the conditions of employment or what is now called social security. The independent farmers and tradesmen who constituted the bulk of the free population in 1776 were more interested in equality of opportunity to subjugate the wilderness and exploit the natural resources of the country than in what we now call social and industrial justice. Instead of a right to work there was a popular demand for the kind of liberty that consists of leveling natural barriers to profitable enterprise rather than organizing the market for labor and regulating the conditions of employment in the interests of a special class of wage earners.[8]

Even today the struggle for freedom from want in America is an uphill battle against the tradition which identifies rights with individual oppor-tunities, in a society guided more by private economic interests than by public policy intended to promote the general welfare.[9]

The history of human rights thought on the continent of Europe is somewhat different. In 1789 the citizens of France were confronted by intractable social and economic forces causing impoverishment and hunger.

Hence the distinctive emphasis on rights more raw and basic than those of individual civic dignity. Economic growth, with more fairness of distribution is the reigning value, and human rights (viewed 'collectively' rather than individualistically) depend upon governmental management, improved for the purpose by ridding itself of archaic involvement with religious preoccupations and institutions.[10]

The French read all of Thomas Paine's *Rights of Man* and not merely the sections which the Americans had embraced.[11] Thus the French Constitution of 1791 provided for public relief for the poor and free public education, rights which were not protected in early American constitutions and which in international law today are described as "economic and social rights."

Thus even within the framework of Western liberal thought, there is diversity as to how the conditions of human dignity are to be realized. Rights are seen to arise in response to particular situations, expressing demands on institutions that certain deprivations be ended. "Hence there can be a recognition of universal rights at the very time there is disagreement on the philosophical foundations of those rights."[12]

Jean-Bernard Marie suggests that human rights "are, quite simply, a way of living together in a society that values human dignity."[13] As all societies fall short of such a vision, one might well conclude that "The movement for human rights is really a movement for world reform."[14] In the West the American and French revolutions stimulated social reforms with different emphases. In the American tradition, liberty or freedom clearly dominated over equality, and thus equality came to mean only equality of opportunity.[15] In the French tradition, equality was as important as liberty, and thus social and economic rights were more readily embraced.[16]

Socialists were quick to point out that Western liberal notions of rights had developed in the particular economic and political circumstances of the seventeenth and eighteenth centuries. As these circumstances changed in the nineteenth century, liberal theory was unable to respond to the need for state action to secure fundamental human rights and freedoms for citizens. Socialist theories of rights, often described as the "second generation" of human rights, emphasize economic, social, and cultural rights. The socialist human rights position was in large part

a response to the abuses and misuses of capitalist development and its underlying, essentially uncritical, conception of individual liberty that tolerated, even legitimated, the exploitation of working classes and colonial peoples. Historically, it is counterpoint to the first generation of civil and political rights, with human rights conceived more in positive ("rights to") than negative ("freedom from") terms, requiring the intervention, not the abstention, of the state for the

purpose of assuring equitable participation in the production and distribution of the values involved.[17]

This development was resisted by those who affirmed liberal notions of natural rights. In the words of Gregorio Peces-Barba, professor of law at the University of Madrid,

> at this very stage of the historical origin of fundamental rights, there is a barrier in positive law to the reception of the philosophy of economic, social and cultural rights when they appear historically, because they presuppose a major factor—one of positive action by the State—which is foreign to that historic origin and to that concept of law.[18]

In the socialist perspective, this historical analysis explains "the assertion of doctrinaire liberalism that equality is incompatible with freedom" and allows for "attempts to correct the discriminatory character" which fundamental rights "have in the liberal conception. . . ."[19]

Peces-Barba speaks of this approach as the "integral reformulation of the concept of fundamental rights" and sees in it great hope for humankind:

> The incorporation into the concept of fundamental rights of the economic, social and cultural rights that assume the egalitarian component which harmonizes, completes and makes freedom more real, also creates a new dimension which is that of solidarity, synonymous in my opinion with the fraternity of the trilogy of the French Revolution. If this is confirmed, the fundamental rights will be the means by which men truly put into practice the banner of liberty, equality and fraternity, which will thus be the patrimony of all and not just of the liberals, and give impulse to historical progress and the liberation of men and their integral development. This is the utopia for which one must struggle as if it were possible to obtain immediately, because the utopia also forms a part of reality, though it be a premature reality anticipated by the dreams of men who have their eyes on a different light.[20]

Thus in a slightly different way than Jean-Bernard Marie, Peces-Barba also sees fundamental rights as central to "the historical development of democratic society," which has as its goal the strengthening of "the freedom of individuals and of the groups they form."[21]

In this sense, Irving Louis Horowitz is correct in asserting that the present debate on human rights

> can be conceptualized in part as a struggle between eighteenth century libertarian persuasions and nineteenth century egalitarian beliefs—that is, from a vision of human rights having to do with the right of individual justice before the law to a recognition of the rights of individuals to social security and equitable conditions of work and standards of living.[22]

This struggle may be seen as an attempt to correct the overemphasis, in liberal notions of civil and political rights, on the rights of the individual over against the welfare of groups and peoples. Yugoslavian scholar Katarina Tomasevski writes: "The second generation (social, economic and cultural rights) emerged as a counter-balance to the dominantly Western concepts, [and was] advocated primarily by the newly founded socialist states."[23]

It is important to recall at this point that the Universal Declaration of Human Rights, in Articles 22-27, affirms

> the right to social security, the right to work and to protection against unemployment; the right to rest and leisure, including periodic holidays with pay; the right to a standard of living adequate for the health and well-being of self and family; the right to education; and the right to the protection of one's scientific, literary, and artistic production.[24]

As noted earlier, these are at least in part an effort to express what President Roosevelt described as "freedom from want." Thus the concept of social and economic rights advanced within the socialist tradition is included in the Universal Declaration and not entirely absent from the liberal tradition.

Similarly, not all second generation rights can properly be described as "positive rights." For instance, the right to free choice of employment, the right to form and to join trade unions, and the right to participate freely in the cultural life of the community may not require action by the state to secure their enjoyment. However, certainly the emphasis of second generation rights is on claims to social equality; and so state intervention is essential in the allocation of resources required to enforce these rights.

Shift at the UN

Antonio Cassese, professor of international law and director of the Post-Graduate School of International Affairs of the University of Florence, describes the years 1960-1973 as the "second phase" in the life of the United Nations.[25] In this phase the socialist countries joined forces with Third World countries to champion the right of peoples to self-determination and to economic and social rights. Rather than resisting the development of human rights instruments, socialists now saw in international law the possibilities of promoting the very concerns for economic and social justice which had prompted their original opposition.

It is no accident that both the International Covenant on Economic, Social and Cultural Rights and the International Covenant on Civil and

Political Rights begin with the same first article: "All peoples have the right of self-determination. By virtue of that right they freely determine their political status and freely pursue their economic, social and cultural development."[26]

Cassese asserts that this right has become "the linchpin of the United Nations strategy toward human rights."[27] He notes that until the middle of the 1970s the struggle in the United Nations was still largely between the Eastern and Western countries, with the developing countries frequently supporting the socialist position. However, since 1974 the Third World countries have come to dominate debate at the UN. Together, the Third World countries have shifted the agenda away from the liberal-socialist controversy to an explicit concern for changing international economic conditions.

The challenge to realize a "third generation of human rights" was first articulated in the 1974 Charter on Economic Rights and Duties of States.[28] It was reiterated in Resolution 32/130, which was proposed by Argentina, Cuba, Iran, the Philippines, and Yugoslavia and adopted by the General Assembly in 1977.[29]

This resolution established two priorities for the future work of the UN Commission on Human Rights. The first priority is to combat violation of the human rights of peoples, with apartheid, racial discrimination and colonialism named as primary concerns. The second priority is the realization of a new international economic order. W. A. Whitehouse comments: "It is fair to observe that the language of human rights has been taken over from the worlds of liberal capitalism and of Marxist socialism and adapted to contend with the collective emergencies of Third World societies."[30]

Resolution 32/130 also affirms that all human rights and fundamental freedoms are indivisible and interdependent and that the realization of civil and political rights is therefore impossible without the enjoyment of economic, social and cultural rights. In addition, all human rights are seen as inalienable and their promotion globally is understood to involve different emphases in different parts of the world. Finally, realization of the new international economic order is identified as essential for the effective protection of human rights.[31]

Third World Crucible

George Shepherd argues that the Third World is the crucible in which a "global consciousness" is being forged, "because it is the center of the anticolonial and development process in which the two streams of individualistic and social human rights flowing from the first two worlds have

met."[32] He suggests that the Third World is developing a conception of human rights which goes beyond both individual and social notions:

> This global view sees rights as both inherent in the individual and socially derived by development. Political freedoms are not possible without primary social development and conflicts are resolved in terms of the welfare of society as a whole.[33]

The basic rights to survival and food are asserted both as qualifying civil and political rights and as depending upon them.

Thus in the Third World human rights are understood to embrace political and religious concepts as well as indigenous traditional values.[34] Human rights are conceived as elements of the right to self-determination, which protects the rights of peoples to their cultural traditions and language, as well as their right to development.

Although socialist concepts may seem to predominate in the Third World, human rights advocates argue that civil and political rights are not subordinated to economic and social rights.[35] For example, the late José W. Diokno of the Philippines, former senator and presidential candidate, argued against the notion that governments in the Third World are inevitably authoritarian either because of the need for rapid economic development or because of indigenous traditions. He characterized the second justification for authoritarianism as "racist" and the first as "a lie" which merely perpetuates an unjust status quo:

> Development is not just providing people with adequate food, clothing, and shelter; many prisons do as much. Development is also people deciding what food, clothing and shelter are adequate, and how they are to be provided.[36]

This is utterly consistent with the assertion by the Sengalese Kéba Mbaye, that the right to development is a "fundamental human right, without which life in a society is not worth living."[37]

In the Third World the right to self-determination, which "is an internationally recognized right of long and dubious standing,"[38] is being given a new shape. This is reflected in the Algiers Declaration of Third World Peoples, adopted on 4 July 1976, which attributes violations of human rights directly to the structures of the international economic system.[39]

Richard Falk argues that the Algiers Declaration is important for at least two reasons. First, as a nongovernmental document it cannot be dismissed as a statement representing only the interests of ruling elites in the Third World. Second, it is an assertion of the principle of popular sovereignty—"that it is the peoples of the world that are the fundamental source of authority":

Somehow statist tendencies have distorted this situation, making it appear as if governments are the ultimate, if not the only source of authority with respect to human rights. The Algiers Declaration, drawing inspiration from the Magna Carta tradition, is a framework of rights asserted by and for the peoples of the world over and against the claims and activities of government, multinational corporations, and international institutions.[40]

In this declaration of human rights it is *every people*, not every individual nor every state, which is said to have the right to existence, respect and self-determination.

The Algiers Declaration was authored largely by "non-Marxist communalists," as David Forsythe describes them, who are convinced that "effective respect for human rights necessarily implies respect for the rights of peoples. . . ."[41] Forsythe suggests that non-Marxist communalists, such as Tanzania's Julius Nyerere, are able to combine liberal and socialist notions of human rights. In 1968 Nyerere asserted:

For what do we mean when we talk of freedom? First, there is national freedom; that is, the ability of the citizens of Tanzania to determine their own future, and to govern themselves without interference from non-Tanzanians. Second, there is freedom from hunger, disease, and poverty. And third, there is personal freedom for the individual; that is, his right to live in dignity and equality with all others, his right to freedom of speech, freedom to participate in the making of all decisions which affect his life, and freedom from arbitrary arrest because he happens to annoy someone in authority—and so on. All these things are aspects of freedom, and the citizens of Tanzania cannot be said to be truly free until all of them are assured.[42]

Forsythe argues that on numerous occasions Nyerere defended individual rights, even as he asserted communal and economic rights as expressions of "working together for the common good instead of competitively for individual private gain."[43]

Louis Henkin agrees that although many of the states of the Third World describe themselves as socialist, most are not essentially Marxist and are only pragmatically socialist in that they stress economic and social development. He argues that while there are many cultural and historical differences,

Almost all Third World states have constitutions including bills of rights, most of which were drafted after World War II on the model of the U. S. Bill of Rights, the French Declaration, the Universal Declaration of Human Rights, or the European Convention on Human Rights.[44]

For instance, the Constitution of the kingdom of Burundi, which had been part of the Belgian Trust Territory of Ruanda-Urundi until 1962,

affirms in the Preamble the King's belief in God and his faith in the high dignity of the human person and his decision to guarantee fundamental human rights, and records that he takes his inspiration from the Universal Declaration of Human Rights and from the Charter of the United Nations.[45]

However, as Henkin readily acknowledges, almost all African constitutions also contain provisions for the suspension or derogation of rights in times of emergency. Therefore, these constitutions do not effectively limit the power of the state.

Affirmations of human rights in the Third World clearly reflect a convergence of Western liberal and socialist traditions and by no means the victory of one over the other.[46] What is also clear is that these reactants are being catalyzed by the cultural values of Third World peoples. Thus in the crucible of the Third World there is not merely a reformulation of liberal and socialist doctrines of human rights—the first and second generations of human rights—but at the same time a reassertion of traditional values. The right to self-determination is seen as the right to shape the future in a way that protects as well as reforms the past.

If diverse cultural contexts in the Third World make the traditional distinctions between individual and group rights seem less clear, the oppressive character of many governments renders the debate between liberals and socialists a luxury. Patricia Weiss Fagen argues in a study of human rights literature in Latin America that "the human rights movement has begun to function in Latin America as a means of keeping politics alive."[47] Against the claims of the ruling elites of Latin America that individual rights must be subordinate to the state, those working for human rights insist "that individual human beings have rights which take precedence over the state's and must be recognized by the state."[48]

Fagen identifies the largest body of this literature as the product of Catholic and Protestant groups working for human rights.

In general, the writing from religious perspectives begins with the assertion that the rights advanced in the UN and inter-American human rights declarations and covenants correspond to accepted religious ethics. Catholic clergy equate human rights principles with the spirit of major theological statements since *Pacem in Terris* (Pope John XXIII).[49]

Thus in Latin America it is understood as natural and necessary for church leaders to defend human rights and for many church programs to be devoted entirely to human rights advocacy.

Fagen concludes that where political systems are open it is not necessary

to appeal exclusively to concepts of human rights in order to struggle, as people always have, for bread, freedom, land, a greater voice in the decisions that direct their lives, and overall human dignity. For the present, the very fact that there are suddenly thousands of people proclaiming and writing about human rights indicates that political systems in most countries are far from open.[50]

In Latin America, as in Africa and Asia, human rights claims are a means of affirming basic moral values in the face of severe oppression.

The breadth of the concept of human rights is an asset in this respect, for it encompasses different social, political and ideological perspectives and "is therefore useful to the political left, right and center, to religious and secular humanitarian associations and to victims of the many forms of repression."[51] Thus the ambiguity of human rights language, as well as its association with established legal and religious institutions, allows a certain amount of protection for those seeking redress for their grievances, as they would be more vulnerable using ideological or political language.

Religious Support

The shift in the last forty years from largely individual notions of human rights to a broader affirmation of social and communal human rights has been strongly supported by leaders of religious communities.[52] At the same time that Third World concerns have become more central in the deliberations of the United Nations, religious leaders from the Third World have become more prominent in the global struggle for human rights.

Mohammed Allal Sinaceur, writing within the Islamic tradition, asserts that

constant concern for human rights, by its role in explaining, justifying and manifesting the values involved, can act as a corrective to individualism and recall society to a sense of duty. It is in this way that the universal awakening to the spirit of justice is regulated, setting the seal of validity on the stubborn aspiration of all individuals and all peoples to attain to a modern mode of life.[53]

Human rights are a means of humanizing the development of modern society, for they preserve the dignity of the human person.

Among Christians this is perhaps clearest in the World Council of Churches. Here advocacy for human rights was first centered on freedom of religion. However, in the middle of the 1970s the consensus of the

WCC listed six human rights, including the right to basic guarantees of life, the right to self-determination, and the right to participate in the decision making of the community, as well as the right to religious freedom.

Jürgen Moltmann clearly recognized the shift in the WCC from liberal concerns for civil and political rights to socialist and Third World concerns for social and basic life interests. He affirmed that the ecumenical church movement had grown with this shift in emphasis and now was fully involved in supporting human rights in the pursuit of the common good of all humanity.

The development of Roman Catholic social teaching can be understood in much the same way. The teachings of the church had resisted individualistic notions of human rights, as formulated in the French and American revolutions. However, in the twentieth century the church began to defend the rights of workers against the obvious injustice of laissez-faire capitalism.

When John XXIII embraced human rights in *Pacem in Terris*, the relationship of rights and obligations within community was clearly articulated. Today in the Roman Catholic tradition human rights are affirmed as the social conditions for human dignity. They are the rights of persons in community, and thus are neither the rights of the individual over against the community nor the rights of the community over against the individual. The goal is "a social order that respects the dignity of the human person and serves the common good."[54]

As with the World Council of Churches, the human rights asserted within Roman Catholic social teaching include social and economic and communal rights, as well as civil and political rights. These human rights are a means of ordering the welfare of the community. Even as human obligations imply rights, so human rights imply obligations. Thus Catholics are taught today that their faith requires the defense of basic human rights, so that the dignity of all human beings might be guaranteed. They are taught not merely to assert their own rights, but to accept the duty to defend the rights of others.

Conservative Protestants are somewhat uncomfortable with the modern affirmation of human dignity, as their theology is based on the biblical notion of the sinfulness of fallen men and women. However, some conservative Protestants have found many areas where they can relate the biblical witness to the modern concern for human rights.

John Warwick Montgomery and Carl F. H. Henry both are troubled by the lack of reference to God in the Universal Declaration of Human Rights, but each as a Christian supports the rights contained within the document. Montgomery derives from the Bible a list of human rights that exceeds in protection the rights affirmed in the Universal Declaration, and

Henry supports these human rights. Moreover, Montgomery specifically supports, on biblical grounds, the call by the Third World nations for a new economic order, so long as civil and political rights are not sacrificed in the process.[55]

The broad support among Christians for human rights struggles in the Third World has been described in detail in chapter 4 of Part I. Christian voices raised to protest human rights violations in the Third World are numerous and vigorous, despite the persecution that may result. In fact, many Christians have already been martyred for human rights.[56] Clearly, more will follow in risking and losing their lives in this witness.

In Part II other religious groups and individuals, as well as Christians, were seen to support human rights. Jews were instrumental in the passage of the Universal Declaration of Human Rights. As a persecuted minority in the Soviet Union and other socialist countries, Jews have stressed civil and political rights. Moreover, because Israel is a minority nation in the Middle East, Jews have felt that Israel is unfairly singled out by Third World nations for accusations of human rights violations.

However, Jews maintain that their tradition supports economic and social as well as civil and political rights. The prophetic witness against the abuse of power by the rulers of a state is well known. Less attention has been given to Talmudic support for the notion of equality of treatment within a community and to the traditional concern for the sojourner and the stranger.

Muslims, too, now generally support the Universal Declaration of Human Rights and are leaders in the Third World in stressing the newer social, economic, and peoples' rights. The basic rights of food, clothing, shelter, education, and employment are stressed by Muslims as long central to their tradition. Moreover, like other religious advocates of human rights, Muslims teach that rights and duties are essentially related aspects of human dignity.

With Christians and Jews, Muslims affirm that human rights are the gift of God. Unlike Christians and more liberal Jews, many Muslims do not affirm the right to religious liberty, as they believe deviance from Islam is opposition to the divine will. However, there is a struggle within the Muslim community over how to interpret scripture in this regard, with some Muslims arguing vociferously for freedom of religion.

Hindus and Buddhists are primarily living in Third World countries, and therefore it is not surprising that they have supported the shift from individual liberties to a greater emphasis on social and communal human rights. However, Hindus also affirm civil and political rights and have written them into their laws. While India's constitution is unequivocal concerning equality of citizenship and the illegality of untouchability, Hindus have yet to reform their caste traditions in the way Gandhi and

others advocated. However, as with other religious supporters of human rights, Hindus argue that sacred duties can only be understood today as implying human rights necessary for the protection of human dignity.

Most Buddhists have been reluctant to identify the *Dharma* with human rights, because they fear that the individualistic connotations of the West will draw attention away from the interdependent nature of reality. However, some Buddhists assert that the human rights to food, clothing, shelter, and justice reflect basic precepts of their tradition. Moreover, in the Third World Buddhists and Christians have joined together to work for justice through the promotion of human rights.

Finally, in Africa and Asia advocates of traditional values have argued strenuously against Western notions that are limited to individualistic formulations of civil and political rights. They assert that traditional values in the Third World protect the basic human rights which are essential for human dignity. Thus they defend the modern synthesis of human rights which sees individual and social rights as expressions of the right to self-determination.

Perhaps noted Chinese scholar Wm. Theodore de Bary offers wise counsel in how to interpret the changes going on in the Third World. He argues that human rights are being translated and adapted into Chinese thought in the same way that Buddhist concepts were assimilated in the early Middle Ages.[57] Therefore, he resists the argument that human rights are intelligible only within Western culture:

> In my own view nothing is to be gained by arguing for the distinctively Western character of human rights. If you win the argument, you lose the battle. That is, if you claim some special distinction for the West in this respect, or assert some inherent lack on the part of Asians, you are probably defining human rights in such narrow terms as to render them unrecognizable or inoperable for others. If, however, you view "human rights" as an evolving conception, expressing imperfectly the aspirations of many peoples, East and West, it may be that, learning from the experience of others, one can arrive at a deeper understanding of human rights problems in different cultural settings.[58]

The synthesis of human rights concepts in the Third World is to be embraced rather than resisted, for it means that the possibility of a truly global standard for human dignity is becoming a reality.[59]

Thus I conclude that around the world religious support for human rights has followed the shift from a narrow conception of human rights, cast largely in the language of Western liberal theory, to a broad and eclectic concept which emphasizes the needs of Third World peoples.[60] Perhaps religious leaders have not simply followed this shift, but have helped to create it. For today throughout the Third World religious advocates are in the forefront of the global human rights movement.

Moreover, despite the obvious violations of human rights there is hope. R. N. Trivedi, director of the Human Rights Institute in Lucknow, India, affirms that

the indomitable spirit of man, phoenix like, has risen from the ashes of despair to refurbish the bastions of hope, to give new meaning to life and make it worth living. . . . *Want* he has sought to banish by unending toil but the lurking *fear* that the fruits of his toil and labor may be snatched away from him has to be dispelled by faith. Faith in the form of awareness of his rights as a human being, individually or in a group, to enjoy life together or alone and to share the bounties of nature beyond the man made barriers—social, economic, political and geographic.[61]

In the Third World, faith in human rights is a way of living, in the face of renewed barbarism and systematic oppression, with hope for the future of the human family.

Notes

1. Hersch Lauterpacht, *An International Bill of the Rights of Man* (New York: Columbia University Press, 1945), 24. Eight pages earlier he asserts: "With isolated, though important exceptions, the idea of the inherent rights of man is the continuous thread in the pattern of history in the matter of that weighty issue of the relation of man and State."
2. See Karel Vasak, *The International Dimensions of Human Rights* (Westport, Conn.: Greenwood Press, 1982).
3. *The New Encyclopedia Britannica* 20, "Macropaedia: Knowledge in Depth" (1985), s.v. "Human Rights," by Burns H. Weston, 715. First published as "Human Rights," *Human Rights Quarterly* 6, no. 3 (August 1984):257-83. See also *Human Rights in the World Community: Issues and Action*, ed. Weston and Richard P. Claude (Philadelphia: University of Pennsylvania Press, 1989).
4. Maurice Cranston, *What Are Human Rights?* (New York: Basic Books, 1964).
5. Jack Donnelly, "What Are Human Rights?: An Historical and Conceptual Analysis" (Ph.D. diss., University of California at Berkeley, 1981), subsequently published as *The Concept of Human Rights* (London: Croom Helm, 1985); Adda B. Bozeman, "The Roots of the American Commitment to the Rights of Man" in *Rights and Responsibilities: International, Social, and Individual Dimensions* (Los Angeles: University of California Press, 1980), 51-102. See also Adamantia Pollis and Peter Schwab, "Human Rights: A Western Construct with Limited Applicability," in *Human Rights: Cultural and Ideological Perspectives*, ed. Pollis and Schwab (New York: Praeger Publishers, 1979); and Clifford Orwin and Thomas Pangle, "The Philosophical Foundation of Human Rights," in *Human Rights in Our Time: Essays in Memory of Victor Baras*, ed. Marc F. Plattner (Boulder, Colo.: Westview Press, 1984). Bruno V. Bitker argues to the contrary that "recognition of human rights is as old as man himself." Bitker, "Applications of the United Nations' Universal Declaration of Human Rights within the United States," *De Paul Law Review* 21, no. 1 (1971):337.
6. James Sellers, "Human Rights and the American Tradition of Justice," *Soundings* 62, no. 3 (Fall 1979):242. Richard Hofstadter was one of the first to suggest that Hobbes and

not Locke was the true guiding spirit of the founding fathers. Hofstadter, *The American Political Tradition* (New York: Vintage Books, 1948), 16. Thomas Paine said, "We have it in our power to begin the world anew." John Locke said, "In the beginning all the world was America. . . ." Perhaps thinking of both of these statements, President Jimmy Carter was later to say, "Human rights invented America." Thomas Paine, *Common Sense* (Penguin Books, 1976), 120; John Locke, *Two Treatises of Government*, ed. Peter Laslett (New York: Mentor Books, 1965), 343. Quoted in Arpad Kadarkay, *Human Rights in American and Russian Political Thought* (Washington, D.C.: University Press of America, 1982), 1 and v.

7.   Quoted in Arthur N. Holcombe, *Human Rights in the Modern World* (New York: New York University Press, 1948), 5. See Douglas Lurton, *Roosevelt's Foreign Policy, 1933-1941: Franklin D. Roosevelt's Unedited Speeches* (Toronto: Longmans, Green, 1942), 324.

8.   Ibid., 32.

9.   See Barbara Jordan, "Individual Rights, Social Responsibility," in *Rights and Responsibilities: International, Social, and Individual Dimensions*, 9-17.

10.   W. A. Whitehouse, "A Theological Perspective," in *Human Rights: Problems, Perspectives and Texts*, ed. F. E. Dowrick (England: Saxon House, 1979), 43. Louis Henkin writes that the "Americans declared what they had; the French declared what they desired." Henkin, "Economic-Social Rights as 'Rights': A United States Perspective," *Human Rights Law Journal* 2, nos. 3-4 (1981):233.

11.   Ibid. Thomas Paine not only argued for democracy and independence, but for economic growth and social security. More recently, Bruce L. Rockwood has argued that American affluence and the myth of limitless resources has prevented Americans from perceiving "the legitimacy of demands for global economic rights as part of the human rights conception. . . ." Rockwood, "Human Right and Wrong: The United States and the I.L.O.—A Modern Morality Play," *Case Western Reserve Journal of International Law* 10, no. 2 (Spring 1978):407.

12.   David P. Forsythe, *Human Rights and World Politics* (Lincoln: University of Nebraska Press, 1983), 158.

13.   Jean-Bernard Marie, *Human Rights or a Way of Life in a Democracy* (Strasbourg, France: Council of Europe, Directorate of Human Rights, 1985), 61.

14.   David P. Forsythe, *Human Rights and World Politics*, 202. He argues that this is perhaps clearest in the "intertwined emphasis on socioeconomic and civil-political rights" which are set forth in the two 1966 human rights covenants.

15.   However, by 1943 David Riesman, Jr. would affirm: "I think it is now generally realized that men who lack productive work under tolerable conditions are not free to speak or otherwise to participate in the community's decisions, not only because they fear for their security, but also because their way of life permits no opportunity for self-development. Thus, the question arises whether or not the rights we cherish are not all parts of a piece, and whether with marginal exceptions, each does not depend upon the other, particularly so as our society becomes more interdependent and more complicated." Riesman, "Report to the Members at the Annual Meeting on the Discussion of the International Bill of Rights Project," ed. William Draper Lewis, American Law Institute (12 May 1943), 7.

16.   See Joachim Kondziela, "*Citoyen* Freedom and Bourgeois Freedom: Religion and the Dialectics of Human Rights," *Soundings* 67, no. 2 (Summer 1984):174-76.

17.   *The New Encyclopedia Britannica* 20, "Macropaedia: Knowledge in Depth" (1985), s.v. "Human Rights," by Burns H. Weston, 715.

18.   Gregorio Peces-Barba, "Reflections on Economic, Social and Cultural Rights," *Human Rights Law Journal* 2, nos.3-4 (1981):282.

19.   Ibid., 282-83.

20.   Ibid., 292- 93. V. N. Kudryavtsev asserts that "The minimum elementary democratic human rights essential for all contemporary civilized societies are affirmed in the Universal

Declaration of Human Rights (1948) and in the international Covenants on Civil, Political, Social, Economic and Cultural Rights (1966), the recognition and ratification of which are obviously vital. All these rights and freedoms are of equal importance." Kudryavtsev, "Human Rights and the Soviet Constitution," in *Philosophical Foundations of Human Rights* (Paris: UNESCO, 1986), 89.

21.   Ibid., 294.

22.   Irving Louis Horowitz, "Foreword—On Human Rights and Social Obligations," *Human Rights and World Order*, ed. Abdul Aziz Said (New York: Praeger Publishers, 1978), viii.

23.   Katarina Tomasevski, "Approaches to Human Rights in the Socio-Economic and Cultural Context of Eastern Europe," in *Frontiers of Human Rights Education*, ed. Asbjørn Eide and Marek Thee (New York: Columbia University Press, 1983), 97.

24.   *The New Encyclopedia Britannica* 20, "Macropaedia: Knowledge in Depth" (1985), s.v. "Human Rights," by Burns H. Weston, 716.

25.   Antonio Cassese, "The Approach of the Helsinki Declaration to Human Rights," *Vanderbilt Journal of Transnational Law* 13 (Spring-Summer 1980):277.

26.   *Human Rights in International Law: Basic Texts* (Strasbourg: Directorate of Human Rights, 1985), 14 and 27.

27.   Antonio Cassese, "The Approach of the Helsinki Declaration to Human Rights," *Vanderbilt Journal of Transnational Law* 13 (Spring-Summer 1980):278.

28.   G.A. Res. 3281, 29 UN GAOR, UN Doc. A/9946 (1974).

29.   G.A. Res. 32/130, 32 UN GAOR, UN Doc. A/32/45 (1978). For the debates preceding the adoption of the resolution, see UN Doc. A/C.3/32/SR. 42-44, 49-52 (1977).

30.   W. A. Whitehouse, "A Theological Perspective," in *Human Rights: Problems, Perspectives and Texts*, 43.

31.   Adolfo Perez Esquivel of Argentina, who received the 1980 Nobel Peace Prize, argues that "we must posit as a fundamental human right the right to life in the context of a just economic and social order." Esquivel, "The Human Right to Justice and Peace," *Breakthrough* 10, nos. 2-3 (Winter/Spring 1989):9. This article, translated from the Spanish by Richard Chartier, is excerpted from a speech to the Forum of Nobel Laureates in Paris in January 1988.

32.   George W. Shepherd, Jr., "Transnational Development of Human Rights: The Third World Crucible," in *Global Human Rights: Public Policies, Comparative Measures, and NGO Strategies*, ed. Ved P. Nanda, James R. Scaritt, and George W. Shepherd, Jr. (Boulder, Colo.: Westview Press, 1981), 215.

33.   Ibid. When he was Secretary-General of the UN in the 1950s, Trygve Lie predicted "that the rise of dependent peoples and the human rights movement will, in the long run, have more significance and give rise to greater events in the second half of the twentieth century than will the present ideological struggle." Quoted in *The United Nations and Our Religious Heritage* (New York: The Church Peace Union, 1953), 44.

34.   Former UN ambassador Andrew Young, noting that the "emerging rights revolution" around the world is often being led by the graduates of Christian missionary schools, concludes that "this emerging movement for human rights is directly related to the Judaeo-Christian tradition and opportunities for higher education." Young, "Human Rights or Necessity," in "Symposium: Development as an Emerging Human Right," *California Western International Law Journal* 15, no. 3 (Summer 1985):441-42.

35.   There is, of course, great diversity of opinion. See "Worlds Apart," *South African Outlook* (December 1987):125-26, reprinted from *One World* (October 1977).

36.   José W. Diokno, untitled lecture, International Council of Amnesty International, Cambridge (21 September 1978), 11-12, mimeo. Quoted in *Development, Human Rights and the Rule of Law*, Report of a Conference held in the Hague on 27 April-1 May 1981, Inter-

national Commission of Jurists (Oxford: Pergamon Press, 1981), 54.

37. Kéba Mbaye, "Chairman's Opening Remarks," in *Development, Human Rights and the Rule of Law* (Oxford: Pergamon Press, 1981), 5. Mbaye defines the right to development as "The recognized prerogative of every individual and every people to enjoy in just measure the goods and services produced thanks to the effort of solidarity of the members of the community."

38. David P. Forsythe, *Human Rights and World Politics*, 29. This right can be traced back to Woodrow Wilson and is mentioned twice in the UN Charter.

39. *Universal Declaration of the Rights of Peoples*, 4 July 1976 (Paris: François Maspero, 1977).

40. Richard Falk, *Human Rights and State Sovereignty* (New York: Holmes and Meier Publishers, Inc., 1981), 192.

41. David P. Forsythe, *Human Rights and World Politics*, 173.

42. Ibid., 175.

43. Ibid.

44. Louis Henkin, *The Rights of Man Today* (Boulder, Colo.: Westview Press, 1978), 78.

45. Egan Schwelb, *Human Rights and the International Community: The Roots and Growth of the Universal Declaration of Human Rights* (Chicago: Quadrangle Books, 1964), 51.

46. Carnes Lord asserts: "there is a very large area of agreement between the various international documents on human rights and moral or legal standards that are widely recognized in the religion, traditions, and customs of non-Western societies." Lord, "Human Rights Policy in a Nonliberal World," in *Human Rights in Our Time*, 131. However, Alwin Diemer believes that in the Third World "the notion of universality expressed in the 1948 Declaration, which used the terms 'human being' and 'human nature', has been abandoned. Each group—however it be defined—is autonomous, 'self-legislating' in and through its culture. Individual cultures and hence the plurality and diversity (!) of cultures are now the basis for determining human rights." Diemer, "The 1948 Declaration: An Analysis of Meanings," in *Philosophical Foundations of Human Rights*, 102.

47. Patricia Weiss Fagen, "Human Rights in Latin America: Learning from the Literature," *Christianity and Crisis* 39 (24 December 1979):328.

48. Ibid., 333.

49. Ibid., 330.

50. Ibid. At least one Latin American novelist, Manlio Argueta, has given his characters a consciousness of human rights, as in the following passage: "And when they [the priests] changed, we also began to change. It was nicer that way. Knowing that something called rights existed. The right to health care, to food and to schooling for our children. If it hadn't been for the priests, we wouldn't have found out about these things that are in our interest." Argueta, *One Day of Life*, trans. Bill Brow (New York: Random House, Vintage Books, 1983), 31. For references to "human rights advocates" and violations of "human rights" see Argueta, *Cuzcatlán*, trans. Clark Hansen (New York: Random House, Vintage Books, 1987), 211 and 214. See also Marjorie Agosin, "So We Will Not Forget: Literature and Human Rights in Latin America," *Human Rights Quarterly* 10, no. 2 (May 1988):177-92. This article was translated by Janice Molloy.

51. Ibid. Hector Fernández-Lesdema, professor of law at the Central University of Venezuela, argues that it is necessary both "to affirm a universal conception of human rights and to develop a Latin American approach for the study of human rights." Fernandez-Lesdema, "The Studying and Teaching of Human Rights in Latin America," in *Frontiers of Human Rights Education*, 73-81.

52. Warren Holleman discusses at length the conflict between the individualistic notion of human rights in the liberal Western tradition and the Christian affirmation that, because

persons are physical and social as well as spiritual beings, they possess social, economic and cultural rights as well as political rights. Holleman, *The Human Rights Movement: Western Values and Theological Perspectives* (New York: Praeger Publishers, 1987), chapters 2-5.

53.   Mohammed Allal Sinaceur, "Islamic Tradition and Human Rights," in *Philosophical Foundations of Human Rights*, 198.

54.   "Building an Authentic World Community," *The Pope Speaks: The Church Documents Quarterly* 33, no. 1 (1988):23.

55.   Baptist Jimmy Carter would seem to agree: "Our definition of human rights should not be too narrow. People have a right to fill vital economic needs—to be fed, housed, clothed, and educated. Civil and political rights must be protected—freedom of speech, thought, assembly, travel, and participation in government. The rights of personal integrity are the most obvious of all—freedom from arbitrary arrest or imprisonment, torture, or murder by one's own government." Carter, "The State of Human Rights in the World," *Human Rights Law Journal* 9, no. 1 (1988):110.

56.   See Rosemary Haughton, "A Christian Theology of Human Rights," in *Understanding Human Rights: An Interdisciplinary and Interfaith Study*, ed. Alan D. Falconer (Dublin: Irish School of Ecumenics, 1980), 235; César Jerez, S.J., "Faith, Hope and Love in a Suffering Church," in *Human Rights: A Challenge to Theology* (Rome: CCIA and IDOC International, 1983), 75; Park Hyung Kyu, "A Letter from a Korean Church Minister," *Asia Link* 7, no. 3 (May 1985):12; Carolyn Cook Dipboye, "The Roman Catholic Church and the Political Struggle for Human Rights in Latin America, 1968-1980," *Journal of Church and State* 24 (1982):524; Mortimer Arias, "Ministries of Hope in Latin America," *International Review of Mission* 71, no. 281 (January 1982):6-9; "Martyrdom in Brazil," in *At/One/Ment* (Garrison, N.Y.: Graymoor Ecumenical Institute, 1986), 3; and the "Martyr Survey" in Penny Lernoux, *Cry of the People: United States Involvement in the Rise of Fascism, Torture and Murder and the Persecution of the Catholic Church in Latin America* (Garden City, N.Y.: Doubleday, 1980), 463-69.

57.   Wm. Theodore de Bary, "Human Rites—An Essay on Confucianism and Human Rights," *China Notes* 23, no. 4 (Fall 1984):307-13. A shortened version of this essay is published as "Neo-Confucians and Human Rights," in *Human Rights and the World's Religions*, ed. Leroy S. Rouner (Notre Dame, Ind.: University of Notre Dame Press, 1988), 183-98.

58.   Ibid., 308. Raimundo Panikkar argues that human rights are not universal but reflect Western values. However, he asserts: "in the contemporary political arena as defined by socioeconomic and ideological trends, the defense of Human Rights [*sic*] is a sacred duty." Panikkar, "Is Human Rights a Western Concept? A Hindu/Jain/Buddhist Reflection," *Breakthrough* 10, nos. 2-3 (Winter/Spring 1989):30-34.

59.   Mihailo Markovic argues, in the words of Paul Ricoeur, that the struggles over human rights "have created a real convergence between the systems." Ricoeur, "Introduction," in *Philosophical Foundations of Human Rights*, 17. See Markovic, "Differing Conceptions of Human Rights in Europe: Towards a Resolution," in *Philosophical Foundations of Human Rights*, 113-30.

60.   For example, the oldest interreligious organization in the world, the International Association for Religious Freedom, in 1978 approved a report affirming that religious freedom must be asserted in relation to other fundamental freedoms. *IARF World*, no. 2 (1989):11.

61.   R. N. Trivedi, "Human Rights, Right to Development and the New International Order—Perspectives and Proposals," in *Development, Human Rights and the Rule of Law*, 132. William L. Bradley affirms: "Common to us all . . . is a pluralistic intellectual heritage of perceptive leaders by whom our civilizations came into being. Common to us all is the prospect of a future that demands rededication to that heritage. Today, as never before, the

heritage of one can become the heritage of all. Therefore, we know that despite our present inability to find solutions to the problems of universal human rights, we must pursue that quest, searching for ways to fashion out of our cultural and historical diversity a world of equity and justice." Bradley, "The Cultural Factor Reappraised," in *The Moral Imperatives of Human Rights: A World Survey,* ed. Kenneth W. Thompson (Washington, D.C.: University of America Press, 1980), 235.

Chapter 13

A GLOBAL FAITH

If the evidence presented in the preceding chapters is circumstantial, nonetheless it is substantial. Faith in human rights may not be affirmed by a majority of the inhabitants of the globe, but it is affirmed in the major religious traditions of the world and on every inhabited continent and in almost every culture.

Understandings of human rights developed in liberal, socialist and Third World contexts may be seen as different emphases within a common tradition of faith. This tradition is grounded in the Universal Declaration of Human Rights, which is accepted by all as the foundation for human rights law. Moreover, this tradition continues to develop, especially due to concerns in the Third World; liberal and socialist concepts of human rights are being recast to reflect indigenous cultural and religious notions of the necessary conditions for human dignity.

Clearly, members of different religious traditions affirm human rights as a part of their faith. To be sure, these affirmations differ; however, these differences occur not only between the traditions but also within a particular tradition. For instance, Christians differ about the justification of human rights not only with Buddhists, but among themselves. However, it is clear that among those who affirm human rights there is considerable agreement as to both the fundamental importance of human rights in the modern world and the content of human rights. Furthermore, the Universal Declaration of Human Rights is affirmed within all the major world religious traditions, and religious leaders and institutions are working cooperatively around the globe for the protection of human rights through law.

Thus faith in human rights is not merely international but interreligious. Faith in human rights, as expressed in the Universal Declaration of Human Rights and as evident in socialist and Third World countries as

well as in Western liberal contexts, is now affirmed within the major religious traditions of the globe.

Is there enough commonality among those who affirm human rights to speak of a global faith? I believe so. History, and not philosophy, will define human rights. As Ludwig Wittgenstein has suggested, "the meaning of a word is its use in the language."[1] The use of the phrase "human rights" is changing in the world, even as I write. For advocacy on behalf of human rights is a sign of the times. Thus we need to heed Wilfred Cantwell Smith's reminder: "words do not themselves mean anything; it is only people that mean something, by the words that they use."[2] The meaning of human rights will be shaped more by people than by the rules of language or logic.

I am not suggesting that there is a single, global philosophy or theology of human rights.[3] Enormous diversity of belief and conviction exists among those who embrace human rights as a standard for law and justice. However, at the level of practice or "action expressing faith," there is surprising and substantial agreement.[4] Despite differences of doctrine, men and women of various religious traditions are in fact working together with those who profess no religious conviction, to secure human rights for all peoples.

This would seem to illustrate the maxim by Wilfred Cantwell Smith that the meaning "the historian finds, incorporates more truth than the doctrine does."[5] There is no single doctrine of human rights, but there is a history of the movement to secure human rights. The different theories of human rights may not suggest a global faith, but the practice of human rights advocacy does.

Faith

The concept of faith is problematic, for it means different things to different people. However, I did not introduce it as a category of analysis in this study. Faith is a central concept within human rights advocacy. It is a fact that people all around the world affirm faith in human rights.

The UN Charter begins: "We the peoples of the United Nations determined . . . to reaffirm faith in fundamental human rights. . . ."[6] The Universal Declaration of Human Rights begins with the same reaffirmation of faith, and the Universal Declaration is affirmed by most if not all those involved in human rights advocacy.[7] Faith here means at least that there are given, universal standards which are to be protected by law if humanity is to be saved from self-destruction. It means that there is a moral order in the universe to which we are to respond.

In the Universal Declaration of Human Rights no argument is made for a philosophical or theological foundation for human rights, nor are legal precedents used to justify human rights law. When it was approved in 1948 there was no consensus about the foundation of justice and law. The drafters of the Universal Declaration of Human Rights might well have concluded, with Max Stackhouse, that "Every philosophy rests not on reason alone, but on fundamental faith assumptions."[8] Thus there is a sense in which faith is a necessary condition for human rights, as for all moral claims. Human rights are not merely derived from deductive argument, but are an expression of faith.

However, it is of greater significance that for some of those who drafted the Universal Declaration, as well as for many who later embraced it, faith in human rights is not merely necessary but compelling. As Prem Kirpal observes: "The ultimate sanction of the true observance of human rights rests in the faith and commitment of societies as reflected in the beliefs and values of individuals."[9]

As early as 1951, Jacques Maritain suggested that the convergence of different traditions was a kind of "secular faith."[10] Cornelius Murphy uses the same phrase in asserting that the Universal Declaration of Human Rights "can be viewed as the expression of a common secular faith in the worth of the human person."[11] Similarly, Earl Warren affirms: "we acquire our faith in the objectives of the nations of the world and of the justification for the United Nations itself" from the Universal Declaration of Human Rights, for it expresses "our faith in humanity, the kind of faith that is based on things not seen."[12]

Vratislav Pechota, Legal Adviser for the Czechoslovak Ministry of Foreign Affairs from 1965 to 1968 and a leader of the Charter '77 movement protesting human rights violations, writes that international human rights

> are a product of the universal human rights culture built on faith "in the dignity and worth of the human person, in the equal rights of men and women and of nations large and small," and on the conviction that respect for the fundamental freedoms of the individual is an indispensable condition for peace.[13]

Hernán Montealegre, writing of human rights education sponsored by churches and other nongovernmental organizations in Latin America, notes that

> The profound commitment displayed by some members of these groups, who bear living witness to their unquenchable faith in the values of human rights, in itself constitutes a form of education, for it sets an example that cannot be matched by any theoretical formulation.[14]

U.S. Supreme Court Justice Thurgood Marshall expresses a faith shared by many human rights advocates: "We shall continue along the lawful road—at all times operating within the law, relying upon the law, and with faith in the democratic processes because time and right are both on our side."[15] Human rights demonstrators in the People's Republic of China assert that "Faith is mankind's spiritual life."[16]

Paul Brietzke quotes the affirmation by Andrei Sakharov, noted Soviet scientist and human rights advocate:

> The ideology of human rights is probably the only one which can be combined with such diverse ideologies as communism, social democracy, religion, technocracy, and those ideologies which may be described as national and indigenous. It can also serve as a foothold for those who do not wish to be aligned with theoretical intricacies and dogmas and who have tired of the abundance of ideologies, none of which have brought mankind a simple happiness. The defense of human rights is a clear path, towards the unification of people in our turbulent world and a path toward the relief of suffering.[17]

Brietzke concludes: "This is the faith that will drive forward the right to development—if the right and its advocates prove worthy."[18]

If the term "faith" is common in affirmations of human rights, other religious images are used even more frequently. Torkal Opsahl, Norwegian legal scholar and member of the European Commission on Human Rights, refers to international human rights law as an ideology "which replaces religion for some of us."[19] And Louis Pettiti, judge of the European Court of Human Rights, asserts that human rights may play an important ethical role in that "They are sometimes, for unbelievers, a substitute for religious motivations, stimulating a will to commit themselves."[20]

The religious nature of human rights was clear to Jimmy Carter, when as president of the United States he spoke to the World Jewish Congress:

> In large measure, the beginnings of the modern concept of human rights go back to the laws and the prophets of the Judeo-Christian tradition. I have been steeped in the Bible since early childhood, and I believe that anyone who reads the ancient words of the Old Testament with both sensitivity and care will find there the idea of government as something based on a voluntary covenant rather than force; the idea of equality before the law and the supremacy of law over the whims of any ruler; the idea of the dignity of the individual human being and also of the individual conscience; the idea of service to the poor and to the oppressed. . . .[21]

Even the late Soviet leader, Leonid Brezhnev, used a religious image in referring to fundamental human rights: "let us place first among all human rights the most sacred of them all—the right to life, and, consequently, to

a lasting peace."[22] And young Chinese refer to "sacred democratic rights."[23]

Peter K. Y. Woo suggests that "moral and religious reflection" is "the true foundation from which human rights can be derived."[24] Louis Henkin speaks of the "theology" of human rights,[25] and John Courtney Murray of the "gospel of human rights."[26] Jeanne Hersch writes of the "incarnation of human rights in history."[27] Terje Wold, chief justice of Norway, affirms "the spiritual fight for human rights."[28] Leo C. Ferrari argues that the Universal Declaration of Human Rights is the first step in checking the "short-sighted, destructive individualism" of the West, for it moves in the direction of "some Great Vision which will lay hold of the very heart of humanity itself and lift it to universal compassion, love and understanding."[29]

It is clear then that Carl Friedrich speaks for many in affirming that "the core of man's dignity is his conviction, his belief, his faith" and that community is "built on faith in human rights."[30] As Jerome Shestack observes: "Most of the laborers in the field of human rights believe that there is a moral inevitability to human rights. I believe that."[31]

Advocates of human rights usually call for more than respect for the law. Commitment, sacrifice and even one's life may be demanded. This call to struggle for human rights as an ultimate concern is rooted in the history of the human rights tradition. The rights considered "natural" in the eighteenth century, though often presented in secular language, reflect a view of nature "derived from Christian ethics."[32] In addition, the doctrine of natural law supports human rights with "a deep and abiding faith in man and his capacity for virtue and self-improvement."[33]

Moreover, human rights are grounded in a rejection of the state's claim to ultimate authority. Even in socialist nations this facade of absolute authority is beginning to crumble.[34] Fundamental to human rights affirmations is "the belief that rights inhere in the individual,"[35] as a member of a community. All around the globe religious and community leaders are struggling with advocates of law and order who deny in practice, if not in principle, that human rights constitute a "higher law."

Of course, David Sidorsky is correct in suggesting that the concept of "human rights" is "the most recent of a series of terms over which semantic battles are waged in order to legitimate competing political and social attitudes."[36] The ideological battle over "human rights" continues to be intense. Furthermore, the fact that human rights are founded on faith is no guarantee against mere rhetoric and "bad faith" among those affirming human rights for political reasons.

However, this does not overcome the evidence already presented of the sincerity and conviction of many who affirm faith in human rights. The fact that human rights are asserted in bad faith does not outweigh the

substantial evidence that many people all over the world affirm human rights in good faith.

For example, William Korey believes the appeal of Soviet Jewish "refuseniks" signifies "an extraordinary faith in the Helsinki Final Act, that somehow this document will finally bring redress, if not salvation, from an intolerable burden."[37] Similarly, in the Third World Samuel Rayan writes: "We see the church taking shape where Jesus-reality is being actualized in history by defense of human dignity and human rights in a struggle even unto death."[38] When many continue to risk and lose their lives for such a faith, it can hardly be discounted as mere rhetoric.

Thus Pavel Litvinov wisely suggests that the struggle to enforce human rights law requires a "healthy skepticism, combined with faith in durable spiritual values," rather than blind faith in utopian ideals.[39] Faith in human rights requires rationality as well as conviction and will.

Results of Survey

The responses to a questionnaire I circulated at the 1987 International Institute of Human Rights in Strasbourg may shed additional light on what faith in human rights in fact means to people today.[40] When participants were asked—after being reminded of the affirmation of faith in human rights in the Universal Declaration—if they had "faith in fundamental human rights," twenty-two of twenty-five respondents answered "Yes." These respondents, from seventeen countries, indicated religious affiliations including Roman Catholicism, several Protestant denominations, Judaism, Islam, Hinduism, and none.[41]

There was less unanimity as to whether this faith in human rights was religious faith. Of the twenty-two respondents who indicated that they had faith in fundamental human rights, seven affirmed that they would describe this faith as "religious" and eleven asserted that they would describe it as "not religious." Many of those responding were not comfortable with such an either/or choice: some checked neither, some checked both, several wrote extended comments explaining their ambivalence.

One Christian respondent wrote: "My 'faith' is not in human rights, per se, but in a transcendent basis." A respondent who affirmed faith in human rights, but indicated no religious affiliation and declined to describe her faith as either "religious" or "not religious," commented: "Personally I also have faith in God's help to make possible the respect of human rights by persons and governments." A Roman Catholic respondent who affirmed faith in human rights, but described his faith as "not religious," wrote: "humanitarian principles are as important as religious matters."

A Jewish student, who described her faith in human rights as both "religious" and "not religious," stated: "[it] stems from my religious as well as non-religious beliefs." A Mennonite student answering in the same way wrote: "As a Christian I consider that everyone is equal. But even if I was a non-Christian I would consider that everyone is equal." A Catholic respondent answering in the same way commented: "I think the protection of faith includes both religious and non-religious belief. I believe in one faith, but do not feel I should impose my belief on others."

A Christian respondent who affirmed faith in human rights, but declined to describe his faith as either "religious" or "not religious," asserted: "I don't believe in human rights by themselves. The only *faith* I can have is in the way of life to which Jesus invites us; but that, of course, is a way in which human rights *are* respected." Another Christian student, who affirmed faith in human rights and described her faith as "religious," affirmed: "Without a divinely given basis for human rights, all statements of rights become arbitrary and a hodge-podge of relativistic, undefinable propositions."

Finally, a Catholic respondent, who indicated her faith in human rights was "not religious," asserted: "I think the value of a human being is inherent in that human quality and not influenced in any way by any religious conviction of the person interpreting or having these rights." And a student without religious affiliation, who affirmed faith in human rights but described her faith as "not religious," commented: "The main thing is people, not whether they confess this or that religion."

Clearly, several respondents to my questionnaire hesitated to describe their faith in human rights as "religious" because of the parochial connotation of the word. Few intimated that faith in human rights which is "not religious" is less ultimate or less important or inconsistent with faith in God. Moreover, those claiming participation in a religious tradition expressed the significance of human rights in terms of their religious faith.

Religious Faith

In considering whether faith in human rights is a kind of religious faith, or is at least strikingly similar, it should be remembered that until quite recently religion and law were not the mutually exclusive concepts they are today. The history of law in the world involves the study of religion, and the elaboration of religious ethics in all traditions involves law. I agree with Harold Berman's assertion that a people cannot live for long without a vision "of the interaction of law and faith."[42] Law is founded on religious vision, which in turn is expressed in law.[43]

A similar conviction moved René Cassin, French statesman and primary author of the Universal Declaration of Human Rights, "to interrelate

religion and human rights" and to affirm "that a direct and powerful relationship existed between the Ten Commandments and the Universal Declaration of Human Rights."[44] The claims of human rights are ultimate, but law by itself cannot make such claims. Thus for Christians the claims of human rights are founded upon religious claims, as they are for Jews, Muslims, Buddhists, and those of other religious traditions.

In addition, the very enterprise of human rights law is "fundamentally different" from the rest of international law in that human rights law is not justified by national self-interest, but subordinates it to the common good of the world community and its individual members.[45] Human rights law has to do with the standards of law itself, with the values that give law moral authority, and with establishing the conditions for life with human dignity. While not a religion, human rights law is a faith. And for many in the world, as demonstrated earlier, this faith is central to their religious convictions.

It is not surprising then that Jews, Muslims and Christians find human rights principles revealed in their scriptures.[46] Many Christians "have long held that the basic freedom and protections of human rights doctrine are divinely revealed in and through the natural order of creation."[47] These rights and freedoms may also be discerned by reason. For many then faith and reason converge in human rights.

For instance, Robert Gordis argues that the prophet Micah's faith in God is not diminished by his "faith in man's capacity to achieve the ideal by the free exercise of his reason and will."[48] Similarly, H. Morren, a Roman Catholic Christian, asserts: "fighting for the respect of Human Rights belongs to the practice of our faith, a Gospel inspired action."[49] Faith in humanity, and thus in the realization of human rights through law, may be the result of faith in God.

If revelation as a source of authority is rejected, as in much of Western liberal thought, nonetheless this Western cultural tradition may be seen to involve faith:

> humanism, idealism, metaphysics, and the idea of rationality, as over the centuries they have been articulated and re-articulated in our life in the legacy that stems from Greece, have provided persons and society with a complex of patterns in terms of which they have been able to organize their lives, and to find them meaningful; to find coherence in the universe, to attain coherence within themselves, and to coordinate these two; to dedicate themselves to goals discerned as worth striving for, with courage and loyalty and discipline strong enough to overcome both external and internal pressures of lesser worth. This, a comparativist well knows, *is the stuff of faith.*[50]

Turning to reason may be as much an act of faith as turning to sources of revelation.

This is evident in statements relating human rights to human aspirations throughout history:

> What is "human rights?" It is everything—life, liberty, human dignity, and justice. It encompasses all that which pertains to mankind in its universal context and is, therefore, universal in scope and application. To those who ascribe to the values of life only things material, this definition may appear esoteric. Beyond that, however, all that which touches upon the quality of life, in an inclusive sense, is ultimately a question of human rights.[51]

On its face this is more a statement of faith in human rights than a rational argument for them. It is more of a declaration of revealed truth than a matter of drawing logical conclusions. When put into practice, it means simply that "true respect for human rights is nothing less than a way of life."[52]

Faith in human rights may be identified with faith in God, as is clearly the case for Christians, Jews and Muslims. On the other hand, Buddhist Masao Abe argues that faith in God is a limitation which is not necessary in affirming human rights. Whether one agrees or not, for many who believe in God it seems "obvious that the basis of human right [*sic*] lies, in the final analysis, in God's plan of creation."[53] Jews and Muslims, as well as other Christians, may agree with Ricardo Antoncich that "Faith in a transcendental God is the best guarantee of human rights because it avoids all idolatrous manipulation of legitimacy and ideologies."[54]

Moreover, at least some Jews as well as Christians and Muslims are clear that faith in God is not the same as mere belief in God.[55] The emphasis in Judaism is upon "conformity in practice, not upon unanimity in belief," because it has a "basic democratic faith" in the "freedom of the human spirit."[56] The Hebrew term *emunah*, which is usually translated "faith," means to trust and applies to acts, not beliefs: "For this reason, Judaism has no symbolic books, no articles of faith. No one has to swear to creedal symbols or subscribe, by solemn oath, to certain articles of faith."[57] Faith in human rights involves struggling for them, not believing anything in particular about God.

It is important also to note that faith may be an important concept within a religious tradition such as Buddhism, which does not even acknowledge a God. Wilfred Cantwell Smith argues that

> The Buddha certainly had faith: a religious faith mighty, contagious, creative; one that has powerfully affected the shape of human history and the personal lives of men and women for now twenty-five centuries. It is a fact that he had faith. Whether we should go on or not to call it faith in God, depends directly on what we think of the universe, *not on what he thought of it.*[58]

Buddhist C. Jinarajadasa affirms that the personality of the Buddha created "the broad platform of a universal Faith."[59] Thus the faith which many affirm in human rights, even if not linked to belief in God, may be comparable to some if not all forms of religious faith.

Mark Juergensmeyer writes, in his study of Gandhi: "Do you believe in human rights? If so, you are affirming a belief in a higher moral order and accepting a conviction of Western thought that parallels Gandhi's insistence on the dignity of all life."[60] This affirmation of a moral reality—what Gandhi called "Truth"—is "largely an act of faith."[61]

I agree with Mark Juergensmeyer and Wilfred Cantwell Smith that faith is not dependent upon a set of beliefs about God, but involves a trusting response to the moral order of the universe. The affirmation of human rights, which involves a commitment to bring into greater realization the moral order which now is corrupted, is faith regardless of what one believes about God. Moreover, I agree with Wilfred Cantwell Smith that much of the humanist tradition in the West affirms just such a transcendent moral order with or without a doctrine of God.[62] In fact, it is clear that human rights have evolved in the West as the "higher law" within such a view of the ultimate order of the universe.

A Global Faith

As the search for a "higher law" is not limited to Western intellectual traditions, I believe that faith in human rights can reasonably be affirmed as a global concept. Clearly, "human rights" and "faith" are not merely Western concepts. Thus whether or not faith in human rights is global is more an empirical question than a matter of philosophical consistency or semantics.

It is useful to note here that the participants in the 1987 International Institute of Human Rights, who in response to my questionnaire affirmed their faith in human rights, are from sixteen countries on six continents and are affiliated with four major religious traditions whose members are spread around the world. Moreover, it is clear from the evidence presented earlier that many others worldwide affirm faith in human rights.[63]

However, certainly one may and many do resist the notion of any universal values or community of faith. The argument for cultural relativism is not easily overcome, for it would seem that exceptions can be found to any generalization about universal standards.[64] It is also extremely difficult to demonstrate that there is in any sense a global community to sustain such values, if in fact they exist. Moreover, it is clear that faith in human rights takes varied forms in different cultures and different times.

Agreement on the Universal Declaration of Human Rights and its centrality in all affirmations of human rights is a significant element of any response to the claims of cultural relativism. The Universal Declaration and its statement of faith in human rights is taught, legislated and affirmed all over the globe.[65] Its principles are applied with varying emphases in vastly different cultures. At times exception is taken to one or more of its principles. However, the Universal Declaration of Human Rights has not been rejected in any culture or religious tradition and is warmly embraced in most.[66]

In addition, it is clear that human rights are evolving as concerned men and women worldwide seek to secure the conditions for human dignity in their own communities. Change and reform of a tradition should not be confused with incoherence or relativism. The development of human rights in law and religious ethics is happening all over the world because men and women with faith in human rights are working and struggling together for human dignity.

Willibald P. Pahr, former Minister of Foreign Affairs of Austria, writes:

> As long as there are different social, economic, cultural and ideological circumstances in the world, as long as there are different traditions, there will be different concepts of Human Rights. In a pluralistic world we must accept pluralism in the field of Human Rights also. But there will be always one basic core to Human Rights: a series of irreducible humanitarian principles determined by human dignity which have to be respected under all circumstances.[67]

Of course, not all agree that a basic core of human rights is well established. Therefore, the objection of cultural relativism must also be answered with empirical data, such as that already presented. In this regard David Sidorsky observes: "While there is evidence of the plurality of moral concepts and attitudes, there is also evidence for universality."[68] Whether or not there are universal patterns in human culture, persons are able to translate concepts from one language and culture to another, to communicate, to persuade, and to change not only their own way of thinking but that of others.

Moreover, lack of agreement today does not mean that there will be no agreement tomorrow. The history of the human rights movement to date suggests that a consensus is developing. Certainly, there is no proof that "the human condition involves an ineradicable inability to recognize and understand moral terms like universal human rights."[69]

Nonetheless, the argument that human rights cannot be meaningfully understood apart from a community which nurtures and sustains them is a major obstacle in asserting that human rights are global. Robin Lovin argues that rights are not derived from governmental declarations, but

"arise out of shared aspirations worked out in a common arena of cultural, political and economic encounters."[70] This is evident in the historical development of nations and, in places such as Europe, of regional organizations as well. However, he argues that "when we reach the scale of global humanity, the patterns of shared life from which commitments to shared rights might grow do not yet exist."[71]

Yet others suggest that world community is becoming a reality.[72] Vratislav Pechota asserts that international human rights "are a product of the universal human rights culture built on faith in human dignity."[73] Moreover, global institutions are functioning, and religious traditions which extend around the world are today drawn more closely together by rapid communication and travel. The Roman Catholic Church is teaching concern for human rights as a part of faith in every part of the world, and Protestant statements on human rights reflect "a growing tradition of human rights concern in modern Protestant Christianity worldwide."[74]

It is true that those working together for human rights are from different communities of faith, as well as different political and social communities. Yet this may not preclude the possibility of a global community of faith in human rights. Robert Gordis suggests that "the contribution of the Vision of Micah to the formulation of human rights is not exhausted by its enunciation of the ideal of peace, nor even by its faith in the destined attainment of this goal," for Micah indicates that the way to peace is through international law which recognizes the rights of different cultures and peoples.[75]

Here then is a vision of faith which allows for different levels of community. To be sure, the bonds of international community are not as strong as the bonds of national community. Yet both may exist together, each shaping the nature of the other. If faith means sharing a vision of the world and entering into the struggle to realize that vision with others, such faith in human rights is now global.

Wilfred Cantwell Smith suggests that "what the religious—and secular—communities of the world have in common historically is an increasingly common awareness of the past, in all its dynamic diversity and cohesion, and an increasingly common involvement in and shared responsibility for an increasingly joint future."[76] I would add that they also have increasingly a common faith in human rights.

The evidence presented of faith in human rights in the legal and religious traditions of the globe reveals a surprisingly cooperative effort by legal and religious advocates, in local as well as international struggles, to realize human rights for the sake of human dignity. People from different communities of religious faith are working with people of no religious faith, in local groups and international organizations and

movements. The result, I am suggesting, is an evolving global community of faith in human rights.[77]

Conclusion

Thus human rights are not merely a matter of political or ethical concern, but a matter of faith: not "blind faith" but faith involving commitment to standards of human dignity, even at risk to one's own life. Such faith involves trusting in these standards of human dignity, despite the inability to prove to the satisfaction of all others that the standards are true. Jerome Hall, employing legal rules of evidence, concludes that "faith is a complex conviction and experience composed of rational and nonrational, but not irrational, factors."[78]

Such faith, more bold than blind, is evident in the lives of many human rights advocates around the globe. In this "action-oriented way of thinking, reason carries faith along with it. . . ."[79]

Faith in this sense is a part of all morality. Christopher Mooney affirms that "morality, unlike ethical reflection, is not a purely rational phenomenon; it is also a product of affectivity, mysticism, and faith."[80] Morality has to do with acting as well as thinking, as does human rights. Thus both morality and human rights involve faith. Huston Smith notes that "Philip Rieff likens faith to the glue that holds communities together. . . ."[81] Perhaps faith in human rights is necessary to hold together the world community.

From the evidence presented, one can conclude that faith in human rights reflects a convergence of the religious wisdom of the world. Huston Smith asserts that "In faith, the West emphasizes what Tillich called prophetic faith (the holiness of the ought) while the East highlights ontological faith (the holiness of the is)."[82] Modern conceptions of human rights are largely the fruits of prophetic faith, and thus it is not surprising that members of the Jewish, Christian and Islamic traditions have historically been more involved in advocating human rights through law. Yet in the crucible of the Third World, human rights are being refashioned to reflect the conditions for human dignity which have long been cherished in cultures of the eastern and southern continents.

Globally then, an interaction is occurring which involves East and West and North and South, and the reforging of both religious and legal traditions, in a process of shaping a new world community and international order. Faith in human rights is an essential element in this process of renewal. The outcome is not yet clear, for violations of human rights are numerous and widespread. However, faith in human rights has been strengthened rather than weakened by oppression, because oppressors

tend to make martyrs of the faithful who become a source of inspiration for others.

There are dangers here, of course, as faith may be false and not saving. Richard John Neuhaus writes that those who

> trust the information issuing from the regime of their choice . . . have, for whatever reasons, made a faith commitment that excludes them from the community of reasonable discourse about human rights. Or, in theological terms, they have, in submitting their reason and conscience to an earthly power, committed the sin of idolatry . . . [and] while they may care about many things, they do not care about human rights.[83]

He argues that to resist the claims of the state "The churches must develop a theology and a piety that undergird our commitment to human rights with a transcendent understanding of the dignity of the person."[84]

Moreover, Neuhaus warns us to guard against placing too much trust in the current enthusiasm for human rights. For the "only devotion to human rights that can be trusted is a long-distance devotion that has pondered the bloody face of our age."[85] He argues that, with those awaiting the Messianic age, "we know that our commitment to human rights does not depend on the consistency with which that commitment can be implemented."[86] Instead: "Our commitment to human rights . . .[depends] on a promise that bestows dignity upon every person and demands of every person a respect—no, a reverence—for the dignity of all others."[87]

Wilfred Cantwell Smith cautions that "To subordinate faith, or to try to subordinate it, to any practical purpose, however worthy, is explosively distorting."[88] Faith in human rights, to be saving, must affirm a moral order which transcends and grounds human endeavors. In the words of Robert Bellah, "only when our action comes from the heart of our faith will it avoid distortion and destruction."[89]

Yet there is hope, for this faith is rooted in reality. One of the most important resources in the world, Alan Paton asserts,

> available to men of faith in their struggle to realize the ideal of human brotherhood is that sometimes powerful, sometimes weak, but always inextinguishable and divine implantment in human nature; the veneration for that which is called personality. This is the common ground on which the most diverse may stand together; on this ground, if the issue is made clear enough, all kinds of men will stand with us.[90]

The truth of this statement is evident today in the worldwide struggle by women and men of faith to secure human rights as the conditions of human dignity in community.

Faith in human rights is a way of affirming a "higher law" which

justifies and limits the lawful power of the state and recognizes the dignity of the human person as the purpose and standard of all law. It is faith that the universe is on the side of freedom and justice and thus, in the words of Martin Luther King, Jr., it is "faith that right defeated is stronger than evil triumphant."[91] It is faith in the power of love, which King described as a "Hindu-Muslim-Christian-Jewish-Buddhist belief about ultimate reality."[92]

Before his assassination, King began calling for an "economic bill of rights" in addition to civil rights, for he saw both as necessary dimensions of "the struggle for human dignity."[93] In accepting the Nobel Peace Prize, he proclaimed an "audacious faith" that "peoples everywhere can have three meals a day for their bodies, education and culture for their minds, and dignity, equality and freedom for their spirits."[94]

With this faith men and women of different religious traditions will be able to labor together to gather in the harvest of justice and peace. With this faith religious and secular leaders will be able to join hands and walk together in the long march for freedom, democracy, and human rights. With this faith people of every color and creed and culture will be able to lift up their voices together to preserve the beauty of the earth and the glory of the skies.

With this faith we will be able to work together with compassion and strive together with courage to secure the conditions of human dignity, not only for ourselves, but for all humankind.

Notes

1.   Ludwig Wittgenstein, *Philosophical Investigations*, ed. G. E. M. Anscombe (New York: Macmillan Company, 1983), 20e.

2.   Wilfred Cantwell Smith, letter to author, 19 June 1987.

3.   John Courtney Murray, S.J. presents a clear and concise argument for a natural law philosophy of human rights over against the alternative theories of "Liberal individualism," Marxism, and "the new rationalism" based on the premises of the autonomy of the human person in a dynamic and evolving world. Murray unmasks this new rationalism as an ethical relativism which merely transforms the "wants" of a given time and place into concepts of "rights." Moreover, he suggests that when this philosophy is combined with scientific technology and the power of the modern state, it tends to absolutize the values and functions of the state. Murray, *We Hold These Truths: Catholic Reflections on the American Proposition* (Kansas City, Mo.: Sheed and Ward, 1960), 320-27.

4.   Jerome Hall affirms that what really counts is not arguments about faith, but "action expressing faith." Hall, "Religion, Law and Ethics—A Call for Dialogue," *The Hastings Law Journal* 29, no. 2 (July 1978):1280.

5.   Wilfred Cantwell Smith, *Belief and History* (Charlottesville: University Press of Virginia, 1977), 19.

6.   Charter of the United Nations, in *Basic Documents on Human Rights*, ed. Ian Brownlie, 2d ed. (Oxford: Clarendon Press, 1981), 3. In declarations of human rights this state-

ment is often included in the preamble, as in the "Declaration of the Rights of the Child," proclaimed by the General Assembly of the UN on 20 November 1959 (G.A. resolution 1386(XIV)): "Whereas the peoples of the United Nations have, in the Charter, reaffirmed their faith in fundamental human rights and in the dignity and worth of the human person. . . ."

7.   In 1988 during its "Human Rights Now!" campaign Amnesty International collected almost three million signatures in support of implementing the Universal Declaration of Human Rights. The appeal was distributed in fifty-eight languages to people in almost every country in the world. While over one million signatures were collected in the United States, support was also strong in some of the Third World countries. For instance, in Uruguay one out of every forty-seven people signed the document. Most of the signers were ordinary citizens, many of whom attended the "Human Rights Now!" concert tour. "A Plea to the Nations: Keep Your Pledge," *Amnesty Action* (November/December 1988):1.

8.   Max L. Stackhouse, "A Protestant Perspective on the Woodstock Human Rights Project," in *Human Rights in the Americas: The Struggle for Consensus,* ed. Alfred Hennelly, S.J. and John Langan, S.J. (Washington, D.C.: Georgetown University Press, 1982), 145.

9.   Prem Kirpal, "The Contemporary Situation—Looking Ahead," in *Philosophical Foundations of Human Rights* (Paris: UNESCO, 1986), 288.

10.   Jacques Maritain, *Man and the State* (Chicago: University of Chicago Press, 1951), 111. V. C. Chukwuloziel, participant in the Adenauer-Foundation and the Muslim-Christian Colloquy in Mohammedia, Morocco in April 1985, discusses Maritain's position in his essay "A Nigerian Viewpoint," in *The Mohammedia Colloquium of 1985* (Selly Oak, Birmingham, U.K.: Center for the Study of Islam and Christian-Muslim Relations, 1985), 1-19.

11.   Cornelius F. Murphy, Jr., "Ideological Interpretations of Human Rights," *De Paul Law Review* 21, no. 1 (1971):290. Within the pluralism of the American context John Courtney Murray, S.J. also argues for a kind of consensus: "The American consensus therefore includes a great faith in the capacity of the people to govern themselves." He finds this faith "not unrealistic," but is concerned that it makes particular laws—such as the two articles of the first amendment—"articles of faith" when they ought only to be "articles of peace." This is as much a temptation for the religious person, Murray argues, as it is for the secularist. Murray, *We Hold These Truths,* 343, 48-56.

12.   Earl Warren, "Address," *The International Observance: World Law Day—Human Rights: 1968* (Geneva: World Peace through Law Center, 1968), 44-45. The reference is most likely to Hebrews 11:1 in the Christian Bible which, in the Revised Standard Version, reads: "Now faith is the assurance of things hoped for, the conviction of things not seen." Similarly, Mohammed Allal Sinaceur argues that in the human rights struggle, "Islam will strengthen and confirm man in his faith in himself, and in the encounter with other men." Mohammed Allal Sinaceur, "Islamic Tradition and Human Rights," in *Philosophical Foundations of Human Rights,* 219.

13.   Vratislav Pechota, "East European Perceptions of the Helsinki Final Act and the Role of Citizen Initiatives," *Vanderbilt Journal of Transnational Law* 13, no. 2 (Spring-Summer 1980):468. He is quoting the Universal Declaration of Human Rights.

14.   Hernán Montealegre, "Institutional Aspects of Human Rights Teaching and Research in Latin America," in *Frontiers of Human Rights Education,* ed. Asbjørn Eide and Marek Thee (New York: Columbia University Press, 1983), 84.

15.   Thurgood Marshall, "Special Message to the 48th Annual NAACP Convention (1957)," *The A.M.E. Church Review* (April-June 1985):51-52. Long before most American civil rights leaders were speaking of human rights, Marshall wrote: "The Fourteenth Amendment and the human rights doctrine inherent in our democracy require the elimination of race and caste as determining factors throughout the United States."

16.   "On Human Rights," from "Enlightenment," in *The Fifth Modernization: China's Human Rights Movement, 1978-1979,* ed. James D. Seymour (Stanfordville, N.Y.: Human

Rights Publishing Group, 1980), 123.

17.   In Osnos, "Review," *Manchester Guardian Weekly* (30 January 1983):18; quoted in Paul H. Brietzke, "Consorting with the Chameleon, or Realizing the Right to Development," in "Symposium: Development as an Emerging Human Right," *California Western International Law Journal* 15, no. 3 (Summer 1985):600.

18.   Paul Brietzke, "Consorting with the Chameleon, or Realizing the Right to Development," *California Western International Law Journal* 15, no. 3 (Summer 1985):600.

19.   Torkal Opsahl, "Introduction to the International Human Rights Protection Systems," International Institute of Human Rights, Strasbourg, lecture 8 July 1987, notes by author.

20.   Louis Pettiti, "The Philosophy of Human Rights as a Means of Fighting against Perversion of the State," *Convergence,* nos. 1-2 (1984):21.

21.   In "U. S. Responsibilities toward Peace and Human Rights," Dept. of State news release (2 November 1977). Quoted in Rockwood, "Human Rights and Wrong: The United States and the I.L.O.—A Modern Morality Play," *Case Western Reserve Journal of International Law* 10, no. 2 (Spring 1987):398. Jimmy Carter affirms: "As the world community recognized more than four decades ago, peace and human rights are closely interconnected. Humanity's yearning for peace and freedom cuts across ideological boundaries and unites the human family." Carter, "The State of Human Rights in the World," *Human Rights Law Journal* 9, no. 1 (1988):108.

22.   Introduction to the first issue of the new Soviet annual publication, "Human Rights, Yearbook" (Moscow: 1983), 8.

23.   James D. Seymour, *The Fifth Modernization,* 254.

24.   Peter K. Y. Woo, "A Metaphysical Approach to Human Rights from a Chinese Point of View," in *The Philosophy of Human Rights: International Perspectives,* ed. Alan S. Rosenbaum (Westport, Conn.: Greenwood Press, 1980), 123. Robert Maynard Hutchins affirmed a half-century ago that education "is an act of faith" and that translating this "faith into reality is our responsibility as educators and concerned citizens of a nation 'conceived in liberty and dedicated to the proposition that all men are created equal'." Quoted in Wilson Riles, "The Relationship of the Rights and Responsibilities of the Individual to Public School Education—Its Meaning for the Nation," in *Rights and Responsibilities: Responsibilities, Interests, Social, and Individual Dimensions* (Los Angeles: University of California Press, 1980), 280-81. Hutchins is quoting from Abraham Lincoln's "Gettysburg Address."

25.   Louis Henkin, *The Rights of Man Today* (Boulder, Colo.: Westview Press, 1978), 51.

26.   John Courtney Murray, S.J., *We Hold These Truths,* 316.

27.   Jeanne Hersch, "Human Rights in Western Thought: Conflicting Dimensions," in *Philosophical Foundations of Human Rights,* 139.

28.   Terje Wold, "Remarks," in *The International Observance: World Law Day—Human Rights: 1968* (Geneva: World Peace through Law Center, 1968) 15.

29.   Leo C. Ferrari, *Human Rights in a Changing World: The Problem of Preserving Human Values in the Upheavals Caused by Science and Technology,* rev. ed. (Fredericton, New Brunswick: The New Brunswick Human Rights Commission, Department of Labor and Manpower, 1977), 74.

30.   Carl J. Friedrich, *Transcendent Justice: The Religious Dimension of Constitutionalism* (Durham, N.C.: Duke University Press, 1969), 115.

31.   Jerome J. Shestack, "The World Had a Dream," *Human Rights* 15, no. 2 (Summer 1988):45.

32.   Ibid., 93.

33.   Ibid., 35.

34.   See F. J. M. Feldbrugge, "The Soviet Human Rights Doctrine in the Crossfire between Dissidents at Home and Critics Abroad," *Vanderbilt Journal of Transnational Law*

13 (Spring-Summer 1980):451-66; Georg Brunner, "Recent Development in the Soviet Concept of Human Rights," in *Perspectives on Soviet Law for the 1980s*, ed. F. J. M. Feldbrugge and William B. Simons (The Hague: Martinus Nijhoff Publishers, 1982); and József Halász, ed. *Socialist Concept of Human Rights* (Budapest: Akadémiai Kiadó, 1966).

35. Margaret E. Crahan, "National Security Ideology and Human Rights," in *Human Rights and Basic Needs in the Americas*, ed. Margaret E. Crahan (Washington, D.C.: Georgetown University Press, 1982), 116.

36. David Sidorsky, "Contemporary Reinterpretations of the Concept of Human Rights," in *Essays on Human Rights: Contemporary Rights and Jewish Perspectives*, ed. Sidorsky (Philadelphia: The Jewish Publication Society of America, 1979), 89.

37. William Korey, "Final Acts and Final Solutions," in *Human Rights and World Order*, ed. Abdul Aziz Said (New York: Praeger Publishers, 1978), 117.

38. Samuel Rayan, "Theological Priorities in India Today," in *Irruption of the Third World: Challenge to Theology*, ed. Virginia Fabella and Sergio Torres (Maryknoll, N.Y.: Orbis Books, 1983), 40.

39. Pavel Litvinov, "The Human-Rights Movement in the Soviet Union," in *Essays on Human Rights*, 124.

40. The annual International Institute of Human Rights in Strasbourg has been described by John Warwick Montgomery as the most "sophisticated human rights teaching program in the world." It was founded in 1969 by French jurist René Cassin, who donated his Nobel Peace Prize to the program. In July of each year over two hundred law students, lawyers, jurists, and scholars meet to examine developing international human rights law. For a description of the 1979 study session, see Montgomery, "Strasbourg: The Capital of Human Values," *Human Rights* 9, no. 1 (Spring 1980):39-41.

41. Study conducted by the author.

42. Harold J. Berman, *The Interaction of Law and Religion* (Nashville, Tenn.: Abingdon Press, 1974), 13.

43. Papers delivered in 1985 at Columbus Law School, the Catholic University of America, in a "Symposium on the Religious Foundations of Civil Rights Law," are very relevant to this discussion. See *The Journal of Law and Religion* 5, no. 1 (1987).

44. John Warwick Montgomery, "Strasbourg: The Capital of Human Values," *Human Rights* 9, no. 1 (Spring 1980):41. See Marc Agi, *René Cassin, Fantassin des Droits de l'Homme* (Paris: 1979), 284-85.

45. Louis Henkin, "Human Rights: Reappraisal and Readjustment," in *Essays on Human Rights*, 72.

46. Arthur Blaser lists eleven religious organizations with major international human rights activity, four Jewish and five Christian. He also mentions the involvement of the World Muslim Congress and the World Federation of Buddhists in human rights activities. Blaser, "The Dialectics of Transnational Human Rights Activity: A Study of NGO's," Ph.D. diss., Ohio State University, 1979, 47 and 61.

47. James M. Childs, Jr., "The Church and Human Rights: Reflections on Morality and Mission," *Currents in Theology and Mission* 7 (February 1980):15.

48. Gordis, "The Vision of Micah," in *Judaism and Human Rights*, ed. Milton R. Konvitz (New York: W. W. Norton and Company, 1972), 281.

49. H. Morren, "Joining in the Promotion of Human Rights: An International Meeting on Human Rights Organized by Pax Romana and the Information Center of International Catholic Organizations in Geneva, 19-21 March 1980," *Convergence*, no. 1 (1982):2.

50. Wilfred Cantwell Smith, "Philosophia, as One of the Religious Traditions of Humankind: The Greek Legacy in Western Civilization, Viewed by a Comparativist," in *Différences, Valeurs, Hiérarchie: Textes Offerts à Louis Dumont et Réunis par Jean-Claude Galey* (Paris: École des Hautes Études en Sciences Sociales, 1984), 268.

51.   M. C. Bassiouni, "The 'Human Rights Program': The Veneer of Civilization Thickens," *De Paul Law Review* 21, no. 1 (1971):271.

52.   Final Document, UNESCO Congress on Teaching Human Rights, September 1978, quoted in David P. Forsythe, *Human Rights and World Politics* (Lincoln: University of Nebraska Press, 1983), title page.

53.   Ricardo Antoncich, S.J., "Evangelization and Human Rights," in *Human Rights: A Challenge to Theology*, 56.

54.   Ibid.

55.   See Wilfred Cantwell Smith, *Faith and Belief* (Princeton: Princeton University Press, 1979); and also Raimundo Panikkar, *The Intra-Religious Dialogue* (New York: Paulist Press, 1978), 8.

56.   Robert Gordis, "The Right of Dissent and Intellectual Liberty," in *Judaism and Human Rights*, 190, 210.

57.   Moses Mendelssohn, "Freedom of Religion—Absolute and Inalienable," in *Judaism and Human Rights*, 184.

58.   Wilfred Cantwell Smith, "The Buddhist Instance: Faith as Atheist?" *Faith and Belief*, 32, 20-32. See also Sung Bae Park, *Buddhist Faith and Sudden Enlightenment* (Albany: State University of New York Press, 1983); Morris J. Augustine, *The Buddhist Notion of Faith*, Ph.D. diss., Graduate Theological Union, 1978; Francis H. Cook, "The Second Buddhist-Christian Theological Encounter: A Report," *The Eastern Buddhist* 19, no. 1 (Spring 1986):133; and Jan T. Erghardt, *Faith and Knowledge in Early Buddhism* (Leiden: E. J. Brill, 1977).

59.   C. Jinarajadasa, *The Reign of Law in Buddhism* (Madras, India: The Theosophical Publishing House, 1948), 38.

60.   Mark Juergensmeyer, *Fighting with Gandhi* (San Francisco: Harper & Row, 1984), 19.

61.   Ibid. Gandhi wrote that "Truth is my God." *Young India*, 8 January 1925. He affirmed "faith in God and human nature." *Harijan*, 15 April 1939. Quoted in *The Essential Gandhi: His Life, Work, and Ideas*, ed. Louis Fischer (New York: Vintage Books, 1983), 199 and 315.

62.   Charles Taylor writes: "Every moral system has a conception of what one might call human dignity, that is to say, of the quality which, in man, compels us to treat him with respect or, in other words, a conception which defines what it is to have respect for human beings." Taylor, "Human Rights: The Legal Culture," in *Philosophical Foundations of Human Rights*, 53.

63.   Harlan Cleveland believes that the idea of human rights "is on its way to universality." Quoted in Jonathan Power, *Against Oblivion: Amnesty International's Fight for Human Rights* (Great Britain: Fontane Paperbacks, 1981), 217.

64.   Rhoda E. Howard and Jack Donnelly argue that history is creating "one international community of modern men and women" and thus is providing a convincing argument for the universality of human rights over against notions of cultural relativism. They see evidence of this in the volume of essays they have edited, in that "Despite the authors' diversity of experience and perspectives, all accept the Universal Declaration of Human Rights as an authoritative international standard." Howard and Donnelly, "Introduction" and "Preface," *International Handbook of Human Rights*, ed. Donnelly and Howard (Westport, Conn.: Greenwood Press, 1987), 18-20 and ix-x.

65.   By the end of 1949 the Universal Declaration was available in nineteen languages, including the five official languages of the United Nations. "It is now printed and circulated in more than 70 languages and copies can be found in almost every nation on earth." "The Universal Declaration: A Living Document," in *40th Anniversary: Universal Declaration of Human Rights, United States Department of State* (December 1988), 11.

66. Alwin Diemer argues to the contrary that the Universal Declaration of Human Rights has been viewed in the Third World as a European document. However, he believes: "we must go back to viewing the 1948 Declaration as a statement of the problem of human rights in universal terms and renounce the tendency to regard it merely as the specific product of a European culture—however that may be conceived. The whole issue must be seen in the context of both universal principles and a worldwide culture." Diemer, "The 1948 Declaration: An Analysis of Meanings," in *Philosophical Foundations of Human Rights*, 111.

67. Willibald P. Pahr, "Human Rights in a Pluralistic World," *Revue des Droits de l'Homme/Human Rights Journal* (December 1985):102. See "Human Rights and Cultural Relativism," in R. J. Vincent, *Human Rights and International Relations* (Cambridge: Cambridge University Press, 1986), 37-57.

68. David Sidorsky, "Contemporary Reinterpretations of the Concept of Human Rights," in *Essays on Human Rights*, 102. Alison Dundes Renteln writes that "the requirement of relativism that diversity be recognized in no way destroys the possibility of an international moral community." Renteln, "The Unanswered Challenge of Relativism and the Consequences for Human Rights," *Human Rights Quarterly* 7, no. 4 (November 1985):540. See Abdullahi A. An-Na'im, "Religious Minorities under Islamic Law and the Limits of Cultural Relativism," 1-18; and Pierre de Senarclens, "The Universality of Human Rights," in *Human Rights Teaching* 2, no. 1 (Paris: UNESCO, 1981), 3-5.

69. Ibid., 103. Leo C. Ferrari asserts that the Universal Declaration of Human Rights is "an expression of the more obvious implications of the common elements in the loftiest religions of mankind." Ferrari, *Human Rights in a Changing World*, 55.

70. Robin Lovin, "Re-examining Human Rights," *The Christian Century* 98 (26 August-2 September 1981):830.

71. Ibid.

72. See *Towards World Community: The Colombo Papers*, ed. S. J. Samartha (Geneva: World Council of Churches, 1975); Wilfred Cantwell Smith, *Towards a World Theology: Faith and the Comparative History of Religion* (Philadelphia: The Westminster Press, 1981); B. R. Singh, "The Phenomenological Approach to Religious Education for a Multi-faith Society," *Churchman* 100, no. 3 (1986):231-48; and Patricia M. Mische, "Human Rights in the Social Dynamics of an Emerging Global Community," *Breakthrough* 10, nos. 2-3 (Winter/Spring 1989):10-12.

73. Vratislav Pechota, "East European Perceptions of the Helsinki Final Act and the Role of Citizen Initiatives," *Vanderbilt Journal of Transnational Law* 13, no. 2 (Spring-Summer 1980):468. R. J. Vincent refers to "the establishment of a global culture" and a "world society." Vincent, *Human Rights and International Relations*, 1, 2 and 105. Kenneth W. Thompson claims international lawyers are more apt to argue for "an embryonic world community" than are diplomatic analysts. Thompson, "Tensions between Human Rights and National Sovereign Rights," in *Rights and Responsibilities*, 131. International lawyer Richard Lillich does indeed speak of the "international human rights community." Lillich, "Discussion," in *United States Ratification of the Human Rights Treaties: With or Without Reservations?*, ed. Lillich (Charlotteville: The University Press of Virginia, 1981), 73 and 78.

74. James M. Childs, Jr., "The Church and Human Rights: Reflections on Morality and Mission," *Currents in Theology and Mission* 7 (February 1980):17.

75. Robert Gordis, "The Vision of Micah," in *Judaism and Human Rights*, 282.

76. Wilfred Cantwell Smith, *Towards a World Theology*, 193.

77. John Courtney Murray, S.J. argues for an American consensus, which is not just "majority opinion" or the "convergent trend of opinion," but "is a doctrine or a judgment that commends public agreement on the merits of the arguments for it." Murray, *We Hold These Truths*, 105. Similarly, I am arguing that there is now in the world a consensus, that fundamental human rights are the necessary conditions for human dignity.

78. Jerome Hall, "Religion, Law and Ethics—A Call for Dialogue," *The Hastings Law Journal* 29, no. 2 (July 1978):1278.

79. Mohammed Allal Sinaceur, "Islamic Tradition and Human Rights," in *Philosophical Foundations of Human Rights*, 199.

80. Christopher F. Mooney, S.J., *Public Virtue: Law and the Social Character of Religion* (Notre Dame, Ind.: University of Notre Dame Press, 1986), 66.

81. Huston Smith, "Does Spirit Matter: The Worldwide Impact of Religion on Contemporary Politics," in *Spirit Matters: The Worldwide Impact of Religion on Contemporary Politics*, ed. Richard L. Rubenstein (New York: Paragon House Publishers, 1987), xiii.

82. Huston Smith, "Another World to Live In: How I Teach the Introductory Course," presentation at "A Teachers' Workshop on the Introductory Course in Religious Studies," Berkeley/Chicago/Harvard NEH Institutes: A Global Approach to the Study of Religion, Graduate Theological Union, Berkeley, Calif., June 1987, 11.

83. Richard John Neuhaus, "What We Mean by Human Rights, and Why," *The Christian Century* 95 (6 December 1978):1180.

84. Ibid.

85. Ibid.

86. Ibid., 1178.

87. Ibid.

88. Quoted in Robert Bellah, "Faith Communities Challenge—and Are Challenged by—the Changing World Order," in *World Faiths and the New World Order: A Muslim-Jewish-Christian Search Begins*, ed. Joseph Gremillion and William Ryan (Washington, D.C.: Interreligious Peace Colloquium, 1978), 150.

89. Ibid.

90. Alan Paton, "Religious Faith and Human Brotherhood," in *Religious Faith and World Culture*, ed. William Amandus Loos (Freeport, N.Y.: Books for Libraries Press, 1951, reprinted 1970), 197.

91. Martin Luther King, Jr., "Letter from Birmingham City Jail," in *A Testament of Hope: The Essential Writings of Martin Luther King, Jr.*, ed. James Melvin Washington (San Francisco: Harper & Row, Publishers, 1986), 300.

92. King, "A Time to Break Silence," in *A Testament of Hope*, 242.

93. King, "Showdown for Nonviolence," in *A Testament of Hope*, 64-72, and "An Experiment in Love," in *A Testament of Hope*, 19.

94. King, "Nobel Prize Acceptance Speech," in *A Testament of Hope*, 226.

INDEX

Robert Traer is General Secretary of the International Association for Religious Freedom in Frankfurt, Germany. He has taught ethics at St. Mary's College of California, Chabot College, and the University of San Francisco and has published in *The Asia Journal of Theology, Human Rights, Christianity and Crisis,* and *The Christian Century.*

D1104332